JOHN MAIN

The Inner Christ

Word into Silence
Moment of Christ
The Present Christ

Foreword by Bede Griffiths

DARTON·LONGMAN+TODD

This collected edition first published in 1987 by
Darton, Longman and Todd Ltd
1 Spencer Court, 140–142 Wandsworth High Street
London SW18 4JJ

Reprinted 1988, 1991, 1994 and 1995

Word into Silence: first published in 1980 by
Darton, Longman and Todd Ltd
© John Main 1980
Distributed in Canada in this collected edition through
special arrangement with the Paulist Press, USA

Moment of Christ: first published in 1984 by
Darton, Longman and Todd Ltd
© 1984 The Executors of John Main OSB

The Present Christ: first published in 1985 by
Darton, Longman and Todd Ltd
© 1985 The Executors of John Main OSB
Introduction © 1985 Laurence Freeman OSB

This collected edition © 1987 Darton, Longman and Todd Ltd
Foreword © 1987 Bede Griffiths OSB

Biblical quotations are taken from the *New English Bible*
© 1970 by permission of Oxford and Cambridge University Presses

British Library Cataloguing in Publication Data

Main, John, *d. 1982*
  The inner Christ
  1. Meditation
  I. Title II. Main, John, *d. 1982*. Word
  into silence III. Main, John, *d. 1982*.
  Moment of Christ IV. Main, John, *d. 1982*.
  The present Christ
  248.3'4   BV4813

ISBN 0-232-51759-2

Printed and bound in Great Britain by
Page Bros, Norwich

Contents

Contents

How to Meditate

Sit down. Sit still and upright. Close your eyes lightly. Sit relaxed but alert. Silently, interiorly begin to say a single word. We recommend the prayer-phrase 'maranatha'. Recite it as four syllables of equal length. Listen to it as you say it, gently but continuously. Do not think or imagine anything—spiritual or otherwise. If thoughts and images come, these are distractions at the time of meditation, so keep returning to simply saying the word. Meditate each morning and evening for between twenty and thirty minutes.

Addresses of meditation centres:

International Centre
World Community for Christian Meditation
23 Kensington Square
London W8 5HN
United Kingdom
Tel: 071 937 4679
Fax: 071 937 6790

Australia
Christian Meditation Network
1 Duncombe Avenue
Brighton
Vic 3186
Tel: 03 593 1360

Belgium
Christelijk Meditatie Centrum
Beiaardiaam 1
1850 Grimbergen
Tel: 02 269 5071

Canada
Meditatio
PO Box 552 Station NDG
Montreal, Quebec H4A 3P9
Tel: 514 768 0475
Fax: 514 937 8178

John Main Centre
470 Laurier Avenue, Apt 708
Ottawa, Ontario K1R 7W9
Tel: 613 236 9437
Fax: 613 230 4901

Christian Meditation Centre
10 Maple Street
Dartmouth
N.S. B2Y 2X3
Tel: 902 466 6691

India
Christian Meditation Centre
1/1429 Bilathikulam Road
Calicut
673006 Kerala
Tel: 495 60395

Ireland
Christian Meditation Centre
4 Eblana Avenue
Dun Laoghaire, Co. Dublin
Tel: 305651

Christian Meditation Centre
58 Meadow Grove
Blackrock, Cork
Tel: 021 357249

New Zealand
Christian Meditation Centre
PO Box 139
Orewa
Tel: 0942 63 891

Philippines
Christian Meditation Centre
5/f Chronicle Bldg., Cor. Tektite Rd,
Meralco Avenue / Pasig, M. Manila
Tel: 02 633 3364
Fax: 02 632 3104

Singapore
Christian Meditation Centre
Holy Family Church
6 Chapel Road
Singapore 1542
Tel: 344 0046

Thailand
Christian Meditation Centre
51/1 Sedsiri Road
Bangkok 10400
Tel: 271 3295

United Kingdom
Christian Meditation Centre
29 Campden Hill Road
London W8 7DX
Tel: 071 937 0014
Fax: 071 937 6790

Christian Meditation Centre
13 Langdale Road
Sale, Cheshire, M33 4EW
Tel: 061 976 2577

Christian Meditation Centre
Monastery of Christ the King
Bromley Road
London N14 4HE
Tel: 081 449 6648
Fax: 081 449 2338

Christian Meditation Centre
29 Mansion House Road
Glasgow G41 3DN
Tel: 041 649 4448

United States
John Main Institute
7315 Brookville Road
Chevy Chase, MD 20815
Tel: 301 852 8635

Christian Meditation Centre
1080 West Irving Park Road
Roselle, IL 60172
Tel: 708 351 2613
Fax: 708 529 4597

Christian Meditation Centre
322 East 94th Street #4B
New York, NY 10128
Tel: 212 831 5710

Christian Meditation Centre
1101 S. Arlington Ave.
Los Angeles, CA 90019
Tel: 213 733 8743

Christian Meditation Centre
2490 18th Avenue
Kingsburg, CA 93631
Tel: 209 897 3711

Hesed Community
3745 Elston Avenue
Oakland, CA 94602
Tel: 415 482 5573

Foreword

I have said that in my experience John Main is the best spiritual guide in the Church today. What is my justification for saying this? It must be understood in the context of the world in which we are now living, where for a great many people the Christian faith has lost its meaning. John Main was acutely aware that there was 'something missing' in the life of the ordinary Christian and that the Church was not answering the need of the majority of people, especially the young of our time. John Main saw the root of the problem to be that people had lost touch with reality, with the reality of themselves and of the world around them. The problem was how to recover this lost dimension, how to recover the sense of an ultimate meaning in life, how to escape from the illusion created both by religion and by the world, and to realize the truth of the self and the world.

Put in these terms one is immediately led to reflect on the oriental view of this world as an illusion and to see why it is that so many people today are turning to the East to find the answer to the problems of their life. I think that it is of profound significance that John Main was led to his discovery of the deeper meaning of life by his contact with a Hindu Swami years before he became a Benedictine monk. It was in Malaya that as a young man he met Swami Satyananda and learned from him the way of the 'mantra', which became for him the means of access to the reality behind the illusion of this world. It seems that contemporary Christianity has to learn this lesson from the religions of the East. A recovery of the depths of the Christian faith can only come when we encounter the profound experience of the inner self, which is India's great gift to the world.

John Main learned through his use of the mantra, taught him by the Hindu Swami, to discover this deeper dimension of his being, but the decisive moment came when he discovered in Cassian, the Christian monk of the fifth century, the same method of the mantra and realized that it was part of the authentic Christian tradition. This tradition derived from the

Fathers of the Desert and had been continued through the Middle Ages especially in the tradition of the Jesus Prayer in the Eastern Church, but also in the beautiful medieval English treatise known as *The Cloud of Unknowing*. It was this tradition, which had been lost in subsequent ages, which John Main saw as his vocation to renew in the Church. But he saw this as by no means confined to the monastic order to which he belonged. It was his genius to discern that it was a way of prayer which was available to every Christian, and to people of no particular religious faith as well.

John Main came therefore with a definite method, the way of the mantra, the repetition of a 'sacred word', which he found to be the ideal method for awakening this deeper sense of reality. People today need a method of prayer. So far the Western Church has virtually has only one method, that of the Exercises of St Ignatius and similar forms of discursive meditation. This method is good so far as it goes, but it does not take you beyond discursive thought and the exercise of the will. It can, of course, lead to a profound conversion and to a deep renewal of Christian life, but this depends on the exercise of the discursive reason. For an oriental, on the other hand, meditation begins with the cessation of all discursive thought. As the Yoga Sutras of Patanjali say, 'Yoga is the cessation of the movements of the mind'. It is the function of the mantra precisely to bring about this cessation of the movements of the mind and to awaken the awareness of the inner self beyond word and thought. It is to silence the mind so that one is brought into direct awareness of the inner self.

What exactly does it mean, to be aware of one's inner self, the self beyond the rational mind? It means to go beyond the ego. The ego, or in Indian terms the *ahamkara*—the I-maker—is the basis of the 'personality', the external self, which works through the senses and the reason. As long as one remains on the level of sense and reason, one remains under the control of the ego. It is only when we go beyond sense and reason that we become aware of our deeper self, that we contact the reality, the real person in us, and at the same time begin to make contact with the reality of the world. It is the paradox which always faces us, that reality is not outside us but within. As long as we live on the surface of life, we see only the surface of the world around us. Only when we enter into our own centre do we find the centre of the world around us.

To go beyond the ego is therefore to find ourselves not in isolation but in communion. It is to realize our intimate relationship with everyone and everything.

John Main had discovered that through the practice of the mantra one can go beyond the ego, the limited human self, and open oneself to others not on the surface but in depth. One begins to discover what he called the 'communion of love'. It is one of the most striking aspects of his method of meditation that it leads to communion, it builds up community, it takes one out of oneself and relates one to the real world. He became acutely aware that people in the Church as well as outside it were living on the surface of life and therefore were becoming isolated and alienated from themselves and from the world. He found in his method of meditation the answer to this human need. I emphasize this matter of method, because I find that most people today need a method. There is a search for God, for truth, for reality going on all over the world, but people need a concrete method to bring them into contact with this reality. In that lies the attraction of Hinduism and Buddhism to multitudes of people in our time, because they teach definite and well-tried methods of meditation. John Main found a method of Christian meditation, which would lead to the same experience of the inner self, the centre of truth and reality.

But it was his special genius to discover how this method of meditation could lead to the experience of the deepest reality of Christian faith. In the Foreword to *Moment of Christ*, which was the last thing he wrote, he described it in this way. To enter into the deep centre of one's being is to enter the consciousness of Christ, or as he puts it, the prayer of Christ. 'I can describe it only', he says, 'as the stream of love which flows constantly between Jesus and the Father. This stream of love is the Holy Spirit.' This takes us to the very heart of John Main's understanding of meditation. It is a participation in the inner life of the Holy Trinity. To enter into the depth of one's own spirit is to encounter the 'love of God, which is poured into our hearts through the Holy Spirit which is given us'. In every human being there is a point of the spirit which is open to the Holy Spirit, and when we enter into deep meditation we experience this outpouring of the Holy Spirit in our hearts, which, as John Main says, is the 'stream of love that flows between Jesus and the Father' or the 'cosmic river of love'. It is this love—the inner life of the Trinity—which sustains the whole creation and flows into every human heart. To meditate is to become aware of this river of love, the spring of water, of which Jesus speaks in St John's Gospel, welling up to eternal life.

There are other methods of meditation than that of the mantra, and there are other ways of experiencing the love of God than that of meditation, but I do not know of any better method of meditation leading to the experience of the love of God in Christ than that of John Main. He has recovered for Christians a way of prayer which links us with the earliest tradition of the Church and at the same time relates us to the most authentic tradition of prayer and meditation in other religions.

BEDE GRIFFITHS

WORD INTO SILENCE

CONTENTS

PREFACE

The beauty of the Christian vision of life is its vision of unity. It sees that all mankind has been unified in the One who is in union with the Father. All matter, all creation, too, is drawn into the cosmic movement towards unity that will be the realization of the Divine harmony. This is not an abstract vision. It is filled with a deep personal joy because within it the value of each person is affirmed. No unique beauty will be lost in this great unification but each will be brought to fulfilment in all. In union we become who we are called to be. Only in union do we know fully who we are.

This is the great controlling vision that has steered the Christian tradition for centuries. Without it we cannot call ourselves His disciples. And yet it is the task of each of us to grow up into this vision in our personal experience, to see it for ourselves, or rather, to see it with the eyes of our Lord. The central task of our life, in the Christian vision, is to come into union, into communion. Putting this from the point of view where most of us start, it means going beyond all dualism, all dividedness within ourselves and beyond the alienation separating us from others. It was dualism that characterized the heresies that threatened to destroy the fine centrality, the balance of the Christian perspective. It is dualism, too, that creates for each of us the impossible, unrealistic 'either-ors' that cause so much unnecessary anguish: God or man, love of self or love of neighbour, cloister or market place.

To communicate the Christian experience of union, the experience of God in Jesus, we have to resolve these false dicho-

5

tomies, first of all, in ourselves. We have to be made one by Him who is One.

It seems to be the nature of dualities to propagate themselves and so to complicate the wholeness and simplicity from which we start and to which deep prayer recalls us. One of the most fundamental of these dualities has been the polarization of the active and contemplative life, and its most harmful effect has been to alienate the majority of Christians from that same deep prayer which transcends complexity and restores unity. We came to think of ourselves as either contemplative or active, and this distinction held for religious as well as the laity. As an active we were among the vast majority whose spiritual life rested on the devotional, or the intellectual, and who made no presumptuous claim to a personal experience of God. As a contemplative, we were part of a small, privileged minority, separated from the main body not only by high walls and strange customs but often by specialized vocabularies or even total non-communication.

Like all heresies this one proved plausible and lasting because it possessed a grain of truth. There *are* some who are called to live in the Spirit on the margin of the world's busyness and whose primary values are silence, stillness and solitude. The contemplative is not a preacher, perhaps, but he must never-theless communicate his experience because his experience *is* self-communicating. His experience is the experience of love and love reaches out to communicate, to share, to widen the realm of its own communion. The conclusion drawn from the false understanding of the Church's contemplative dimension distorted the explicit teaching of the New Testament, namely, that the call to sanctity is universal. The call of the Absolute is made to each of us and it is only this call that gives us ultimate meaning; our ultimate value is the freedom we are given to respond to it. The exclusion of the majority of Christians from this call had deep and major effects on both Church and Society. If our ultimate value and meaning is denied, how

6

can we expect a human reverence for each other to be the guiding principle of our ordinary relations?

There is no greater need in the Church and in the world today than for the renewed understanding that the call to prayer, to deep prayer, is universal. Unity among Christians as well as, in the long term, unity among different races and creeds rests upon our finding the inner principle of unity as a personal experience within our own hearts. If we are to realize that Christ is indeed the peace between us, we have to know that 'Christ is all and is in all'. And we in Him. The authority with which the Church communicates this experience will be the degree to which we, the Church and Christ's Body, have realized it personally. Our authority has to be humble, that is, it has to be rooted in an experience that takes us beyond ourselves into full personhood. Our authority as disciples is our closeness to the Author, far removed from authoritarianism or that complex of fear and guilt by which power is used by man against man. The Christian, in his prayer, renounces his own power. He leaves self behind. In so doing he places absolute faith in the power of Christ as the only power that increases the unity among men because it is the power of love, the power of union itself. As Christian men or women of prayer open their hearts to this power they enlarge the capacity of all men to find the peace that lies beyond their ordinary understanding.

It is not a new idea that Christians should pray. The really contemporary challenge is that we should recover a way of deep prayer that will lead us into the experience of union, away from surface distractions and self-conscious piety. The questions today have always been there: How do we pray at this level? How do we learn the discipline it involves? How do we concentrate ourselves, in a wholly natural way, in the deepest reality of our faith? How do we make the essential transition from imagination to reality, from the conceptual to the concrete, from notional assent to personal experience? It is not enough to approach these questions as intellectual problems. They are far more urgent than that. They are challenges to our existence and so they can only be answered, not by ideas, but with our life.

The simplest way to answer the question, 'How do we pray?' can be found in St Paul's statement – 'We do not even know how we ought to pray, but the Spirit prays within us.' The Christian has been given freedom from all problematical questions about prayer by the revelation that what he calls 'his prayer' is nothing less than an entry into the prayer-experience of Jesus himself, the Spirit, the bond of union with the Father. It is this personal experience of Jesus that is the present, the eternally present reality at the heart of every human consciousness. All our seeking for secret knowledge, hidden ways or teaching has been rendered unnecessary because the ultimate secret has been revealed: 'the secret is this – Christ in you'. So, in prayer we are not striving to make something happen. It has already happened. We are simply realizing what already is, by travelling deeper into the unified consciousness of Jesus, into the wonder of our own creation. The prison of self-fixation that prevents our making this journey can no longer hold those who can understand that 'we possess the mind of Christ'.

When we understand that the centre of prayer is in Christ, not ourselves, then we can ask 'How?' and receive a useful answer. The journey we make to this point of departure is a first stage, and perhaps it will be a difficult, lonely journey. But at this moment in our life we awaken to ourselves within the community of all those others who have come to this same point and have travelled on. Our own experience leads us into the tradition; in our acceptance of the tradition we make it live and pass it on to those who follow us. What is important is that we recognize and embrace the opportunity to make our own experience fully real.

The tradition of Christian meditation is a simple and, above all, practical response to this question and yet within it is concentrated the rich and profound experience of the saints, known and unknown. It is a tradition rooted in the teachings of Jesus, the religious tradition in which he lived and taught, the Apostolic Church and the Fathers. Very soon in the Christian Church it became a tradition associated with monks and monasticism and ever since has been a principal channel through which it has spread into the whole Body and nourished it. I do not think there is anything mysterious about this. Monks are essentially people whose first priority is practice rather than theory, whose inner and outer poverty is designed to facilitate the 'experience-in-itself' rather than reflection upon the experience. It is then only natural, indeed inevitable, that meditation should be found at the heart of monasticism. And, because it is found there, monasticism is important to the Church and to the world.

Such a monasticism, clear as to its own priority, will be an inclusive rather than an exclusive movement in the Church. It will know that the experience has only to be really lived to be communicated. Where the path is being followed by a few, others will be drawn to it. Something will have to be said, written or discussed. But the profoundest teaching and the end of all words will be a participation in the creative moment of prayer. It is the silence of monks that is their true eloquence.

People sometimes express concern about the availability of the monastic tradition of meditation. In communicating it, they wonder, are monks not saying that this is the only way? Behind this, very often, is the fear that too absolute a demand is being made on 'ordinary Christians', the 'non-contemplatives'. But this is the demand, the opportunity, presented by the Gospel to all men and women in every age and culture. It was to 'all' that Jesus revealed the condition for following him. The irony is that 'ordinary' people have been seeking this way outside the Church in their thousands, people who could not find this spiritual teaching in the Church when they went to find it, and so have looked to the East or to forms of Eastern religion imported to the West. When such people hear of their own Western, Christian tradition of meditation they express astonishment: 'Why has this been kept from us?' they ask. The meeting of East and West in the Spirit, which is one of the

9

great features of our time, can only be fruitful if it is realized on the level of deep prayer. This, surely, is also true of the union of the different Christian denominations. The precondition is that we rediscover the richness of our own tradition, and have the courage to embrace it.

But is all this merely religious utopianism? This book is based on the faith that it is not. And the faith is based on the experience we have had as a monastery in communicating and sharing this tradition as a living reality. In our Community here in Montreal we have as our priority four periods of meditation each day that are integrated with our Office and Eucharist. Beyond that, our work is to communicate and share our tradition with whoever wishes to be open to it. The majority of those coming to our weekly meditation groups or of those coming to stay with us as guests or to meditate with us at our communal times of prayer, are people with families, careers, the normal and demanding responsibilities of life. Yet meditation has spoken to them, created a space of silence in their lives each morning and each evening and provided them with structure and discipline in their search for depth and rootedness in Christ. To label them 'active' or 'contemplative' would be ludicrous. They are people who have heard the Gospel and who seek to respond at the deepest level of their being to the infinite gift they have received in the love of God that comes to us in Jesus. They know that this response is a journey into the endless depths of God's love. They have simply begun to make that journey.

This book was stimulated by the response of these people to meditation. The substance of it is a set of tapes we made some years ago in England as an introduction to meditation and a means of encouragement to those who have begun to meditate, especially for those who could not visit or stay long with us. It began therefore with the spoken word and I think that remains the ideal means of communicating this tradition. The mystery into which meditation leads us is a personal mystery, the mystery of our own personhood, which finds its completion in the person of Christ. And so, the more personal the way it is communicated, the closer it is to its source and its goal.

So, I ask you to remember that the words printed in this book originally came to life as spoken words and I hope, in remembering this, they will speak to you from a tradition that must always come alive in our own experience.

The Benedictine Priory   John Main O.S.B.
Montreal
June 1980

INTRODUCTION

Learning to meditate is not just a matter of mastering a technique. It is much more learning to appreciate and respond directly to the depths of your own nature, not human nature in general but your own in particular. Ideally, you should find a teacher who will help to guide you on your pilgrimage. This little book may inspire you to do that.

Being Restored to Ourselves

First we must understand the Christian context of meditation. I am using the term meditation in this instance synonymously with such terms as contemplation, contemplative prayer, meditative prayer, and so on. The essential context of meditation is to be found in the fundamental relationship of our lives, the relationship that we have as creatures with God, our Creator. But most of us have to take a preliminary step before we can begin to appreciate the full wonder and glorious mystery of this fundamental relationship. Most of us have to get into touch with ourselves first, to get into a full relationship with ourselves before we can turn openly to our relationship with God. Putting this another way, we can say that we have first to find, expand, and experience our own capacity for peace, for serenity, and for harmony before we can begin to appreciate our God and Father who is the author of all harmony and serenity.

Meditation is the very simple process by which we prepare

ourselves, in the first instance, to be at peace with ourselves so that we are capable of appreciating the peace of the Godhead within us. The view of meditation that many people are encouraged to take as a means of relaxation, of retaining inner peacefulness throughout the pressures of modern urban life, is not essentially wrong in itself. But if this is all it is seen as being, the view is very limited because, as we become more and more relaxed in ourselves, and the longer we meditate, the more we become aware that the source of our new-found calm in our daily lives is precisely the life of God within us. The degree of peace we possess is directly proportional to our awareness of this fact of life, a fact of human consciousness, common to every man and every woman in the world. But to realize this fact as a present reality in our lives, we have to decide that we want to be at peace. This is the reason for the psalmist's saying: 'Be still and know that I am God.'[1]

This deep inner peacefulness is in a sense more freely available for us today than it was for the Hebrew poet who wrote that psalm, even if our problems are greater and our pace of life faster than his were; and this is because of the great fact of Jesus.

The great conviction of the New Testament is that Jesus by giving us His Spirit has dramatically transformed the fabric of human consciousness. Our redemption by Jesus Christ has opened up for us levels of consciousness that can be described by St Paul only in terms of a totally new creation. As a result of all that Jesus has accomplished for the humanity into whose being He fully entered, we have been quite literally re-created. In Chapter 5 of Paul's letter to the Romans he writes about what God has accomplished in the person of His Son, Jesus:

Therefore, now that we have been justified through faith, let us continue at peace with God through our Lord, Jesus Christ, through whom we have been allowed to enter the

1. Ps. 46:10

14

sphere of God's grace, where we now stand. Let us exult in the hope of the divine splendour that is to be ours . . . because God's love has flooded our inmost heart through the Holy Spirit He has given us.[2]

Just think about this language for a moment and consider the quite staggering claim it is making. 'We have been allowed to enter the sphere of God's grace, where we now stand.' 'God's love has flooded our inmost heart through the Holy Spirit He has given us.' St Paul was no mere theorist. He was a passionate announcer of a real event that he was trying to make all men realize, and his words were urgent indicators of this event as a reality shared by all men. His great conviction is, that the central reality of our Christian faith is the sending of the Spirit of Jesus; indeed our faith is a living faith precisely because the living Spirit of God dwells within us, giving new life to our mortal bodies.

The all-important aim in Christian meditation is to allow God's mysterious and silent presence within us to become more and more not only *a* reality, but *the* reality in our lives; to let it become that reality which gives meaning, shape and purpose to everything we do, to everything we are.

Meditation is a learning process. It is a process of learning to pay attention, to concentrate, to attend. W. H. Auden made the point well when he said that schools were places that should be teaching the spirit of prayer in a secular context. This they would do, he maintained, by teaching people how to concentrate fully and exclusively on whatever was before them, be it poem, picture, maths problem, or leaf under a microscope, and to concentrate on these for their own sake. By the 'spirit of prayer', he meant selfless attention.[3]

In learning to meditate, then, we must pay attention firstly

2. Rom. 5:1–5
3. W. H. Auden, 'A Certain World' (*A Commonplace Book*, Viking Press, New York, 1970), p. 306

to ourselves. We must become fully aware of who we are. If we can really apprehend for a moment the truth that we are created by God, we can begin to sense something of our own potentiality. We have a divine origin. God is our Creator. And in the Christian vision we know that God is not only a once-for-all Creator who creates us and then leaves us to ourselves; but He is also equally our loving Father. This is the truth about ourselves that we commemorate, pay full attention to in meditation. It is only because we forget this fundamental truth that we treat ourselves so trivially for so much of the time, our lives slipping through our fingers while we are either too busy or too bored to remember who we are. The reason why we can become so trivial, and why we can find ourselves and our lives so boring, is simply that we do not pay enough attention to our divine origin, our divine redemption by Jesus who has redeemed us from both triviality and boredom. Nor do we pay attention to our own holiness as temples of the Holy Spirit.

Meditation is the process in which we take time to allow ourselves to become aware of our infinite potential in the context of the Christ-event. As St Paul puts it in Chapter 8 of Romans: 'And those whom He called, He has justified, and to those whom He justified, He has also given His splendour.'[4]

In meditation we open ourselves up to this splendour. Put another way, this means that in meditation we discover both who we are and why we are. In meditation we are not running away from ourselves, we are finding ourselves; we are not rejecting ourselves, we are affirming ourselves. St Augustine put this very succinctly and very beautifully when he said: 'Man must first be restored to himself that, making in himself as it were a stepping-stone, he may rise thence and be borne up to God.'[5]

It is probable that most of us will be familiar with all that I have written so far. We know that God is our Creator. We

4. Rom. 8:30
5. *Retractions* 1 (viii) 3 (Migne PL XXXII)

16

know that Jesus is our Redeemer. We know too that Jesus has sent His Spirit to dwell within us, and we have some sort of idea about our eternal destiny. But the great weakness of most Christians is, that although they know these truths on the level of theological theory, the truths do not really live in their hearts. In other words, these truths that are thought are not realized. We know them as propositions propounded by the Church, by theologians, by preachers from pulpits, or in magazines, but we have not realized them as the grounding truths of our lives, as the sure basis which gives us conviction and authority.

There is nothing essentially new or modern therefore about the Christian context of meditation. Its aim is to turn to our own nature with total concentration, to experience our own creation first-hand and, above all, to turn to and experience the living Spirit of God dwelling in our hearts. The life of that Spirit within us is indestructable and eternal and, in this sense, the truths that make the Christian context of meditation are always new and permanently modern.

In meditation we do not seek to think about God nor do we seek to think about His Son, Jesus, nor do we seek to think about the Holy Spirit. We are trying rather to do something immeasurably greater. By turning aside from everything that is passing, everything that is contingent, we seek not just to think about God, but to be with God, to experience Him as the ground of our being. It is one thing to know that Jesus is the Revelation of the Father, that Jesus is our Way to the Father, but quite another to experience the presence of Jesus within us, to experience the real power of His Spirit within us and, in that experience, to be brought into the presence of His Father and our Father.

Many people today are finding that they have to face the fact that there is an all-important difference between thinking about these truths of the Christian faith and experiencing them, between believing them on hearsay and believing them from our own personal verification. Experiencing and verifying these truths is not just the work of specialists in prayer. St Paul's inspiring and exultant letters were not written to members of an enclosed religious Order, but to the ordinary butchers and bakers of Rome, Ephesus and Corinth.

These are truths that each one of us is called to know for himself, and in meditation we seek to know them.

Learning to be Silent

We now need to take a closer look at the sort of silence that is needed for meditation. Meditation is not the time for words, however beautifully and sincerely phrased. All our words are wholly ineffective when we come to enter into this deep and mysterious communion with God whose own Word within us is before and after all words. 'I am the Alpha and the Omega,' says the Lord.

In order to enter into this holy and mysterious communion with the Word of God dwelling within us, we must first have the courage to become more and more silent. In a deep creative silence we meet God in a way that transcends all our powers of intellect and language. We are all basically aware that we cannot apprehend God by thinking about Him. What the philosopher Alfred Whitehead said of human investigation of time could apply equally to human thought of God. He wrote: 'It is impossible to meditate on time and the mystery of the creative passage of nature without an overwhelming emotion at the limitations of human intelligence.'[1]

The experience of this 'overwhelming emotion' at our own limitations leads us into a silence where we have to listen, to concentrate, to attend rather than to think. The mystery of our relationship with God is one that embraces such a vast canvas that only by developing our capacity for awe-filled and reverential silence will we ever be able to appreciate even a fraction of its wonder. We know that God is intimately with us and we know also that He is infinitely beyond us. It is only through deep and liberating silence that we can reconcile the polarities of this mysterious paradox. And the liberation that we experience in silent prayer is precisely liberation from the inevitably distorting effects of language when we begin to experience God's intimate and transcendent dominion within us. Anyone who has experienced this liberating work of the Spirit knows

1. cf. G. H. Whitrow, *The Nature of Time* (Penguin 1975), p. 144

exactly what St Paul means when he writes to the Romans in Chapter 8: 'It follows, my friends, that our lower nature has no claim upon us; we are not obliged to live on that level.'[2]

He puts it with the same wonderful confidence in His letter to the Colossians in Chapter 1: 'He rescued us from the domain of darkness and brought us away into the kingdom of His dear Son.'[3]

It is because this kingdom is established and is present within us that we can be made free of the limitations of language and thought.

Our attempt to achieve this silence may be difficult. It will almost certainly be prolonged. It is not just a matter of keeping our tongues still but much more of achieving a state of alert stillness in our mind and heart, which is not a state of consciousness familiar to most Westerners. We tend either to be alert or relaxed; rarely are the two states combined in most of us. But in meditation we come to experience ourselves as at one and the same time totally relaxed and totally alert. This stillness is not the stillness of sleep but rather of totally awakened concentration.

If you look at a watchmaker about to perform some deft movement with a fine pair of tweezers, you will notice how still and poised he is as he scrutinizes the inside of the watch through his eyeglass. His stillness, however, is one of complete concentration, serious absorption in what he is doing. Similarly in meditation our stillness is not a state of mere passivity but a state of full openness, full wakefulness to the wonder of our own being, full openness to the wonder of God, the author and the sustainer of our being, and a full awareness that we are at one with God.

Here are some very simple and practical hints. To meditate well you should adopt a comfortable sitting posture; it must be comfortable and relaxed, but not sloppy. The back should be

2. Rom. 8:12
3. Col. 1:13

as straight as possible with the spine in an upright position. Those who possess a fair degree of suppleness and agility may sit on the floor in a cross-legged position. If you sit in a chair, make sure it is one that is upright with comfortable arm-rests. Your breathing should be calm and regular. Allow every muscle in your body to relax. And then, put the mind in tune with the body. The interior dispositions you need are a calm mind and a peaceful spirit, and it is here that the challenge of meditation lies. It is easy enough to sit still, and we must learn to sit quite still, but the real task of meditation is to achieve the harmony of body, mind and spirit. That is what we mean when we talk about the peace of God, a peace that passes all understanding.

The Indian mystic Sri Ramakrishna, who lived in Bengal in the nineteenth century, used to describe the mind as a mighty tree filled with monkeys, all swinging from branch to branch and all in an incessant riot of chatter and movement. When we begin to meditate we recognize that as a wonderfully apt description of the constant whirl going on in our mind. Prayer is not a matter of adding to this confusion by trying to shout it down and covering it with another lot of chatter. The task of meditation is to bring all of this mobile and distracted mind to stillness, silence and concentration, to bring it, that is, into its proper service. This is the aim given us by the psalmist: 'Be still and know that I am God.' To achieve this aim we use a very simple device. It is one that St Benedict drew to the attention of his monks as long ago as the sixth century by directing them to read the *Conferences* of John Cassian.[4]

Cassian recommended anyone who wanted to learn to pray, and to pray continually, to take a single short verse and just to repeat this verse over and over again. In his Tenth Conference, he urges this method of simple and constant repetition as the best way of casting out all distractions and monkey chatter from our mind, in order that it might rest in God.[5]

4. *Rule of St Benedict* 42:6, 13; 73:14
5. Cassian, *Conference* 10:10

21

When I read Cassian on this, I am immediately reminded of the prayer that Jesus approved of when He tells us of the sinner who stood at the back of the temple and prayed in the single phrase: 'Lord, be merciful to me a sinner, Lord be merciful to me a sinner.' He went home 'justified', Jesus tells us, whereas the Pharisee who stood at the front of the temple in loud eloquent prayer did not.[6] The whole of the teaching of Cassian on prayer is based on the Gospels: 'In your prayers do not go on babbling like the heathen, who imagine that the more they say, the more likely they are to be heard. Do not imitate them. Your Father knows what your needs are before you ask him.'[7]

As I have suggested, prayer is not a matter of talking to God, but of listening to Him, or being with Him. It is this simple understanding of prayer that lies behind John Cassian's advice that if we want to pray, to listen, we must become quiet and still, by reciting a short verse over and over again. Cassian received this method as something which was an old, established tradition in his own day and it is an enduring universal tradition. A thousand years after Cassian, the English author of *The Cloud of Unknowing* recommends the repetition of a little word: 'We must pray in the height, depth, length, and breadth of our spirit, [he says] not in many words but in a little word.'[8]

As this idea may be a novel one, and indeed even sound rather strange, let me repeat the basic technique of meditation. Sit down comfortably, relax. Make sure you are sitting upright. Breathe calmly and regularly. Close your eyes and then in your mind begin to repeat the word that you have chosen as your meditation word.

The name for this word in the Eastern tradition is *mantra*. So from now on I will use the phrase 'saying the mantra'. Choosing your word or mantra is of some importance. Ideally,

6. Luke 18:9–14
7. Matt. 6:7–8
8. *The Cloud of Unknowing*, ch. 39

22

again, you should choose your mantra in consultation with your teacher. But there are various mantras which are possible for a beginner. If you have no teacher to help you, then you should choose a word that has been hallowed over the centuries by our Christian tradition. Some of these words were first taken over as mantras for Christian meditation by the Church in its earliest days. One of these is the word 'maranatha'. This is the mantra I recommend to most beginners, the Aramaic word 'maranatha' which means, 'Come Lord. Come Lord Jesus.'

It is the word that St Paul uses to end his first letter to the Corinthians,[9] and the word with which St John ends the book of Revelation.[10] It also has a place in some of the earliest Christian liturgies.[11] I prefer the Aramaic form because it has no associations for most of us and it helps us into a meditation that will be quite free of all images. The name Jesus would be another possibility as a mantra, and so would the word that Jesus Himself used in His prayer, namely, 'Abba'. This is again an Aramaic word which means 'Father'. The important thing to remember about your mantra is to choose it, if possible in consultation with a teacher, and then to keep to it. If you chop and change your mantra you are postponing your progress in meditation.

John Cassian speaks of the purpose of meditation as that of restricting the mind to the poverty of the single verse. A little later, he shows his full meaning in an illuminating phrase. He talks about becoming '*grandly poor*'.[12] Meditation will certainly give you new insights into poverty. As you persevere with the mantra, you will begin to understand more and more deeply, out of your own experience, what Jesus meant when He said, 'Blessed are the poor in spirit.'[13] You will also learn in a very

9. 1 Cor. 16:22
10. Rev. 22:20
11. *Didache* 10:6
12. *Conference* 10:11
13. Matt. 5:3

concrete way the meaning of faithfulness as you persevere in fidelity to the repetition of the mantra.

In meditation, then, we declare our own poverty. We renounce words, thoughts, imaginations and we do so by restricting the mind to the poverty of one word, and thus the process of meditation is simplicity itself. In order to experience its benefits, it is necessary to meditate twice a day and every day, without fail. Twenty minutes is the minimum time for meditation, twenty-five or thirty minutes is about the average time. It is also helpful to meditate regularly in the same place and also at the same time every day because this helps a creative rhythm in our life to grow, with meditation as a kind of pulse-beat sounding the rhythm. But when all is said and done, the most important thing to bear in mind about meditation is to remain faithfully repeating the mantra throughout the time put aside for it, throughout the time of what the author of *The Cloud of Unknowing* called 'the time of the work'.[14]

14. *The Cloud of Unknowing*, ch. 4–7, 36–40

The Power of the Mantra

All Christian prayer is basically the experience of being filled with the Spirit, and so, in any talking or thinking about prayer we should fix the spotlight firmly on the Spirit not ourselves. In Romans 8, Paul puts it this way: 'We do not even know how to pray, but through our inarticulate groans the Spirit Himself is pleading for us, and God who searches our inmost being knows what the Spirit means.'[1]

This experience of prayer, of being filled with the Spirit, increases our capacity for wonder and our capacity for understanding the transcendent potential of our own being. There is a sense in which we can say that before prayer our principal conviction about reality is of its limitations. We see everything in its transient dimension passing away from us. We feel ourselves caught in the Buddhist *samsara*, the unavoidable cycle of birth and death. But after prayer our principal conviction about ourselves and the whole of creation is of the infinite capacity in everything to mediate the wonder and splendour of God.

A marvellous thing then happens. With this growing sense of wonder at God's power within us there comes an ever-deepening awareness of the harmony, the creative wholeness that we possess, and we begin to feel that we know ourselves for the first time. But the truly transcendent nature of this discovery is that we do not begin to appreciate our own personal harmony alone, but we begin to experience it as a new capacity for true empathy, a capacity to be at peace with others, and indeed at peace with the whole of creation.

In meditation our way forward to this growing awareness of the Spirit praying within us lies simply in our deepening fidelity to the saying of the mantra. It is the faithful repetition of our word that integrates our whole being. It does so because it brings us to the silence, the concentration, the necessary level

1. Rom. 8:26–7

25

of consciousness that enable us to open our mind and heart to the work of the love of God in the depth of our being.

To understand the process once more, begin by sitting down comfortably and calmly and then start to say your mantra in the silence of your mind: Maranatha, Ma-ra-na-tha. Repeat the word calmly, serenely, and above all faithfully for the full time of your meditation, that is for about twenty to thirty minutes. We begin by saying the mantra in the mind. For modern Western man who has so restricted himself to the mental modality, there is no other way to begin. But as we progress with simple fidelity, the mantra begins to sound not so much in our head but rather in our heart. That is, it seems to become rooted in the very depths of our being.

The spiritual masters of the Orthodox Church have always emphasized the essential importance of what they call the 'prayer of the heart'. They see the fundamental consequence of the fall as the separation of mind and heart in man, and indeed this sense of inner division pervades Western man's self-understanding. The twentieth-century word for sin is alienation. If we ponder the wide spectrum of meaning that word has for us, the Marxist sense, the sense of powerlessness, meaninglessness, self-estrangement, the failure to find adequate norms for social or personal relationships, and if we ponder these conceptions we have of ourselves, we will realize how deeply divided we are. In the context of meditation all these many alienations resolve into that one basic division between mind and heart. The mind is our organ for truth; the heart our organ for love. But they cannot work independently of each other without filling us with a sense of failure, dishonesty, deep boredom or frenetic evasion of ourselves through busyness.

The truly religious understanding of man is not found in terms of reward and punishment, but in terms of wholeness and division. The supreme religious insight in East and West is that all our alienations are resolved, and all our thinking and feeling powers united, in the heart. One of the *Upanishads* says that the mind must be kept in the heart.[2] St Paul proclaims the same vision of unity in man when he gives love the supremacy over every other dimension and activity.[3] The holy men of the Orthodox Church see the essential task of the Christian life as being to restore this unity to man with a mind and heart integrated through prayer. The mantra provides this integrating power. It is like a harmonic that we sound in the depths of our spirit, bringing us to an ever-deepening sense of our own wholeness and central harmony. It leads us to the source of this harmony, to our centre, rather as a radar bleep leads an aircraft home through thick fog. It also rearranges us, in the sense that it brings all our powers and faculties into line with each other just as a magnet drawn over iron filings pulls them into their proper force fields.

In starting to meditate, we have three preliminary aims. The first is simply to say the mantra for the full duration of the meditation. It will probably take some time to achieve this first stage and we will have to learn patience in the meantime. Meditating is an entirely natural process for all of us, for just as our physical growth takes place in its own natural rhythm, with variations for each individual, so does our prayer life develop quite naturally. We cannot force anything to happen but must simply say the mantra without haste, or expectation.

The second aim is to say the mantra throughout the meditation without interruption, while remaining quite calm in the face of all distractions. In this phase the mantra resembles a plough that continues resolutely across the rough field of our mind, undeflected by any obtrusion or disturbance.

And the third of these preliminary aims is to say the mantra for the entire time of the meditation, quite free of all distractions. The surface areas of the mind are now in tune with the deep peacefulness at the core of our being. The same harmonic sounds throughout our being. In this state we have passed

2. *Maitri Upanishad* 6:24
3. I Cor. 13:13

beyond thought, beyond imagination, and beyond all images. We simply rest with the Reality, the realized presence of God Himself dwelling within our hearts.

As you read this, you may think that it is a very ambitious endeavour. But it is an endeavour we make in response to the invitation of Jesus to leave all things and to follow Him.[4] Leaving all these thoughts and imaginations, we seek to follow Him in the purity of our heart. Meditation in this sense is a purifying process. In Blake's phrase: 'If the doors of perception were cleansed, everything will appear to man as it is, infinite.'[5] By means of the mantra we leave behind all passing images and learn to rest in the infinity of God Himself. St Paul urges us to do just this when he implores us in Romans 12:

> . . . by God's mercy to offer your very selves to Him: a living sacrifice, dedicated and fit for His acceptance, the worship offered by mind and heart. Adapt yourselves no longer to the pattern of this present world, but let your minds be remade and your whole nature thus transformed.[6]

This transformation of our nature is put before us as a real and an immediate possibility. It is also the essential Christian experience, the experience of being born again in the Holy Spirit, being born again when we realize the power of the living Spirit of God within us. By becoming aware of Its presence within us we, as it were, set It free to work freely within us, to transform us. The mantra is simply the device which leads us to this central Christian experience, leading us to know from our own experience that God's love has flooded our inmost heart through the Holy Spirit He has given us.[7]

It is so easy for a modern Christian to read words like those of St Paul with veiled hearts and closed minds, never knowing

4. Luke 9:23
5. *A Memorable Fancy: The Ancient Tradition*
6. Rom. 12:1–2
7. Rom. 5:5

for himself what Paul so exultantly knew from within and tried to communicate to us. We may accept it all notionally. We may even preach it. But if we lack authority and confidence and courage, it is because we have not ourselves experienced its immediate and enduring reality. 'Know it', Paul tells us, 'though it is beyond knowledge.'[8] We have to prepare our hearts to receive the wonderful message of the Gospel in all its fullness. And until we have expanded our consciousness, we will be incapable of taking in anything of the grand scale of the message of our redemption, and we will be incapable too of knowing what the traditional religious language we use really means. Until an expansion of our consciousness takes place our minds and hearts will be too limited, too absorbed in day-to-day trivia. Meditation is precisely the way we need to follow in order to expand our hearts, broaden our vision and, as Blake said, 'cleanse the doors of our perception'.

This should give you some idea of the perspective which regular meditation can open up. There are, of course, stages we pass through en route to the full realization of the Kingdom of God within us. But we should not waste time and energy worrying about what stage we have reached. 'Unless you become like little children, you cannot enter the Kingdom of Heaven.'[9] What we must do is to begin to meditate, to begin to open ourselves up to the love of God and its power. To do this, all we need to do is to begin to say the mantra, lovingly and in a deep spirit of faith.

The stages of our progress in meditation will come about in their own time. God's own time. We in fact only hinder this progression by becoming too self-conscious about our stage of development. This is where a teacher is of immense help for keeping you on a straight course. But basically your teacher has only one instruction to give you and that is: to say your mantra. More than this is simply encouragement and comfort

8. Eph. 3:18
9. Mark 10:15

29

until the mantra is rooted in your consciousness. The path of enlightenment is one we tread for ourselves. Each person wins wisdom for himself. The teacher is there to keep you steadily going forward. The word 'guru' itself, dispeller of darkness, means the one who is steady.

The greatest temptation of all is to complicate ourselves. 'Unless you become like little children. . .' Meditation simplifies us, simplifies us to the point where we can receive the fullness of truth and the fullness of love. It prepares us and enables us to listen with childlike attention to the Spirit of Jesus within us. As we persevere in meditation, we enter ever more deeply into relationship with this Spirit, with God who is love dwelling in our hearts, enlightening us and vitalizing us.

The Fullness of Life

When a person looks at meditation for the first time from the outside, he often mistakes it for just another form of fashionable egocentric introversion. It often appears to the outsider that the meditator goes into himself so much, so often, that he is rather tastelessly betraying a deep-rooted and unhealthy narcissim. That it should appear like this is really quite understandable, because, as we have seen in St Augustine's phrase, man must first be 'restored to himself that he might rise thence to God'. In meditating we do affirm our faith in the gift of our own creation. We recognize the wonder of our own being, and we are prepared to spend time and to persevere in coming to terms with it. For Jesus has told us that His mission was to bring us fullness of life: 'I have come that men may have life, and may have it in all its fullness.'[1] In making this declaration. He assures us in the same Gospel of St John, that it is He Himself who is the Way to this fullness. He tells us that He is the Light of the world and, 'no follower of mine shall wander in the dark; he shall have the light of life.'[2] In beginning to meditate we are declaring a courageous acceptance of this invitation of Jesus and we enter into our meditation on each occasion as the twin process of vitalization and enlightenment.

What emerges so triumphantly from the teaching of Jesus, and from the understanding of that teaching by the early Church, is that this Life and this Light are quite literally to be found within each of us. St Paul writes, not to specialists, nor to a group of Carthusians or Carmelites, but to the ordinary citizens of Rome: 'Moreover, if the Spirit of Him who raised Jesus from the dead dwells within you, then the God who raised Christ Jesus from the dead will also give new life to your mortal bodies through his indwelling spirit.'[3]

1. John 10:10
2. John 8:12
3. Rom. 8:11

Meditation summons us to open our hearts to this light and to this life by the very simple expedient of paying attention; that is, paying attention to their presence within us. We pay attention to our own true nature, and by becoming fully conscious of the union of our nature with Christ, we become fully ourselves. By becoming fully ourselves we enter the fullness of life Jesus has brought us. We come to appreciate, in the reverent silence of our prayer, that we are infinitely holy as temples of God's own Spirit. We learn to remember who we are, and that our vocation is to look upon and contemplate the Godhead itself and thus to be ourselves divinized. As the third Eucharistic prayer expresses it: 'On that day we shall see You our God as You are and we shall become like You.' The great masters of prayer in the Christian tradition have understood prayer in this way as a discovery of self that takes us far beyond narrow self-consciousness, a discovery made by making of ourselves a stepping-stone. The twelfth-century Scot, Richard of St Victor, expresses it so clearly and simply:

The rational soul finds in itself the chief and principal mirror for seeing God. Let him who desires to see God wipe his mirror and cleanse his heart. When the mirror has been cleansed and examined a long time carefully, a brightness of the divine light begins to shine through to him and a great beam of illumination not known hitherto appears before our eyes.[4]

Saying the mantra is just this process of polishing the mirror, the mirror within us, so that our heart becomes fully open to the work of God's love for us, fully reflecting the light of that love. We must understand very clearly that the first step in this process is to set our own house in order. Meditation is thus a process of self-discovery. By faithfulness to the twice-daily

4. Richard of St Victor, *Selected Writings on Contemplation*, ed. Kirchberger. (Faber & Faber 1957), p. 102

meditation we find that in the Christian tradition self-discovery and self-affirmation are the realizations of our own true grandeur and true splendour in Christ. St Catherine of Genoa put it this way: 'My me is God nor do I know my selfhood save in Him.'[5] In the Indian tradition the same understanding finds expression in the assertion that our first task is the discovery of our own true inner self, the Atman, which is the means of becoming aware of union with the ultimate universal self, which is Brahman, which is God.

Similarly, in the Christian perspective, we see the great task of prayer as the realization of our intimate union with God, our Father, through Christ in the Spirit. St Gregory wrote of St Benedict that, 'he dwelt within himself always in the presence of his Creator and not allowing his eyes to gaze on distractions.'[6] There is something extraordinarily attractive about the description. It reveals an understanding of the Father of Western Monasticism as above all a man of prayer. 'He dwelt within himself.' That tells us that, in Gregory's view, Benedict had realized a wholeness and harmony that had dispelled all false ideas, all illusions about himself, illusions which are necessarily outside of ourselves.

The task we have is to find our way back to our creative centre where wholeness and harmony are realized, to dwell within ourselves, leaving behind all the false images of ourselves such as what we think we are or what we think we might have been, because these have an unreal existence outside of us. Remaining within ourselves in this sense of illusion-shattering honesty and simplicity, leads us to remain always in the presence of our Creator. This is where the mantra is a device of such importance. As we learn to root it in our consciousness, the mantra becomes like a key that opens the door to the secret chamber of our heart. At first, in the set times of our meditation, both morning and evening, saying the mantra is work. We

5. cf. E. Underhill, *The Mystics of the Church*. (James Clarke 1975), p. 51
6. *Dialogues* (Book II) ch. 3

have to learn to become thoroughly familiar with it. But as we progress, as we begin to sound it and to listen to it, then, each and every time we recite it, we enter into and remain in our heart. Thus, by merely calling the mantra to mind at other times of the day, we enter straight away into the presence of the Creator who dwells within us; 'I am with you always,' says the Lord.[7]

Learning to pray is learning to live as fully as possible in the present moment. In meditation we seek to enter as fully as we can into the now, and in entering into the now to live as fully as possible with the now-risen and ever-loving Lord Jesus. To be thus fully committed to the present moment is to find ourselves, to enter into ourselves, to dwell within ourselves; and this we do by renouncing thought and image. In meditation we are not thinking about the past, neither our own past nor anyone else's, nor are we thinking about the future, our own nor anyone else's. In meditation we are wholly inserted into the present, and there we live to the fullness of our capability, our consciousness expanding as we entertain the Lord of Life. The experience of this being wholly conscious is an experience of unity and simplicity.

First of all, we are conscious of our own wholeness and unity, and as we stay in this state of consciousness we experience a growing awareness of our unity with all persons, with all creation, with our Creator. As we rest in this state of heightened consciousness we begin to understand more and more of what St Paul meant when he wrote such words as these to the Ephesians: 'So may you attain to fullness of being, the fullness of God Himself.'[8] We begin to understand that to be, is to be here and now.

This is a journey we have to make, a pilgrimage which is a pilgrimage to our own heart. It is a pilgrimage that requires a certain amount of nerve. As Eliot put it in *The Four Quartets*:

7. Matt. 28:20
8. Eph. 3:19

34

'Human kind cannot bear very much reality.'[9] Meditation is our way of leaving behind all the illusions about ourselves, about others, and about God, which we have either created for ourselves or received from the past.

As we advance into the silence we begin to experience the true meaning of the words of Jesus: 'The man who would find his life must first lose it.' And again. 'Anyone who wishes to be a follower of mine, must leave self behind.'[10] It requires nerve to become really quiet. To learn just to say the mantra and turn away from all thought requires courage. But as we persevere we discover that the poverty of the mantra leads us to a really radical simplicity that makes this courage possible, for we are capable of greater courage than we usually believe of ourselves. But meditation is the prayer of faith, because we have to leave ourselves behind before the Other appears and with no pre-packaged guarantee that He will appear. The essence of poverty consists in this risk of annihilation. This is the leap of faith from ourselves to the Other. This is the risk involved in all loving.

There comes a delicate moment in our progress when we begin to understand the totality of the commitment involved in self-surrendering prayer, when we see the total poverty involved in the mantra. This is a moment again where the help of a teacher could be critical. But in essence the invitation to meditate is a simple one. We meditate simply to prepare ourselves to receive that fullness and life and light for which we were created.

9. From 'Burnt Norton I', *The Four Quartets*. Faber & Faber 1979
10. Mark 9:34–6

MEDITATION: THE CHRISTIAN EXPERIENCE

THE SELF
I Corinthians 2:14

'Know then, thyself; presume not God to scan. The proper study of mankind is man.' When Alexander Pope wrote those lines in his *Essay on Man* he enjoyed a far greater trust in Man's essential reasonableness than prevails today, and his confidence in mankind was something more than a merely rational humanism. It assumed a common faith in the essential goodness of man, in the fundamentally positive meaning of life and a common sense of the presence of an order in the affairs of men and of a harmony in the unfolding energies of the cosmos. Modern man's confidence in himself is much less secure. He is more likely to see himself as having unleashed powers he can no longer control and of having exploited his natural resources so wantonly that he is in danger of exhausting them by the time his grandchildren have reached maturity.

But perhaps the primary cause of his confusion and alienation is that he has lost the support of a common faith in man's essential goodness, reasonableness and inner integrity, indeed of any common faith at all. Where he finds his community, his community of thought, and of feeling (and find it or concoct it he must) is much more likely to be in self-recrimination and prophecies of doom; or in protest, which is usually a protestation against and seldom a witness for. Now this is perhaps a part of our fallen nature that we have to live with, namely, that much common sympathy between people is built upon this negative base of sharing the same fears and the same prejudices. But it is possible to enjoy a deeper, more positive fraternity which is rooted in a common awareness of the potential of the human spirit rather than the limitations of human life. It is the specifically Christian task to sink the roots of this awareness deep into modern man's understanding of himself and his world.

If our Christianity is more than just another ideology on a comparative religion programme, if it is a life we receive and mediate, we have to ask ourselves a question: 'Why is it that the power of this risen life of Jesus is not being mediated through us to transform the negative energies of modern man's self-rejection into the positive awareness of the depth and richness of his own spirit?'

In the ancient myth of the Fisher King, the land has been blighted by a curse that has frozen all the waters and turned the earth to stone. No power in the land can lift the curse and the king sits silently fishing through a hole in the ice, despondent, waiting. One day a stranger approaches and asks the king the redemptive question. Immediately the waters thaw and the earth softens.

Religious people have so often pretended to have all the answers. They have seen their mission as being to persuade, to enforce, to level differences and perhaps even to impose uniformity. There is really something of the Grand Inquisitor in most religious people. But when religion begins to bully or to insinuate, it has become unspiritual because the first gift of the Spirit, creatively moving in man's nature, is freedom and frankness; in Biblical language, liberty and truth. The modern Christian's mission is to resensitize his contemporaries to the presence of a spirit within themselves. He is not a teacher in the sense that he is providing answers that he has looked up in the back of a book. He is truly a teacher when, having found his own spirit, he can inspire others to accept the responsibility of their own being, to undergo the challenge of their own innate longing for the Absolute, to find their own spirit.

To be able to do this work of inspiration, it is not enough to be courageous, though courage is needed. Moses cried to God in fear, 'But they will never believe me; they will say, "the Lord did not appear to you." '[1] Nor is it enough to be eloquent, though eloquence will be given. No human quality can of itself undertake to ask the redemptive question. Whenever a man discovers himself acting as an instrument of the Word, it is when he knows himself directed by the Spirit. And to know this is to have seen his own spirit; it is to have glimpsed the depths of his own spirit and to have known that his spirit is of God.

To know this, though as St Paul said, it is beyond knowledge, is to be born over again in Spirit, and to undergo the seminal Christian experience which ignited the early Church and burst into the preaching of St Paul and of the saints down the ages. It is the experience that begins in the silent encounter within ourselves. For it, only one condition needs to be fulfilled, namely, that we subject everything else to it: possessions, possessiveness, desire and honour, body and mind. We renounce everything in order to attain to that complete simplicity that demands not less than everything, which opens our eyes to the living presence of the loving Lord Jesus within us and His Spirit ever returning into communion with the Father. 'If a man does not possess the Spirit of Christ, he is no Christian,'[2] St Paul tells us. The redemptive question the Christian asks to set his contemporaries free rises from the depths of his experience of spirit and inspires the unspiritual to discover those same depths within themselves. We can only talk though of what we have seen. The Gospel of John reminds us that it is only spirit that can give birth to spirit.[3]

1. Exod. 4:1
2. Rom. 8:9
3. John 3:6

Few generations have been so introverted and self-analytical as our own, and yet modern man's study of himself is notoriously unproductive. The reason for this, as I have been suggesting, is that it has been radically unspiritual; that is, it has not been conducted in the light of the Spirit, it has not taken account of that real and fundamental dimension of man's nature. Without spirit there is no productivity, no creativity, no possibility of growth. The Christian's duty is to point this out, and to be able to do so with the authority of one who really knows what spirit is, but only because he knows his own spirit and that infinite expansion of man's spirit that takes place when it responds to the presence of the Spirit of God, from whom it derives its being.

Such a Christian possesses power, the power of the Risen Lord, and it is a power that consists in the liberation of spirit that is achieved through the cycle of death and resurrection, through our participation in the dying and rising of Jesus. What dies as we persevere in opening ourselves to the Spirit is our narrow limited ego and all the petty concerns and ambitions with which it boards over the shaft of our being; what dies is the fear we experience as we see the light emerging from this shaft; what dies is everything that obstructs us from realizing life, life in all its fullness. This discovery of our own spirit, our real self, is an experience that consists of an indescribable joy, the joy of liberation. But the loss of self which makes it possible, the erosion and the shedding of long familiar illusions require those qualities which have so important a place in St Paul's teaching: boldness, courage, faith, commitment and perseverance. It is these qualities, mundane rather than heroic, which enable us to persevere in the daily commitment to the pilgrimage, the fidelity to the twice-daily meditation and the 'grand poverty' to which the mantra leads us. These are not home-grown qualities, they are given to us by love, gifts from the Spirit to lead us to Himself, to deeper love. There is no way to truth or to the Spirit that is not the way of love. God is love.

In discovering his own spirit, man is led to his creative centre whence his essence is being emanated and renewed by the loving overflow of the life of the Trinity. Man finds his own spirit fully only in the light of the One Spirit, just as he is sustained and expanded by the love of his fellow-men and knows himself when he allows himself to be known by them. To see himself, a man must look at another, for the way to selfhood is the way of otherness.

It is not enough to concur with these statements merely as conceptual realities. Our rational process can, of course, by the guidance of the Spirit itself, begin the process of our rebirth in Spirit. It can lead us to uncover and expand our own spirit, but no merely conceptual expression is in itself the experience of our true self. No intellectual self-analysis can substitute for real self-knowledge in the ground of our being. There are many words and terms from many traditions in which we can try to express the purpose of meditation, of prayer. Here I am suggesting only this preliminary purpose, that in the silence of our meditation, in our attentiveness to the Other, in our patient waiting, we find our own spirit.

The fruit of this discovery is very rich. We know then that we share in the nature of God, that we are called ever deeper into the joyous depths of His own self-communion, and this is no peripheral purpose of the Christian life. In fact, if it is Christian and if it is alive, our life must place this at the very centre of all we do and aim to do. 'Our whole business in this life', said St Augustine, 'is to restore to health the eye of the heart whereby God may be seen.'[4] This eye is our spirit. Our first task, in the realization of our own vocation and in the expansion of the kingdom among our contemporaries, is to find our own spirit because this is our life-line with the Spirit of God. In doing so, we come to realize that we participate in the divine progression and that we share the dynamic essence of God's still point: harmony, light, joy and love.

4. *Serm. (de Script, N.T.)* 88 v 5.

To fulfill this destiny we are called to transcendence, to that continuous state of liberty and perpetual renewal, that complete passing into the other. In our meditation we begin to enter this state by our renunciation of words, images, thoughts and even self-consciousness, everything which is in itself contingent, ephemeral, tangential. In meditation we must have the courage to attend solely to the Absolute, the abiding and the central. To find our own spirit, we must be silent and allow our spirit to emerge from the darkness to which it has been banished. To transcend we must be still. The stillness is our pilgrimage and the way of the pilgrim is the mantra.

THE SON
2 Corinthians 5:17

'It is better to be silent and real than to talk and be unreal,' wrote St Ignatius of Antioch in the first century,[1] and our contemporary situation must surely bear this out. Authority, conviction, personal verification, which are the indispensable qualities of the Christian witness are not to be found in books, in discussions or on cassettes, but rather in an encounter with ourselves in the silence of our own spirit.

If modern man has lost his experience of spirit, pneuma or essence in which his own irreducible and absolute being consists, it is because he has lost his experience of and capacity for silence. There are few statements about the spiritual reality which can claim a universal agreement. But this one has received the same formulation in almost all traditions, namely, that it is only in accepting silence that man can come to know his own spirit, and only in abandonment to an infinite depth of silence that he can be revealed to the source of his spirit in which multiplicity and division disappear. Modern man is often deeply threatened by silence as what Eliot called, 'the growing terror of nothing to think about,'[2] and everyone has to face this fear when they begin to meditate.

First, we must confront with some shame the chaotic din of a mind ravaged by so much exposure to trivia and distraction. Persevering through this in fidelity to the mantra, we then encounter a darker level of consciousness, of repressed fears and anxieties. The radical simplicity of the mantra clears this too. But our first inclination is always to retreat from the dawn of self-knowledge and, as Walter Hilton very graphically expressed it, 'this is not surprising, for if a man came home to his

1. Eph. ch. 15
2. 'East Coker III', *The Four Quartets*

house and found nothing but a smoking fire and a nagging wife, he would quickly run out again.'[3]

In entering upon these first two levels, of surface distractions and subconscious anxiety, we risk being bruised. But in entering into the next, into our own silence, we risk everything, for we risk our very being: 'So I said to my soul, "Be still."' The stillness of mind and body to which the mantra guides us is a preparation for entering this silence, and for our progression through the spheres of silence to see with wonder the light of our own spirit, and to know that light as something beyond our spirit and yet the source of it. This is a pilgrimage through our spheres of silence that we undertake in faith, putting our entire trust in what is only a dim apprehension of the authentic, the real, yet confident in doing so because it is authentic.

In saying the mantra, we lay down our life for the sake of Him we have not yet seen.[4] Blessed are they who believe and act on their belief though they have not yet seen. In saying the mantra we are plunged into a silence that explores our infinite poverty of mind and spirit, revealing our absolute dependence on another. We are led from depth to depth of purifying simplification until, having contacted the very ground of our being, we find the life we laid down and the self we surrendered in the Other.

St Paul claimed to carry the dying of Christ within himself and it was because of the authenticity of that perception that his witness to Christ was radiant with risen life.[5] It is precisely in this dying of Jesus that we all participate. St Luke's Gospel emphasizes that Jesus called upon all to renounce self and to take up their cross daily.[6] To that call we respond when we meditate every day. We mislead ourselves and others if we try to play down the extremity of the Christian vocation and the

3. *The Scale of Perfection* (see Bibliography)
4. I Pet. 1:8
5. 2 Cor. 4:10
6. Luke 9:23

total demand it makes. If we have been directed by the Spirit to undertake this pilgrimage, and every Christian is chosen to do so, then it must be with the mature understanding of what is at stake. As we enter the silence within us, having allowed ourselves to become aware of its presence in the first place, we are entering a void in which we are unmade. We cannot remain the person we were or thought we were. But we are, in fact, not being destroyed but awakened to the eternally fresh source of our being. We become aware that we are being created, that we are springing from the Creator's hand and returning to Him in love.

In the silence, we are being prepared for this awakening which is an encounter with the fullness and the splendour of Jesus in that fully awakened state to which the Resurrection led Him, because no one comes to the Father of all except through the Son in whom all creation comes into being. But even if we know intellectually that this is the purpose of the silence, at the time our actual experience is of the void. In the beginning, we know reduction not expansion, a shedding of qualities and a contraction to the point of pure being in pure poverty of spirit, a cataclysmic simplicity.

The Christian carries this dying within him as he goes about his daily routine, not in a self-dramatizing or self-obsessed way, but with a joyful awareness that more and more deeply suffuses his whole being, that the degree to which he dies to himself in this void is the degree to which he is revivified in the transcendent life of the completely free man, Jesus. 'Though our outward humanity is in decay, yet day by day we are inwardly renewed.'[7] Within the structure of our daily life, this inward renewal of which St Paul speaks is the purpose and fruit of our twice-daily meditation. We are literally made new in the fact of entering into the ever-deeper centres of being, and of knowing ever more fully the harmony of all our qualities and energies in that ultimate centre of our being which is the centre and

7. 2 Cor. 4:16

44

source of all being, the centre of the Trinitarian love. 'When anyone is united to Christ', Paul wrote to the Corinthians, 'there is a new world.'[8]

As the Christian enters into the cycle of death and resurrection more thoroughly, he becomes more aware of its universal truth, that it is the model of all being. He begins to appreciate what Mystery is. In order to become fully opened to the force of this universal cycle, we need to understand that it is completed at every level of every life, and in all of the countless ways in which we can examine or apprehend the meaning of our own life. It is, for example, the cycle upon which each half-hour of meditation is based, a death to the possessiveness and triviality occupying our ego and a rising to the liberty and significance that dawn when we find ourselves by looking fully at the Other. It is, too, the cycle upon which a whole lifetime of prayer can be seen on a larger scale. We are dying and rising to new life every day as we participate in the evolution of God's plan for each of his creatures.

Yet it is also true that there is only one death and one rising, that which Jesus underwent for all creation. The Word proceeds from silence and it returns to the unfathomable silence and limitless love of the Father, the cycle of issuing and return upon which every life-cycle in creation is based, the cycle in which creation exists at every moment, could it but see this with a pure heart. But the Word does not return under the same conditions. In revealing Himself to man in the depths of man's own being, which are the depths of God, the Word fulfils the purpose of the Father from whose silence He and, in Him, creation proceed. It is the purpose of our being of which we have read a thousand times in Paul's words to the Ephesians and yet can never fully fathom:

In Christ He chose us before the world was founded, to be dedicated, to be without blemish in his sight, to be full of

8. 2 Cor. 5:17

45

love; and He destined us, such was His will and pleasure, to be accepted as His sons through Jesus Christ, in order that the glory of His gracious gift, so graciously bestowed upon us in His Beloved might redound to His praise.[9]

It is a stupefying claim that our meaning is somehow involved in the meaning of God Himself, and we need to have the courage that only utter simplicity affords in order to accept it. No egoism or complexity can awaken to this revelation: 'Unless you become like little children, you cannot enter the kingdom of Heaven.' We know that this claim is authentic because of our communion with the Word, the Son. All things and all men return to the Father through the Son and of the Son, St John tells us that: 'Through Him all things came to be; no single thing was created without Him.'[10] So just as He is the prime and ultimate expression of the Father, Jesus is also the hinge upon which the universe and all being swings back to the Father, its source. It is through our incorporation in the body of Christ in this swing-back to the Father that we are destined to be accepted as sons of God.

In its essential significance, the aim of meditation is just this: the realization of our total incorporation in Jesus Christ, in the cycle of his utterance by, and return to, the Father. The qualities we need in this fundamental encounter between ourselves and the ground of our being are attentiveness and receptivity. In order to realize our complete incorporation with the Word, we have not only to listen to its silence, the silence within us, but also to allow the cycle of its life to be completed in us and to lead us into the depth of its silence. There in the silence of the Word we share His experience of hearing Himself eternally spoken by the Father.

This is why the life of Jesus is of such meaning and why Scripture's record of His life is of such value. The experience

9. Eph. 1:4–6
10. John 1:3

of Jesus of Nazareth in awakening to Himself, entering the spheres of silence within Himself, finding His own Spirit and the source of His Spirit, this experience is the experience of every man reborn in spirit. And it is, within the unimaginable design of the Father, the self-same experience. The wonder of creation is found, not in a succession of awakenings, but in the single all-inclusive awakening of Jesus, the Son, to the Father.

Our language is wholly inadequate and our thought too self-conscious to reflect the simplicity and actuality of this cycle of dying and rising. But it is not language or thought we need. We need only to become aware of the mystery within us, the silence in which we see our own spirit. Our path into this silence is the one little word of the mantra.

THE SPIRIT
I Corinthians 6:19

The Gospel of Jesus is different from every other programme of salvation precisely because it is personal. Jesus is a person, not a symbol or an archetype, and the way of salvation is our personal encounter with the person of Jesus in experiencing His all-redemptive love.

Because this is so, we know that we are called to become full persons, to become fully ourselves so that our encounter with Jesus may be fully personal, fully mature. There is, of course, nothing narrowly individualistic about growing into full personhood. The human race is formed in such a way that the whole of humanity reaches its fulfilment in the individual, while the individual is realized only by knowing himself incorporate in the whole. In the mystery of all personhood there is this central truth, that the fully realized individual participates in the life of the whole. The communal corporate authority of the Church is derived from this truth, that is, from the depth to which her members have become persons, have actually experienced their own salvation in terms of the depth of the redemptive love of Jesus within them. We are all summoned to this experience here and now and it is our pre-eminent task to dispose ourselves for it. In our own day, this means transferring our conscious hopes for a renewal of the Church's relevance and effectiveness in the world from politics to prayer, from mind to heart, from committees to communities, from preaching to silence.

In fact, of course, the priority of prayer, of personal authentication, is a perennial one. 'To this end are celebrated the holy mysteries, to this end, the Word of God is preached, to this end, are the moral exhortations of the Church made,' wrote St Augustine.[1] And 'this end', as we have seen was 'to restore to health the eye of the heart whereby God may be seen'.

1. *Serm. (de Script. N.T.)* 88 V 5; vi, 6

48

Every personal loving relationship has its source in the movement from lover to beloved, though it has its consummation in a wholly simple communion. If the Christian mystery depended upon the strength of our desire for God for its authenticity, it would be no more than a nostalgia for the numinous. But the actuality of our faith derives from the initiative that God has taken. 'The love I speak of', wrote St John, 'is not our love for God, but the love He showed to us in sending His Son.'[2] As long as our faith is seen as comprising a movement from man to God, we can only remain self-centred, earthbound. But in apprehending it as the movement from God to man we discover ourselves caught up in that movement, in its own depths, self-transcending and returning to the Father through the Son. Another name for this movement is love.

The first step in personhood then is to allow ourselves to be loved. It was to facilitate this that the Holy Spirit was sent into the human heart, to touch it, to awaken it, to draw man's mind into its redemptive light. The sending of the Spirit was a resurrection event and so continues as freshly today as it did 'late that Sunday evening', as St John tells us, when the disciples were together behind locked doors and Jesus came and breathed on them saying: 'Receive the Holy Spirit.'[3] The natural lethargy and self-evasiveness of man, his reluctance to allow himself to be loved are, like the locked doors, no impediments to the Holy Spirit. The Spirit has been sent into the human heart, and it lives out the divine mystery there for as long as God sustains man in being. In the heart of the utterly evil man, were there such a man, the Holy Spirit would still be crying: 'Abba, Father', without ceasing.[4]

In His resurrection and return to the Father, Jesus, the man, our brother, transcended every limitation of the human condition, the limitations of fear and ignorance, no less than those

2. I John 4:10
3. John 20:19–22
4. Gal. 4:6

49

of time and space. He rose to a universal presence in the centre of all things. In man He achieved a living personal presence at the centre of man's being which we know as the heart; and in man His presence is different from His presence in matter without consciousness. In us He lives as in a conscious being capable of expansion of consciousness, and of recognizing and responding on the level of the personal. The presence of Jesus within us, His Holy Spirit, calls out to us to become fully conscious of this level of our being. In the twinkling of an eye, we awaken to ourselves, to the Spirit dwelling in us, and thence to consciousness of the communion within God Himself in which we are called to share. And so, we awaken not to a platonic aloneness but to a complete communion of all beings in Being itself.

We begin with a dim awareness of the stirring of the Spirit in our heart, the presence of Another by which we know ourselves. In awakening to its full reality, in listening to our heart, we awaken to the living proof of our faith justifying that first dim awareness, that first hope. And, as St Paul told the Romans: 'This proof is the ground of hope. Such a hope is no mockery because God's love has flooded our inmost heart through the Holy Spirit He has given us.'[5] The intoxication of Paul's language is the intoxication of his personal awakening to the Reality of the Spirit, to the experience of the joy released, pressed down and flowing over, which Jesus preached and communicates through His Spirit. It is the intoxication of prayer.

We have come to think of prayer largely as our movement to God, as an activity that we are responsible for, a duty we perform to please God or to appease Him. There can be an element of charm, of childish sincerity in this, but true prayer eschews the sentimental. We have been summoned to a spiritual maturity in which, as St Peter tells us, we are 'alive with

5. Rom. 5:4, 5

the life of God'.[6] Now if he, St Paul, and the New Testament as a whole deserve to be taken seriously, we are led to say that prayer is something greater than our talking to God, or imagining God, or imagining holy thoughts. Indeed, as St Paul said, this cannot be a real explanation of prayer if it is true that we do not even know how to pray. But as he goes on to say, 'the Spirit is pleading for us in our inmost being beyond words, beyond thoughts, beyond images, with sighs too deep for words'.[7]

Prayer then, is the life of the Spirit of Jesus within our human heart: the Spirit through whose anointing we are incorporate in the Body of Christ and by which, in turn, we are returning fully awakened to the Father. We are praying when we are awakening to the presence of this Spirit in our heart. If this is so, there can be no forms or methods of prayer. There is only prayer, the stream of love between the Spirit of the risen Jesus and His Father, in which we are incorporate. If this is so, there is no part-time or partial prayer as if the Spirit were not always alive in our heart. But there are times, our twice-daily meditation, when we make a complete turn of consciousness towards this ever-present reality. There comes a level of awakening to which St Paul was clearly directing the Thessalonians when he told them to 'pray without ceasing',[8] when our awareness of this reality is constant throughout the most diverse activities or concerns.

Just as the Eucharist is both a commemoration and an actual present event so the mantra spans levels of consciousness and dimensions of time. It is, in a sense, our echoing response to the love-cry of the Spirit, to the whole life of Jesus returning to the Father, a response not at any level of conceptual reasoning but an absolute, an unconditional response. Insofar as we are aware of it, it is a response at the deepest level of our being

6. I Pet. 4:6
7. Rom. 8:26
8. I Thess. 5:17

where we acknowledge and experience our complete poverty and complete dependence upon the sustaining love of God. Our response achieves this absolute value, travels to this source level of our being to the extent that we say the mantra with complete simplicity and persevere in our renunciation, at the time of our meditation, of our thoughts, imaginations, of our very self-consciousness. As the mantra becomes rooted more deeply and thoroughly integrated with our consciousness, so does our whole being participate in our response to the Spirit. Its purpose is that integration of all our levels of being with the source of our being, the source that calls the whole person back into itself, awakened through the Spirit of Jesus.

Our aim is the realization of our whole being and this is why we are impelled to transcend all qualities and faculties to find the ground of our being wherein our essential unity, the essence of our personhood, consists. There is no doubt of the absolute demand of the mantra. In essence it is our acceptance of the absoluteness of God's love flooding our heart through the Spirit of the risen Jesus. Our death consists in the relentless simplicity of the mantra and the absolute renunciation of thought and language at the time of our meditation.

This is not an esoteric doctrine or method. The mantra has been in the Christian tradition of prayer from the beginning and the understanding that prayer is beyond the operations of the mind is to be found in every authoritative statement. St Bonaventure wrote that, 'if this passover is to be perfect, we must set aside all discursive operations of the intellect and turn the very apex of our soul to God to be entirely transformed in Him.'[9] Bernard Lonergan has drawn a distinction between what is conscious and what is known. By 'conscious' he means the experience in itself, by 'known' our understanding and evaluation of the experience.[10] Now just as the *Spiritual Exercises* of St Ignatius demand a clear distinction between prayer and

9. *Journey of the Soul to God* VII
10. cf. B. Lonergan, *Insight*. Darton Longman & Todd 1978

review,[11] so this distinction of Lonergan's indicates how we must arrange our priorities. Of course, the Christian mystery contains both our experience and our understanding of the experience. Jesus is the whole man summoning us to wholeness, but unless we accept the distinction between the conscious and the known, between prayer and review, we have not admitted our own essential creatureliness. Hence, we remain bound by the limitations of that creatureliness; we have not transcended ourselves.

Again, it is not enough to give this notional assent. It must be a truth of our being apprehended by our whole being. The mantra creates the possibility of such an integration. It prepares us as a living sacrifice to the Lord. It leads us in all simplicity to the seminal Christian experience of the prayer of the Spirit in our heart. The fruits of that experience are the fruits of the Spirit, and perhaps the first discovery we make that opens the way to all these gifts of the Spirit is that of our own personal and infinite loveableness. We cannot manufacture or anticipate the experience; we can only learn to be still, to be silent and to wait with an ever-growing sense of our own harmony. Nor can we forge the gifts of the Spirit within a fabricated joyfulness, within dogmatism rather than authority, or uniformity rather than liberty. For these are mere imitations of the true Christian qualities, and they contradict the very Gospel they purport to proclaim.

The authentic Christian qualities, the fruits of the Spirit, are given with and grow out of the experience of the Spirit of Jesus, flooding our hearts with God's personal love and summoning us to the fullness of our personhood in our personal encounter with Jesus: 'By their fruits you shall know them.' The renewal and enrichment of the Church and its reinstatement as an authoritative voice in men's lives depends upon its members' receiving this experience in the depths of their own hearts.

11. cf. B. O'Leary, 'Repetition and Review', *The Way*, Supplement 27, pp. 48–58.

Each member of the Church is called to this awakening as a present reality. Each will receive it in the way suited to his own unique personhood, within the plan for his fulfilment held in the mysterious love of God.

I do not wish to imply that meditation is the only way, but rather that it is the only way I have found. In my own experience it is the way of pure simplicity that enables us to become fully, integrally aware of the Spirit Jesus has sent into our heart; and this is the recorded experience of the mainstream of the Christian tradition from Apostolic times down to our own day.

THE FATHER
Romans 8:15

If the Gospel of Jesus were ever to be established as the basis of a political system, man would have achieved one of his perennial ideals, the self-renewing revolution. But first it would have to become a reality in the personal life of men for the Kingdom of God on earth begins in the human heart: 'Be converted in heart and believe the gospel.' This is the lynchpin of all idealism, that it has first to be realized in the individual life and then, and then only, can it be presented as the means of general salvation.

This means that we have to be able ourselves to recognize the life of God in all situations and peoples, to identify it for a sceptical generation looking for signs elsewhere, and then to place it in the context of that ultimate revelation of God's life which Jesus brought to man in His own person. To see God in the world, in other faiths, in our lonely cities and dismal suburbs, we have first to have found the image of God in ourselves. We are then free to accept the generosity of God's love wherever it overflows from the depths of His own being. We need that sensitive spirit of liberty of which St Paul wrote to the Galatians: 'If you are led by the Spirit, you are not under the law.'[1]

I have been suggesting in this book that meditation affirms the essential naturalness of spiritual growth. Because Jesus has already passed beyond the veil in His human form and nature, it remains for us only to realize the life He has made available to us, to activate our potential by the enlightenment and enlargement of our consciousness. The light that enlightens us bathes the whole of creation but it enters us through a narrow aperture. 'The gate that leads to life is small and the road is narrow,'[2] said Jesus. It is narrow because it is the product of

1. Gal. 5:18
2. Matt. 7:13

concentration, the focusing of our whole being, all our energies and faculties upon a single point.

Sartre wrote that, 'the only thing that counts is total commitment.' It is certainly the only thing that authenticates our efforts and proves our sincerity. The way to fullness of life is just this way of total commitment of our personhood to the Other, the complete and harmonious concentration of mind, body and spirit upon the centre of our being. The beliefs and values we take with us into the silence of this commitment are, as Thomas Merton often said, of limited importance because they are largely the familiar compounds of language and imagination. But every man knows in his heart that the riddle of his existence is solved beyond these compounds, by focusing upon the centre of his being where he in some way knows his source and meaning to lie.

We cannot, strictly speaking, achieve or acquire this integral condition of commitment and concentration. As St Paul said we do not know how to pray. There are no tricks or devices that will get quick results, no instant mysticism, or at least none that will not overload an unprepared and undisciplined psyche. But there is a way for us to prepare ourselves for the emergence, in a natural process which is itself the gift of God, of the light of the Spirit. The mantra stills the mind and summons all our faculties to the resolution of a single point; that point we know as the condition of complete simplicity which demands not less than everything.

It is only when we have focused everything, surrendered everything that we are able to receive everything. Until then, the real generosity, the superabundance of the Gospel message does not strike us as credible. We are numbed by the extravagance of the claims put by the New Testament writers and we read them as metaphor or tone them down in safe theological formulae. But the essence of the message of Jesus is an unlimited generosity, a complete self-giving of the infinite God. This is proclaimed throughout the New Testament: 'He who unites himself with the Lord becomes one Spirit with Him';[3] 'Then I shall know fully, even as I have been fully understood';[4] 'Here and now we are God's heirs. What we shall be like has not yet been disclosed, but we shall be like Him for we shall see Him as He is.'[5]

If Jesus had not Himself told us that whatever He has received from the Father He gives to us, we could never have dared to believe it. Indeed, few want to believe it because, at least at the conceptual level (that is, before the beginning of personal verification) it seems to suggest the swallowing up of the person in God. It is only when we are led by the Spirit, when we take our first steps in the actual experience that we begin to understand what Teillhard de Chardin meant in saying that, 'in every domain, union differentiates'. In the superabundance of love we become the person we are called to be.

Jesus explained His own mission as the proclamation of the Father: the revelation to men of the person whom He encountered in the depths of His own human heart. His union with men, His calling us friends and brothers, His loving all-embracing universalization through the Spirit: all these considerations serve to confirm what He Himself assured us of, that we are called to the same knowledge and the same communion with the Father, the same completion and verification of our being that He enjoyed as man and communicates to us as the incarnate Word. When He sends the Spirit into our hearts, Jesus transmits to us everything that He receives from the Father.[6] He withholds nothing, neither any secret nor intimacy of personal love. By His very nature He is impelled to give all of Himself, and the power, the urgency of the love-impulse radiating from the Father make it impossible for Jesus to retain any area of special privilege, of non-communication. The build-

3. I Cor. 6:17
4. Rom. 13:12
5. I John 3:2
6. John 15:15

ing up of the Body of Christ is precisely the consuming desire of Jesus to flood every part of our human consciousness with His Spirit. Nothing can prevent that desire from being satisfied except man's own unwillingness to receive, to acknowledge, to awaken to this gift of God's personal love.

The heart of the Christian mystery, of the life of Jesus Himself, is the mysterious paradox of life proceeding from death. But to avoid being overwhelmed by the unresolvable paradox and lapsing into either extreme of superstition or cynicism, we need a personal inner balance, what Scripture calls one of the gifts of the Spirit: self-control. This is precisely the fruit of meditation, the middle way, the centring process of silent prayer. But this is very different from mere passivity or quietism. The awakening of our own spirit to the Spirit of Jesus cannot be received by us passively, as if it were a pre-packaged experience imported from outside, or as if we were not persons created in the image of God but objects masquerading as persons. Our awakening is, in itself, the awareness of our participation in the life of God, of God as the source of our personhood, the very power by which we are enabled to accept His gift of our being. It is therefore a free response, an utterly personal communication, a free acceptance.

Our beginning and our end lie in the infinite generosity of God, that extravagance of love in which He transcends Himself in every manifestation of Himself. The human mind is not constituted to be able to make complete sense of this. We can, it is true, glimpse the nature of transcendence by our sensitivity to paradox. But we always return to the fact of His unimaginable generosity, such generosity which, even in the human experience, is the source of liberty and joy. Man indeed is most God-like when he gives himself without measure, when, that is to say, he loves; and it is without measure that God gives Himself to us.[7] He has 'lavished' His Spirit upon us; His love has 'flooded' our hearts.

7. John 3:34

If it keeps this vision central to its work, any theological investigation must lead to a sense of awe, of wonder, of joy, and to a humility that liberates us from all our own petty self-importance; for it should lead men to an awareness of the God who is both infinitely beyond us and yet closer to us than we are to ourselves. Any discussion about God has value to the degree that it is truly a revelation. This, I think, is what Evagrius Ponticus meant when he said that, 'if you are a theologian you truly pray, if you truly pray you are a theologian.'[8]

Meditation is not a technique of prayer. It is, though, an incredibly simple means of leading us into an integral awareness of the nature of our own being and of the central, authenticating fact of our being which is the Spirit praying 'Abba, Father' in our heart. I say 'simple' not 'easy'. The way of simplicity soon becomes a pilgrimage in which we will experience the difficulty of laying down our lives. But we are not alone on the pilgrimage. We have both the community of the faithful and persevering, and the guidance of the Spirit in our heart. To the degree that we lay ourselves down, to the same degree and a hundredfold will we be restored to ourselves. The fruit of the radical simplicity of the mantra is a joy beyond description and a peace beyond understanding

The multiplicities of thought and the mobility of words all find their resolution in the one little word, the mantra. John Cassian described it as 'embracing all the feelings implanted in human nature' and as 'comprising all our thoughts'.[9] When it is rooted in us, the mantra leads us to that point of unity where we become simple enough to see, to receive, and to know the infinite gift of God's personal love. It leads us to that joy promised by Jesus to those who persevere on the pilgrimage to simplicity, the same joy St Paul wished to the Philippians: 'I wish you all joy in the Lord, I will say it again: all joy be yours.

8. *Chapters on Prayer* 60
9. *Conference* 10:10, 12

Let your magnanimity be manifest to all. . . The grace of our Lord Jesus Christ be with your spirit.'[10]

10. Phil. 4:4–5, 23

TWELVE STEPS FOR MEDITATORS

This section is intended to help you prepare for the silence of meditation. It is designed to help you bring your mind to a state of peacefulness, to concentration. It is meant to point you in the direction you need to be facing for your meditation, which is centrewards, to help you to move on and also to set out once more with faith and love and openness on your pilgrimage with the freshness of a new start. In meditation we are all beginners.

There are twelve separate pieces here, and my recommendation is that you read just one of them at a time, and then begin your meditation.

Remember, to meditate well you need the quietest place you can find. You need a good posture, with your spine upright and calm, and regular breathing. Then begin to say your mantra calmly, peacefully, and with complete simplicity. To meditate you need only to repeat your mantra with persevering faithfulness.

These pieces are not designed to provide you with something to think about during your meditation, but are meant as an encouragement for you to persevere and to be faithful. If you can concentrate on each one for five minutes or so you will be preparing yourself in the art of meditation, which is also essentially concentration. But in your meditation you will not then be concentrating on ideas or images. You will be concentrating on the mantra and the silence to which it will lead you.

The Tradition of the Mantra I

I have often found when I have talked to people about meditation that it is the non-Christian, even the person with no
religion, who first understands what meditation is about. To
many ordinary churchgoers and many priests, monks and sisters, the mantra seems at first a suspiciously new-fangled technique of prayer or like some exotic trick-method, or some kind
of therapy that may help you to relax, but has no claim to be
called Christian. This is a desperately sad state of affairs. So
many Christians have lost touch with their own tradition of
prayer. We no longer benefit as we should from the wisdom
and experienced counsel of the great masters of prayer. All
these masters have agreed that in prayer it is not we ourselves
who are taking the initiative. We are not talking to God. We
are listening to His word within us. We are not looking for
Him, it is He who has found us. Walter Hilton expressed it
very simply in the fourteenth century. He wrote: 'You, yourself, do nothing, you simply allow Him to work in your soul.'[1]
The advice of St Theresa was in tune with this. She reminds us
that all we can do in prayer is to dispose ourselves; the rest is
in the power of the Spirit who leads us.

The language in which we express our spiritual experience
changes. The reality of the Spirit does not change. So it is not
enough to read the masters of prayer; we have to be able to
apply the criterion of our own experience, limited though it
may be, in order to see the same reality shining through different testimonies. For example, what Hilton and St Theresa
are showing us is the same experience of prayer as that which
led St Paul to write that 'we do not even know how to pray,
but the Spirit prays within us.'[2] What this means in the language
of our own day is that before we can pray we have first to
become still, to concentrate. Only then can we enter into a

1. *The Scale of Perfection*, Bk II, ch. 24 (see Bibliography)
2. Rom. 8:26

loving awareness of the Spirit of Jesus within our heart. Now many Christians would still say at this point, 'Very well, but this is for Saints, for specialists in prayer,' as if stillness and silence were not universal elements of the human spirit. This type of obstinate false humility is based on a plain unawareness of who St Paul was writing to in Rome and Corinth and Ephesus. He was not writing to specialists, to Carmelites and Carthusians, but to husbands, wives, butchers and bakers. It shows too an unawareness of the specific teaching on prayer by later masters.

St Teresa of Avila, for example, was of the opinion that if you were serious about prayer, you would be led into what she called 'the prayer of quiet' within a relatively short time, six months or a year. Abbot Marmion saw the first year's novitiate in the monastery as being designed to lead at the end of it to what he called 'contemplative prayer'. St John of the Cross said that the principal sign of your readiness for silence in prayer was that your discursive thinking at the time of prayer was becoming evidently a distraction and counter-productive. Yet there is a kind of self-important posing humility that makes us stand aloof from the call of the redemptive love of Jesus. Very often we are reluctant to admit that we are the sick and sinful Jesus came to heal, and very often we prefer our self-protecting isolation to the risk of our face-to-face encounter with the Other in the silence of our own vulnerability.

In meditation we turn the searchlight of consciousness off ourselves and that means off a self-centred analysis of our own unworthiness. 'If memories of past actions keep coming between you and God', says the author of *The Cloud of Unknowing*, 'you are resolutely to step over them because of your deep love for God.'[3] In prayer we come to a deeper awareness of God in Christ. Our way is the way of silence. The way to silence is the way of the mantra.

3. *The Cloud of Unknowing*, ch. 6

The Tradition of the Mantra II

Jesus summons us to fullness of life, not to a self-centred reluctance to realize the true beauty and wonder of our being. The mantra is an ancient tradition, the purpose of which is to accept the invitation Jesus makes.

We find it in the ancient Jewish custom of 'blessing the Lord at all times'. We find the mantra in the early Christian Church. We may find it, for example, in the Our Father which was a series of short rhythmic phrases in the original Aramaic. We find it too in the Orthodox tradition of the Jesus Prayer, the prayer that Jesus Himself commended: 'Lord, be merciful to me, a sinner.'[1] The prayer of Jesus Himself as recorded in the Gospel leads to the same conclusions. 'Lord, teach us to pray,' his disciples asked Him. His teaching was simplicity itself: 'When you pray do not be like the hypocrites . . . but go into a room by yourself, shut the door and pray to your Father who is there in the secret place. . . Do not go babbling on like the heathen who imagine that the more they say, the more likely they are to be heard. Your Father knows what your needs are before you ask him.'[2] In the Garden of Gethsemani Jesus is described as praying over and over again 'in the same words'[3] and whenever He addresses the Father for the sake of the crowd, the word, 'Abba', is always on His lips, the same word which St Paul describes the Spirit of Jesus eternally crying in our hearts.

Time and again the practical advice of masters of prayer is summed up in the simple injunction: 'Say your mantra'; 'Use this little word'. *The Cloud of Unknowing* advises, 'and pray not in many words but in a little word of one syllable. Fix this word fast to your heart so that it is always there come what

1. Luke 18:13
2. Matt. 6:5–8
3. Mark 14:39, Matt. 26:44

may. With this word you will suppress all thoughts.'[4] Abbot Chapman, in his famous letter of Michaelmas 1920 from Downside, describes the simple, faithful use of a mantra which he had discovered more from his own courageous perseverance in prayer than from teachers. He had rediscovered a simple enduring tradition of prayer that entered the West through Monasticism, and first entered Western Monasticism through John Cassian in the late fourth century. Cassian himself received it from the holy men of the desert who placed its origin back beyond living memory to Apostolic times.

The venerable tradition of the mantra in Christian prayer is above all attributable to its utter simplicity. It answers all the requirements of the masters' advice on how to pray because it leads us to a harmonious, attentive stillness of mind, body and spirit. It requires no special talent or gift apart from serious intent and the courage to persevere. 'No one', Cassian said, 'is kept away from purity of heart by not being able to read nor is rustic simplicity any obstacle to it for it lies close at hand for all if only they will by constant repetition of this phrase keep the mind and heart attentive to God.'[5] Our mantra is the ancient Aramaic prayer, 'Maranatha, Maranatha'. 'Come Lord. Come Lord Jesus'.

4. *The Cloud of Unknowing* ch. 7, 39
5. *Conference* 10:14

Saying the Mantra I

Learning to meditate is learning to say the mantra, and because it is as simple as this, we should be quite clear in our understanding of the process of saying the mantra.

We must grow in our fidelity to the mantra and in the same proportion the mantra will grow more and more deeply rooted in us. As you know, the mantra I recommend you to say is the word 'Maranatha', the ancient Aramaic prayer which means, 'Come Lord, Come Lord Jesus'. I suggest that you articulate it in your mind silently, with equal stress on each of the four syllables. Ma-ra-na-tha. We usually begin by saying the mantra, that is, it seems as though we are speaking it with our mind silently, somewhere in our head, but as we make progress the mantra becomes more familiar, less of a stranger, less of an intruder in our consciousness. We find less effort is required to persevere in saying it throughout the time of our meditation. Then it seems that we are not so much speaking it in our minds as sounding it in our heart, and this is the stage that we describe as the mantra becoming rooted in our hearts.

No metaphor is really very satisfactory in this matter but it is sometimes helpful and reassuring to know that one's own experience in meditation is also the general experience of the faithful. So, at this stage of sounding the mantra in our hearts, we might describe it as similar to pushing lightly a pendulum that needs only a slight stimulus to set it swinging in a calm, steady rhythm. It is at this moment that our meditation is really beginning. We are really beginning to concentrate away from ourselves because from now on, instead of either saying or sounding the mantra, we begin to listen to it, wrapped in ever-deepening attention. When he described this stage of meditation, my teacher used to say that from this moment on it is as though the mantra is sounding in the valley below us while we are toiling up the side of a mountain.

Meditation is in essence the art of concentration precisely because, the higher we toil up the mountain side, the fainter becomes the mantra sounding in the valley below us, and so the more attentively and seriously we have to listen to it. There then comes the day when we enter that 'cloud of unknowing' in which there is silence, absolute silence, and we can no longer hear the mantra.

But we must always remember that we cannot attempt to force the pace of meditation in any way or to speed up the natural process in which the mantra roots itself in our consciousness by means of our simple fidelity in saying it. We must not be self-consciously asking ourselves, 'How far have I got? Am I saying the mantra or sounding it or listening to it?' If we try to force the pace or to keep a constant self-conscious eye on our progress we are, if there is such a word, non-meditating because we are concentrating on ourselves, putting ourselves first, thinking about ourselves. Meditation requires complete simplicity. We are led to that complete simplicity, but we begin and continue by saying the mantra.

Saying the Mantra II

I need to stress here the importance of continuing to say the mantra because, when we start to meditate we can often come quite quickly into realms of peacefulness and experience a sense of pleasant well-being, even euphoria; saying the mantra can then be made to appear a distraction. We do not want to lose this pleasant plateau and so we try to stay where we are, to strike camp and make no further progress up the mountain side. We stop saying the mantra. Many people are led into long, unnecessarily long, and uncreative periods when they make no progress for this very reason. They barter the potential of an expanding consciousness and a deepening awareness of the Spirit for a kind of floating piety, a kind of religious anaesthesia.

The great fourth-century master of prayer, our master, John Cassian, had already noted this danger in alluding to what he called, the '*pax perniciosa*', the pernicious peace. His graphic phrase points out something that needs to be remembered if we ever think that we can just say, 'So far and no further, this will do'. *Perniciosa* means what it says, namely, destructive or fatal. I am myself convinced that many people do not make the progress they should in prayer, and do not become as free as they are called to be in prayer, simply because they opt for this destructive lethargy, they give up too soon in their toilsome pilgrimage up the mountain side; they abandon the constant saying of the mantra.

When we begin to meditate we must say the mantra for the whole twenty or thirty minutes of our meditation, regardless of whatever mood we are in or whatever reaction we seem to be having. As we progress in fidelity in saying it, we must then sound it for the whole time of our meditation, whatever the distractions or feelings that may arise. Then, as the mantra becomes rooted in our heart, we must listen to it with our whole attention without ceasing.

I repeat this to re-emphasize what is the essential and perhaps the only advice worth giving about meditation, which is simply: *to say your mantra*. This is not an easy doctrine to accept, nor is it easy to follow. We all hope when we first begin to meditate for some instant mystical experience, and we tend to over-estimate the first unusual experiences that the process of meditation brings to us. But this is not important. The important thing is to persevere with the mantra, to stabilize ourselves by our discipline which makes us ready for the higher slopes of the mountain.

We need not be over-concerned with our motives to begin with. It is not we, but the Lord who takes the initiative. As John Cassian puts it: 'He, Himself, has struck the small spark of good will out of the hard flints of our hearts.' So now, begin your meditation in simplicity of heart and be faithful to your humble task of saying the mantra without ceasing.

Leaving Self Behind

These are the words of Jesus taken from St Mark's Gospel: 'Anyone who wishes to be a follower of mine must leave self behind; he must take up his cross and come with me.'[1] Now we meditate to do just that: to obey that absolutely fundamental call Jesus makes, which is the basis of all our Christian faith, to leave self behind in order that we can indeed journey with Christ in His return to the Father.

Saying the mantra is a discipline which helps us to transcend all the limitations of our narrow and isolated self-obsession. The mantra leads us into an experience of the liberty that reigns at the centre of our being. 'Where the Spirit is there is liberty,'[2] said St Paul. It introduces us to this liberty by helping us to pass over into the Other, by helping us to take our minds off ourselves. This is what Jesus means by leaving self behind.

In our own day we have perhaps lost our understanding of what it really means to renounce self. Self-renunciation is not an experience with which our contemporaries are familiar or which they even understand very clearly, mainly because the tendency of our society is to emphasize the importance of self-promotion, self-preservation, self-projection. The materialism of our consumer society puts 'What I want' at the centre of our life, and it renders 'the other' merely an object which we see in terms of our own pleasure or advantage. But the other is only really Other if approached with reverence for itself and in itself. We must learn to pay complete attention to it and not to its effect upon us. If we begin to objectify the other then its reality, its uniqueness, and essential value escape us and it becomes not the other, but a projection of ourselves.

Many people today and in the past have confused self-renunciation with self-rejection. But our meditation is no running away from, no attempt to evade the responsibility of our own

1. Mark 8:34
2. 2 Cor. 3:17

70

being or the responsibilities of our life and relationships. Meditation is rather an affirmation of ourselves, not however of the self that is involved in this particular responsibility alone, nor the self that wants this or wants that. These aspects of our self are illusory; they become little egos when we isolate them from the central point of our being where our irreducible selfhood exists in complete harmony with the Other, the Other being the source of our being and the sustainer of our selfhood. It is this whole self, the real self which we affirm in the silence of meditation.

We cannot affirm it however by trying to lay violent hands on it or by trying to possess or control it. If we do so, we are in the absurd position of our ego trying to command the self, or unreality dictating to reality, or of the tail wagging the dog. This is what Niebuhr meant when he said: 'The self does not realize itself fully when self-realization is the conscious aim.' In meditating we affirm ourselves by becoming still, by becoming silent, we allow the reality of our real self to become more and more apparent; we allow its light to diffuse throughout our being in the course of the natural process of spiritual growth. We do not try to do anything. We simply let ourselves be. When we are renouncing self, we are in that condition of liberty and receptivity that allows us to be in relationship with the Other, which is the condition that makes it possible for us to decide positively for the Other, to say, though not in words, 'I love you.'

But we can only turn to the Other, we can only make this movement of self, if we leave self behind, that is, if we take our consciousness away from its involvement with me and direct it on the thou. Self-obsession is the means of restricting and limiting the self. Self-renunciation, on the other hand, is the means of liberating the self for its real purpose which is loving the Other. Meditation is a simple and natural process. It is the process that reveals our real being as a state of open-hearted receptivity to the Spirit of Jesus who dwells in our hearts. This revelation dawns when we renounce, step aside from, the external manifestations of our consciousness such as thoughts, words and images and when instead we move into the level of consciousness itself. We then become silent because we have entered silence and we are wholly turned towards the Other. In this fully conscious, fully free silence, we naturally open ourselves to the Word that proceeds from the silence, God's own Word, in whom we are called into being, and in which we ourselves are spoken by the Creator.

This is the living Word within us. Our faith tells us that we are wholly incorporate in this Word, but we need to know it fully, in the height, length, depth and breadth of our spirit, to know it though it is beyond knowledge. The silence brings us to this knowledge that is so simple that no thought or image could ever contain or represent it. By renouncing self we enter the silence and focus upon the Other. The truth to be revealed is the harmony of our Self with the Other. In the words of the Sufi poet: 'I saw my Lord with my heart's eye and said: "Who art Thou Lord?" "Thyself," He replied.'

John Cassian

We would not still be reading the Gospels or St Paul today, were it not true that the human experience of the Spirit is essentially the same at all times and in all traditions, because it is, in essence, the same encounter with the redemptive love of God in Jesus Christ, who is the same yesterday, today and forever. The importance of this truth for us today is that although no one can make another's pilgrimage for him, we can nevertheless benefit from the experience and the wisdom of those who have made the pilgrimage before us. In his own day and for his contemporaries, Jesus was seen as just such a teacher who had reached enlightenment through His fidelity and perseverance.

Throughout Christian history, men and women of prayer have fulfilled a special mission in bringing their contemporaries, and even succeeding generations, to the same enlightenment, the same rebirth in Spirit that Jesus preached. One of these teachers, John Cassian, of the fourth century, has a claim to be one of the most influential teachers of the spiritual life in the West. His special importance as the teacher and inspirer of St Benedict and so of the whole of Western Monasticism, derives from the part he played in bringing the spiritual tradition of the East into the living experience of the West.

Cassian's own pilgrimage began with his own search for a teacher, for a master of prayer, a master he could not find in his own monastery in Bethlehem. Just as thousands of young people today make their pilgrimage to the East in search of wisdom and personal authority, so Cassian and his friend Germanus journeyed to the deserts of Egypt where the holiest and most famous men of the spirit were to be found in the fourth century. In his *Institutes* and *Conferences* Cassian himself hardly comes across as a distinct personality, no more than St Benedict does in his Rule which is so heavily indebted to John Cassian. But we do feel that we are encountering a spirit in Cassian:

one which, like St Benedict's, has achieved the object of its own teaching, the transcendence of self.

Cassian's special qualities, that give him such authority and directness, are his capacity to listen and his gift of communicating what he has heard and made his own. It was in listening with total attention to the teaching of the Holy Abbot Isaac that Cassian was first fired with an enthusiasm for prayer and the firm resolve to persevere. Abbot Isaac spoke eloquently and sincerely but, as Cassian concludes in his first *Conference*: 'With these words of the holy Isaac we were dazzled rather than satisfied, since we felt that though the excellence of prayer had been shown to us still we had not yet understood its nature and the power by which continuance in it might be gained and kept.'[1]

His experience was clearly similar to that of many today who have heard inspiring accounts of prayer but are left uninstructed as to the practical means of really becoming aware of the Spirit praying in their hearts. Cassian and Germanus humbly returned to Abbot Isaac after a few days with the simple question: 'How do we pray? Teach us, show us.' His answer to their question which can be found in Cassian's tenth *Conference*, had a decisive influence on the Western understanding of prayer down to our own day. It shows, firstly, that prayer is both the acknowledgement and experience of our own poverty, our own utter dependence on God who is the source of our being. But it is also the experience of our redemption, our enrichment by the love of God in Jesus. These related aspects of prayer, of poverty and redemption leads Cassian to call the condition we enjoy in prayer a 'grand poverty'. 'The mind should unceasingly cling to the mantra', Cassian writes, 'until strengthened by continual use of it, it casts off and rejects the rich and ample matter of all kinds of thought and restricts itself to the poverty of the single verse. . . . Those who realize this poverty arrive

1. *Conference* 9:36

with ready ease at the first of the beatitudes: "Blessed are they who are poor in spirit for theirs is the Kingdom of Heaven." [2]

The spiritual life for Cassian, the serious perseverance in the poverty of the single verse, is a passover. By persevering we pass from sorrow to joy, from loneliness to communion. And, unlike many of the Egyptian ascetics who saw mortification as an end in itself, Cassian clearly teaches that it is merely a means to an end and that end is the unbroken awareness of the life of the Spirit continually renewing us, giving new life to our mortal bodies. Similarly, he sees the religious community as a means of leading each individual to an awareness of his communion with all in Jesus. Just as the mantra is the sacrament of our poverty in prayer, so in the community absolute honesty and frankness in our relationships with one another and above all with our teacher are the signs and means of making the passover from fear to love.

One of the recurrent themes of Cassian is the absolute importance of personal verification. We must know for ourselves in the depth of our own being. We must perform rather than teach, be rather than do. Above all, we must be fully awake to the wonder and beauty of our being, to the mystery of the personal life of Jesus in our heart. Relentlessly, we must avoid the pitfall of half consciousness, the drowsy state of what he calls pernicious peace, *pax perniciosa*, a lethal sleep, the *sopor letalis*. His importance as a teacher in our own day is his simplicity and directness, for his are noble sentiments, inspiring ideals. But how do we fulfil the command of Jesus, 'to stay awake and pray'?[3] Cassian brought the answer to the West from the ancient tradition of Christian prayer. By knowing ourselves to be poor and by deepening in prayer our experience of poverty in complete self-renunciation. The simple practical means he teaches is the unceasing use of the mantra. He wrote that the Christian has as his principal aim the realization of the

2. ibid. X:11
3. Matt. 26:41

Kingdom of God, the power of the Spirit of Jesus in his heart. But we cannot achieve this by our own efforts or think our way into it and so we have a simpler more immediate goal which he calls 'purity of heart'.[4] This is all we should concern ourselves with, he teaches. The rest will be given to us. And the way to purity of heart, to full and clear awareness, is the way of poverty, the 'grand poverty' of the mantra.

4. *Conference* 1:4

Set Your Mind on the Kingdom

If most of us were asked why we thought we were not fulfilled, why we were not simply happy, we would probably not answer using terms such as essential harmony, awareness, consciousness or spirit. We would be much more likely to point to particular features of our life such as work, relationships, or health, and to attribute our unhappiness or anxiety to one or all of these. Many people, indeed, would not even see all these different aspects of their life as having any common point of contact. To so many of us the activities of our day are like parallel lines and many actively resent one area's impinging on another. The result of this is that modern life so often lacks a centre, a point of convergence, a source of unity. Consequently, men and women lose the sense of their own creative centre and as a result they have no contact with their real selves.

The understanding of prayer that makes it merely a matter of telling God what we want or need and reminding Him of our sins of omission only compounds our alienation from reality. For this was the liberating message Jesus came to bring: 'I bid you put away anxious thought about food and drink to keep you alive and clothes to cover your body. Surely life is more than food, the body more than clothes.'[1] What Jesus is advocating here is not an irresponsible or fanatical indifference to the external aspects of our life, but rather He is urging us to develop a spirit of trust; of absolute trust, in the Fatherhood of the God who not only created us, but sustains us in being from moment to moment. 'Do not be anxious about tomorrow; tomorrow will look after itself,' He taught.[2] Realize yourself, that is, in the present moment because your happiness and fulfilment are here and now.

To trust another is to renounce self and place your centre of gravity in the other. This is liberty and this is love. 'All these

1. Matt. 6:25
2. ibid. 6:34

77

things', said Jesus of the material concerns of life, 'are for the heathen to run after, not for you, because your heavenly Father knows that you have need of all of them.' The trust which He calls on His followers to have in the Fatherhood of His Father is not the immature, childish presumption of getting what you want simply because you want it. To trust in God means to have turned ourselves fully towards another and if we have done that we have transcended both ourselves and our wanting. In this experience of transcendence itself we receive more than we could ever have asked for or ever have dared even to want: 'Set your mind on God's Kingdom before everything else, and all the rest will come to you as well.'[3]

The proper ordering of our external activities can only be achieved once we have re-established conscious contact with the centre of all these activities and concerns. This centre is the aim of our meditation. It is the centre of our being. In St Teresa's words, 'God is the centre of the soul.' When our access to this centre is opened up, the Kingdom of God is established in our hearts. That kingdom is nothing less than the present power and all-pervasive life of God Himself permeating all creation. In the words of John Cassian: 'He who is the author of eternity would have men ask of Him nothing that is uncertain, petty or temporal.'[4] This is not because He does not want us to enjoy the good things of life, but because we can fully enjoy them only when we have received His gift of Himself, of Himself from whom all good things come, who is goodness itself. The proof of His generosity is also what St Paul calls, 'The ground of our hope'. It is: 'The love of God flooding our inmost hearts through the Holy Spirit He has given us.'[5]

This is not an experience reserved for the selected few. It is a gift available to all men and women. To receive it we must return to the centre of our being where it enters us to the

3. ibid. 6:33
4. *Conference* 9:24
5. Rom. 5:5

source of our being where we find the infusion of God's love through the Spirit of Jesus.

Realizing Our Personal Harmony I

One of the most distinctive features of our time is the almost universal feeling among people that they must somehow get back to a basic level of personal confidence, to the ground or bed-rock of their life. An almost universal fear is the fear of slipping into non-being, losing touch with ourselves, living at a certain distance from ourselves. James Joyce said of one of his characters that 'he lived at a certain distance from his body'. It was a marvellously simple but accurate diagnosis of what we have come to know as alienation.

The reasons for our sense of alienation from ourselves, from others, and from nature are no doubt legion, but there are perhaps two particular causes. The first is our evasion of personal responsibility. We are out of touch with ourselves because we allow someone or something else to take our personal decisions for us. How often do we say of someone when they act unconventionally, 'He has gone off the rails,' with the underlying assumption that society lays down the course that every life must follow. A second reason is the way we are trained and encouraged to think of ourselves. We are trained to compartmentalize our lives too rigidly into, for example, school, work, home, family, entertainment, church and so on. As a result we lose a sense of our own personal wholeness. The whole person is involved in any activity or responsibility we undertake, just as the personal presence of God is total everywhere and cannot be made into a partial or a limited presence.

Modern man is in a state of deep confusion because the complexity and fractionalization of his life seem to have destroyed his personhood. The question he asks himself, which is asked by all modern men and women and not just by religious people, is: 'How can we get back into touch with ourselves? How do we recover a sense of confidence in ourselves, the confidence of knowing that we really do exist in our own right?' It is a question we must ask and answer, because without this basic confidence in our own existence we have not the courage to go out from ourselves to meet the other, and without the other we do not become fully ourselves.

There is also a kind of universal instinct that warns us that the answer to this question is not found in the way of cerebral self-analysis. To discover our essential harmony and wholeness, which is what finding oneself means, we cannot concentrate on just one limited part of our being. The particular rediscovery that modern man is making, though it is also a new discovery, is that reality can be known only as a whole, not in parts, and that this total apprehension can be realized only in silence. We see this truth being discovered in many areas of life and thought today. Abstract art, for example, defies or renounces any meaningful linguistic equivalent. We cannot talk about different shades of maroon on canvas. Wittgenstein, perhaps more than any other writer, has brought us to the brink of saying that language cannot be trusted to represent the truth. Speech is a kind of infinite regression for words only really refer to other words. This is a liberating discovery for each of us, provided that we can have the courage to follow it through and become truly silent. If we can do so one of our first rewards will be the awareness of our own essential harmony, the harmony we find through whole-hearted attention in prayer, and that attentiveness is something more profound, more real, than anything that thought, language or imagination can achieve. The whole man who rejoices in life, in the gift of his own life, is the man who can enjoy himself as a unity: 'I thank thee Lord for the wonder of my being,' sings the psalmist.[1]

Our task in meditation is to allow our unity to be restored and for our scattered parts to move back into their proper harmonious alignment to the centre of our being. To do this we must not scatter ourselves further. We have to concentrate, to move towards our centre. When our consciousness truly awakens to that centre, in silence, then a power is released which is the power of life, the power of the Spirit. In that

1. Ps. 138:13

power we are reformed, reunited, re-created. 'When a man is united to the Spirit there is a new world,'[2] said St Paul. The mantra leads us straight to this centre.

2. 2 Cor. 5:17

Realizing Our Personal Harmony II

In the last piece I wrote about modern man becoming more and more aware of the insufficiency of language as a means of leading him back to himself. There is nothing anti-intellectual about this. It does not suggest that language is not an essential means of communication between people. Indeed this book would be something of an anachronism if it did suggest that. Language may not be able to lead us into the ultimate communion, but it is the atmosphere in which we first draw the breath of consciousness. It expands our consciousness and leads us to silence, but only in and through silence do we become fully conscious.

As an example of this somewhat abstract point, let me return to the idea of our personal harmony. As an idea we have to talk about it in language. Language uses words. Words have meaning to the extent that they do not mean something else and so to talk about personal harmony we must analyse, distinguish, separate. By personal harmony I mean the integration, the perfect co-operation of mind and heart, body and spirit. But when I talk about them like this, as separate entities, am I not suggesting that they actually work independently of each other? Of course you know and I know that they do not work for themselves but they work for the whole. If I hear some joyful news I feel that joy in my body, I know it in my mind and it expands my spirit. All these things happen, they are altogether my response, my involvement in what is happening to me. It is not that my body is telling my mind something or that my mind is communicating something to me through body language. I am a whole person and I respond wholly.[1]

We know that we are this whole person, this harmony and yet we do not know it because this knowledge has not yet become fully conscious. Perhaps we could say that the con-

1. cf. 1 Cor. 12:12–26

scious harmony that lives in perfect joy and liberty at the centre of our being has not yet expanded and spread itself throughout our being. To allow it to do so we must simply remove the obstacle of narrowly self-conscious thought, self-important language. In other words we must become silent. If a man really did know himself as body-mind-spirit, as the harmony of these three, then he would be on the way to making that knowledge fully conscious throughout his whole being. But modern man, at any rate, has lost the knowledge of his spirit and confounded it with his mind. As a result he has lost that sense of his own balance and proportion as a creature which should lead him into the creative silence of prayer. It is only when we have begun to recover our awareness of spirit that we begin to understand the intelligent mystery of our being. We are not just an extreme of body and an extreme of mind co-existing. We have a principle of unity within our being, in the centre of our being and it is this, our spirit, which is the image of God within us.

The fourteenth-century author of *The Cloud of Unknowing* writes: 'I tell you the truth when I say that this work [of meditation] demands great serenity, an integrated and pure disposition in soul and body . . . God forbid that I should separate what God has coupled: the body and the spirit.'[2] The way to become fully conscious of this essential harmony of our being is to be silent. And to meditate is to be silent. The harmony of our essence, our centre, then, as it were blossoms and diffuses itself throughout every part and molecule of our being. *The Cloud* puts it very charmingly: 'When grace draws a man to contemplation it seems to transfigure him even physically so that though he may be ill-favoured by nature he now appears changed and lovely to behold.'[3]

The diffusion of our essential harmony throughout our being is another way of saying that the prayer of the spirit of Jesus

2. *The Cloud of Unknowing*, ch. 41, 48
3. ibid. ch. 54

wells up in our hearts, floods our hearts and overflows through-out us. This is the amazing gift we have been given by Jesus sending us His Spirit. But He does not force it on us. It is for us to recognize it and accept it, and this we do, not by being clever or self-analytical, but by being silent, by being simple. The gift is already given. We have merely to open our hearts to its infinite generosity. The mantra opens our hearts in pure simplicity. 'Do you not know', wrote St Paul to the Corinthians, 'that your body is a shrine of the indwelling Holy Spirit, and the Spirit is God's gift to you?'[4] Meditation is simply our way to knowing it.

4. 1 Cor. 6:19

A Present Reality

Someone once argued that there would be no morality and no conscience if we did not have a sense of the future. If we could see only the present and lived wholly in the present moment we would achieve goodness here and now because we would be unable to postpone the moment of conversion to some indefinite future time.

Perhaps part of the explanation of the phenomenal religious impact which Judaism had on the world is that in the Hebrew language there was no future tense. This sense of the eternal presentness of God pervades both the Old and New Testaments. To Moses, God is described as calling Himself: 'I AM. Tell them that I AM sends you.'[1] Jesus not only preached the Kingdom of Heaven as already arrived among men, but said of Himself: 'Before the prophets were "*I am*".'[2] This sense of the presentness of the kingdom suffuses the testimony that St Paul proclaimed: 'Now is the day of salvation; now is the acceptable time.'[3] Now read these words from the opening paragraph of Chapter 5 of Romans and pay special attention to the tenses he uses:

> Now that we have been justified through faith, let us continue at peace with God through our Lord Jesus Christ, through whom we have been allowed to enter the sphere of God's grace, where we now stand. Let us exult in the hope of divine splendour that is to be ours.[4]

You will see that the main effect of this passage is to draw our attention to what condition we are in now, to draw our minds into a steady concentration on the present moment.

1. Exod. 3:14
2. John 8:58
3. 2 Cor. 6:2
4. Rom. 5:1–2

The extraordinary dynamism of these words and the whole of St Paul's writing is that the marvel, the splendour, the unimaginable reality of the condition we are in here and now is so overwhelming that we can hardly keep our concentration steady. We have been allowed to enter the sphere of God's grace where we now stand. Jesus has blazed the trail for us and through His own experience has incorporated us in His present state which is His glorious communion with the Father in His risen life, a life that now pervades the whole of creation. We stand in the sphere of God's grace because we are where He is and He is where we are. We are in Him and His Spirit is in us.

And yet, that passage I quoted ended with the words: 'Let us exult in the hope of the divine splendour that is to be ours.' Why do we now seem to have returned to a postponement of our entering the sphere of God's grace? Is Paul's rhetoric tripping him up and leading him to contradict himself? No, what he is saying is what Jesus was saying: 'The Kingdom of Heaven is upon you, is within you.' But you must realize this. You must let your consciousness expand and your awareness develop. We are already in the sphere of God's grace because the Spirit has been sent into our hearts. But because we have been created in the image of God we are called to self-awareness. We ourselves must become aware of what Jesus has achieved for us. We must realize the persons we already are. This is the purpose of our meditation to lead us to a full awareness of who we are, where we are, to stop hovering in the realms of eternal postponement. We must touch down in the concrete reality of the present moment where our divine splendour is revealed. We must become still. We have to learn how to pay attention steadily and continuously to the reality of our being in the here and now. Père de Caussade called this 'the sacrament of the present moment', and this is what the mantra leads us into, a full awareness of the divine splendour of the eternal present. The mantra is our sacrament of the present moment.

87

Christian Community I

If we Christians fail today to proclaim the Gospel of Jesus with sufficient conviction and enthusiasm, it is due above all to our forgetting that the very essence of our meaning is to exist for others. The Church does not exist to perpetuate itself, to guard itself against injury, to increase its own security. It exists to lead others into an awareness of the redemptive love of God in Jesus and, insofar as it does really exist for the other, the Church is invulnerable, triumphant. 'You are the light for all the world,' Jesus told His disciples. 'When a lamp is lit it is not put under the meal-tub, but on the lamp-stand, where it gives light to everyone in the house. And you, like the lamp, must shed light among your fellows, so that, when they see the good you do, they may give praise to your Father in heaven.'[1]

If the world does not believe what we say about Jesus, what we say about the reality of the human spirit, is it not mainly because they do not believe that we really believe it and know it? It is not enough to turn our minds to changing the image of the Church in the world, to be constantly thinking what effect will this have, what impression will that make. We have to begin not by changing the image of the Church, but by rediscovering ourselves as the image of God.

There is only one way to do this and it is the essential means of shedding the light with which the Church is entrusted upon every one in the house. This is the way of prayer. The means, in this matter as in all, have to be conformable to the end. Our Christian communities do not exist for themselves, but for others and ultimately for the Other. In our prayer we have to discover ourselves existing for the Other because it is in prayer that we experience ourselves being created and sustained by Him.

In our prayer then, we let God be; we rejoice in His being as He is; we do not try to manipulate Him, to harangue Him

1. Matt. 5:14

88

or to flatter Him; we do not dispel Him with our clever words and formulae but we worship Him, that is, we acknowledge His value and worth and in doing this we discover that we, created in His image, share in His value and worth as sons of God.

Everyone has experienced at some time in their life, when they were with the person they loved, or perhaps at a time of deep sorrow or pain that there is a peculiar power in silence. Silence comes naturally at times of great significance in our life because we feel we are coming into a direct contact with some truth of such meaning that words would distract us, and prevent us from fully entering into that meaning. The power that silence has is to allow this truth to emerge, to rise to the surface, to become visible. It happens naturally in its own time and fashion. We know that we are not responsible for making it appear, but we know it has a personal meaning for us. We know it is greater than we are and we find a perhaps unexpected humility within ourselves that leads us to a real attentive silence. We let the truth be.

But there is also something in all of us that incites us to control others, to defuse the power we dimly apprehend in a moment of truth, to protect ourselves from its transforming power by neutralizing its otherness and imposing our own identity upon it. The crime of idolatry is precisely creating our own god in our own image and likeness. Rather than encounter God in His awesome difference from ourselves, we construct a toy model of Him in our own psychic and emotional image. In doing this we do not harm Him, of course, as unreality has no power over Him, but we do debase and scatter ourselves, surrendering the potential and divine glory of our humanity for the false glitter of the golden calf. The truth is so much more exciting, so much more wonderful. God is not a reflection of our consciousness but we are His reflection, His image, by our incorporation with Jesus, His Son, our Brother. Our way to the experience of this truth is in the silence of our meditation.

Christian Community II

Just as we can cut God down to our own size, impose our identity on him, so we can do this with other people. Indeed, if we do it to God we inevitably do it to other people, and if we do it to them, we inevitably do it to God. This is the obverse of saying what St John said: 'If a man says "I love God" while hating his brother, he is a liar. If he does not love the brother whom he has seen, it cannot be that he loves God whom he has not seen. And indeed this command comes to us from Christ Himself: that he who loves God must also love his brother.'[1] Let us be quite clear what St John is saying, namely that we cannot love God *or* our neighbour. We love both or neither. And what love means is rejoicing in the otherness of the other because the depth of this awareness is the depth of our communion with the other. In this communion the discovery of our own true self and that of the other is the same discovery. So, in the people we live with we find not objects to be cast in our own superficial likeness but, much more, we find in them our true selves, for our true selves only appear, only become realized, when we are wholly turned towards another.

In meditation we develop our capacity to turn our whole being towards the Other. We learn to let our neighbour be just as we learn to let God be. We learn not to manipulate our neighbour but rather to reverence him, to reverence his importance, the wonder of his being; in other words, we learn to love him. Because of this, prayer is the great school of community. In and through a common seriousness and perseverence in prayer we realize the true glory of Christian community as a fraternity of the anointed, living together in profound and loving mutual respect. Christian community is in essence the experience of being held in reverence by others and we in our turn reverencing them. This reverence for each other reveals the members of the community as being sensitively attuned one

1. I John 4:19–21

to the other on the wavelength of the Spirit, the same Spirit that has called each of us to fullness of love. In others I recognize the same Spirit that lives in my heart, the Spirit that constitutes my real self. In this recognition of the other person, a recognition that remakes my mind and expands my consciousness, the other person comes into being as he really is, in his real self, not as a manipulated extension of myself. He moves and acts out of his own integral reality and no longer as some image created by my imagination. Even if our ideas or principles clash, we are held in unison, in dynamic equilibrium, by our mutual recognition of each other's infinite lovableness, importance and essential unique reality.

Thus the mutually supporting and suffering dynamic of Christ's mystical body has just this creative aim: the realization of each other's essential being. True community happens in the process of drawing each other into the light of true being. In this process we share a deepening experience of the joy of life, the joy of Being, as we discover more and more of its fullness in a loving faith shared with others. The essence of community then is a recognition of and deep reverence for the other. Our meditation partakes of this essence because it leads us to turn wholly towards the Other, who is the Spirit in our heart. The full revelation of otherness, and our communion with all is achieved in reverential silence. So complete is our attention to the other that we say nothing ourselves but wait for the other to speak. The mantra guides us into a deeper consciousness of the silence that reigns within us, and then supports us while we wait.

SUGGESTED READING

This is a deliberately short list of suggested reading. Its aim is simply to inspire you to begin the pilgrimage of meditation and to persevere.

Ideally, this is done within the context of a teacher and a community. But it is important, too, to realize that the pilgrimage is followed within a universal community and one that has passed on its accumulated wisdom and insight to successive generations. The aim of these masters of prayer, whose works are recommended here, was not to provide a vicarious experience but to lead us as directly as possible into a fully personal response to the call addressed to each of us.

1. The most succinct, practical and balanced guide to meditation in the English mystical tradition is the anonymous four-teenth-century treatise *The Cloud of Unknowing*. The original English is brisk and vivid and has an untranslatable flavour. The best modern translation is by William Johnston in an edition that includes the same author's other work, *The Book of Privy Counselling*. It has an excellent introduction.
2. The best general introduction to the religious and historical context of *The Cloud of Unknowing* is David Knowles' *The English Mystical Tradition*.
3. Underlying this tradition and the whole of the Western Christian tradition of prayer are the fifth-century *Conferences* of John Cassian. They retain a real vitality and contemporary relevance to the needs of our own day. The essence of Cassian's teaching on prayer is contained in the

two brilliant 'Conferences of Abbot Isaac', *Conferences* 9 and 10.

4. One of the most inspired books of our time is *Saccidananda* by Abhishiktananda, a Benedictine monk who lived the Christian experience of prayer in India until his death in 1973. The book proclaims with unmistakable personal authority both the fully personal and fully universal nature of the Christian experience.

BIBLIOGRAPHY

Useful editions of some of the books cited are:
1. Abhishiktananda, *Saccidananda* (a Christian Approach to Advaitic Experience). I.S.P.C.K., Delhi 1974.
2. *Rule of St Benedict*. Latin text critical edition Cuthbert Butler, Herder, Freiburg 1912. There are many modern translations.
3. New English Bible, Oxford University Press with Cambridge University Press 1970.
4. John Cassian, *Institutes* and *Conferences*, translated by E. Gibson in 'A Select Library of Nicene and Post-Nicene Fathers of The Christian Church', Second Series, Volume XI. Wm B. Eerdmans Publishing Co., Michigan 1973.
5. *The Cloud of Unknowing*, ed. E. Underhill. Stuart and Watkins, London 1970 (original). Tr. William Johnston, Image Books, New York 1973.
6. Walter Hilton, *The Scale of Perfection*. Translated by Leo Sherley-Price, Penguin, 1957. A good modern selection is by Illtyd Trethowan O.S.B, Geoffrey Chapman, London 1975.

Moment of Christ

The Path of Meditation

Contents

Preface

Perhaps because it was the last thing he wrote, not many weeks before his death, I have re-read Fr John's foreword to this book many times. Although we did not fully understand how close to death he was, it seems to me that he knew it would be his last written message and so he compressed into a few hundred words an experience of prayer and a zeal to lead others into it which, to me, is the essence of wisdom's grand simplicity.

Over my years of discipleship with him I had learned to understand both his own simplicity and the simplicity of his teaching. When he spoke to the groups who came to meditate with us at the monasteries in London and Montreal, groups composed of widely differing types of people, the authority of his simplicity together with his considerable genius for language, anecdote and humour kept the group in profound attention and prepared them, as he intended, not for speculation but for silence.

During the last few years we recorded these talks at each session and then published them as cassettes in our 'Communitas' series. These will continue to be published and to nourish and inspire individuals and groups around the world for some years to come. So it is important to understand the context in which these written words were spoken. The groups met (and still do) at eight o'clock in the evening. One of the community meets newcomers to the Monday night introductory group and shows them down to the meditation-lecture room where people assemble and where music is playing. A few minutes before eight o'clock Fr John enters and sits on a chair near the stereo. He is facing anywhere between forty and a hundred people, some sitting on cushions on the floor, others on chairs lining the walls. The people come from all walks of life, ages and backgrounds. The clock chimes upstairs and, shortly after, Fr John gets up to remove the record. He sits again and sometimes has to be reminded to attach the small microphone to the front of his habit. He quietly clears his throat and begins the talk. There is always a quotation from the New Testament, sometimes opening, sometimes closing the talk. He plays some more quiet music, often Bach or plain-chant, closes it after a few moments ('so that we can leave behind all the words I have been using and enter into the silence of the one word') and resumes his seat for half an hour of meditation. After that he plays some more music and invites questions. Sometimes there are many, sometimes none. In either case he smiles, says a word of farewell and leaves the room, usually to be caught and questioned by people in the hall.

The atmosphere of these groups, with a sizable proportion of people coming straight from work, is extraordinary, silent and attentive and deeply serious. But there is no solemnity, no gimmicks, no rituals, because of the simplicity of what is being taught.

It is important to understand what these talks were designed to do and what Fr John hoped they could still do, even in print. Their aim is to persuade people of the importance and simplicity of the Christian tradition and practice of meditation. They are not therefore theological or philosophical statements. This kind of exposition of the teaching is to be found in his other books such as *Word into Silence*[1] and *Letters from the Heart*[2]. These talks are not designed to stimulate discussion but to inspire a desire for silence and personal discipline.

They are communicating ideas, of course, but also much more than ideas. As everyone who heard these talks in person could testify, they communicated an energy and extraordinary spirit. To be in that room was to know you were in the presence of a man who knew the Presence, was filled with it, joyfully, humorously and profoundly, and who embodied it. It is not very useful to try to describe this, of course. It always struck me how much of this spirit he conveyed by setting people free,

1. Darton, Longman and Todd, 1980.
2. Crossroad, New York, 1982.

not only to be silent but, afterwards, to laugh. It is important to know something of this special presence, if these talks are going to be read in the spirit they were heard in.

Fr John edited most of them, and I the rest. We left in a certain colloquial flavour and quite a lot of repetition. I would advise you not to skip the sentences where you see repetition. Rather I would advise you to read them twice. They are saying the same thing, but if you listen to them you will hear it differently and more deeply each time. I listened to the basic teaching many hundreds or perhaps some thousands of times. It never struck me as monotonous, because each time it was brilliantly set off in a new context, a new facet of the 'many-faceted diamond of God'.

A woman once told me of her experience of coming back to the groups after a year in the north of Canada. She had continued to meditate faithfully through the solitude and difficulty of the year. When she returned to Montreal she suddenly realized to her surprise how frightened she was to come back to the group. What, she thought, if I have been doing this meditation for the last year and now go to hear the talk and find a new teaching and find the old one discarded. Nevertheless, she came and was not betrayed. She could not describe her joy at hearing repeated the same teaching she had committed herself to. And yet she said, it sounded brand new and it was as if she were hearing it for the first time.

A teacher, a true master of the spiritual life like Fr John (who would have smiled at such a solemn title), teaches by gaining the attention of the whole person, not just by addressing the mind with ideas or the feelings with emotions. To be taught like this is itself an experience of the spiritual reality, although like all such experiences it can sound incredibly uninspiring when we come to describe it. I feel these talks in print can lead the reader into the same or a qualitatively similar experience of being in the presence of a great teacher who was filled with the wisdom love gives. If, I suppose, the reader is prepared not only to read but to listen as well.

Benedictine Priory,   LAURENCE FREEMAN, OSB
Montreal.

101

Foreword

Our purpose in publishing these Communitas talks is to make available the teaching that we give to the groups who come to our monastery on Monday and Tuesday evenings each week.

The essential content of each talk is very simple and is meant to serve as an encouragement to those who are following the path of meditation and to help them to follow that path with greater fervour.

It will be seen that meditation affects every part of our living and dying, and we have tried to include a wide cross-section of the talks that we give.

The usefulness of publishing the talks is that the book can serve as a source for spiritual reading by allowing the reader to turn to any of the talks according to the subject matter. The text is not a continuous narrative but can be entered into at any point.

Perhaps it might be useful to say a general word of introduction to our way of meditating.

It is our conviction that the central message of the New Testament is that there is really only one prayer and that this prayer is the prayer of Christ. It is a prayer that continues in our hearts day and night. I can describe it only as the stream of love that flows constantly between Jesus and his Father. This stream of love is the Holy Spirit.

Again it is our conviction that it is the most important task for any fully human life that we should become as open as possible to this stream of love. We have to allow this prayer to become our prayer, we have to enter into the experience of being swept out of ourselves – beyond ourselves into this wonderful prayer of Jesus – this great cosmic river of love.

In order for us to do this we must learn a way that is a way of silence – of stillness, and this by a discipline that is most demanding. It is as though we have to create a space within ourselves that will allow this higher consciousness – the consciousness of the prayer of Jesus – to envelop us in this powerful mystery.

We have got used to thinking of prayer in terms of 'my prayer' or 'my praise' of God, and it requires a complete re-thinking of our attitude to prayer if we are going to come to see it as a way through Jesus, with Jesus, and in Jesus.

The first requirement is that we begin to understand that we must pass beyond egoism, so that 'my' prayer just doesn't become even a possibility. We are summoned to see with the eyes of Christ and to love with the heart of Christ, and to respond to this summons we must pass beyond egoism. In practical terms this means learning to be so still and silent that we cease thinking about ourselves. This is of critical importance – we must be open to the Father through Jesus, and when we are at prayer we must become like the eye that can see but that cannot see itself.

The way we set out on this pilgrimage of 'other-centredness' is to recite a short phrase, a word that is commonly called today a mantra. The mantra is simply a means of turning our attention beyond ourselves – a way of unhooking us from our own thoughts and concerns.

Reciting the mantra brings us to stillness and to peace. We recite it for as long as we need to before we are caught up into the one prayer of Jesus. The general rule is that we must first learn to say it for the entire period of our meditation each morning and each evening and then to allow it to do its work of calming over a period of years.

The day will come when the mantra ceases to sound and we are lost in the eternal silence of God. The rule when this happens is not to try to possess this silence, to use it for one's own satisfaction. The clear rule is that as soon as we consciously realize that we are in this state of profound silence and begin to reflect about it we must gently and quietly return to our mantra.

Gradually the silences become longer and we are simply absorbed in the mystery of God. The important thing is to have the courage and generosity to return to the mantra as soon as we become self-conscious of the silence.

It is important not to try to invent or anticipate any of the experiences. I hope that, reading these talks, it will become clear that each of us is summoned to the heights of Christian prayer – each of us is summoned to fullness of life. What we need however is the humility to tread the way very faithfully over a period of years so that the prayer of Christ may indeed be the grounding experience of our life.

Montreal,   JOHN MAIN, OSB
October 1982

The Way of the Mantra

The most important part of our time together in our groups is that time we spend being silent together. Silence is the best preparation for meditation. When you begin to meditate, spend a couple of moments getting really comfortable. If you want to sit in a chair, sit in an upright one. If you sit on the floor, sit in a comfortable position. Then try to be as still as you can for the entire time of the meditation. It isn't all that easy for most of us when we start, but meditation involves coming to a still-ness of spirit and a stillness of body. It gives you an awareness of yourself as one, as still, as whole. So you have to learn to sit as still as you can. When you are seated and are still, close your eyes and then begin to repeat, interiorly and silently in your heart, the word *Maranatha*. In some traditions, this is called a 'mantra', in others, a 'prayer phrase' or 'prayer word'.

The essence of meditation and the art of meditation is simply learning to say that word, to recite it, to sound it, from the beginning to the end of the meditation. It is utterly simple – say it like this: 'Ma-ra-na-tha'. Four equally stressed syllables. Most people say the word in conjunction with their breathing, but that isn't of the essence. The essence requires that you say the word from beginning to end and continue to say it right throughout your meditation time. The speed should be some-thing that is fairly slow, fairly rhythmical – 'Ma-ra-na-tha'. And that is all you need to know in order to meditate. You have a word, and you say your word, and you remain still.

The purpose of meditation for each of us is that we come to our own centre. In many traditions, meditation is spoken of as a pilgrimage – a pilgrimage to your own centre, your own heart, and there you learn to remain awake, alive and still. The word 'religion' means a 're-linking', being 'rebound' to your own centre. The importance of meditation is to discover from your own experience that there is only one centre and that the life task for all of us is to find our source and our meaning by discovering and living out of that one centre.

I think that what we have to understand is that returning to our centre, discovering our own centre, is the first task and the first responsibility of every life that is to become fully human. Again, in meditation, in the discipline of it, you will discover from your own experience that to be at one with our own centre means that we are at one with every centre.

The truly spiritual man or woman is one who is in harmony, one who has discovered that harmony within themselves and *lives* this harmony with creation and with God. What we learn in meditation is that to be in our own centre is to be in God. This is not only the great teaching of all Eastern religions but it is the fundamental insight of Christianity. In the words of Jesus, 'The kingdom of heaven is within you.' And the kingdom, in the teaching of Jesus, is an experience. It is an experience of the power of God. It is an experience of the basic energy of the universe. And, again in the vision of Jesus, we understand that this basic power, out of which we are invited to live our own lives vitally, is love. The Christian experience is learning to live at this level of reality. St John of the Cross expressed this when he said that he knew that God was the centre of his soul. Each one of us is invited to discover the validity of that statement from our own experience. The invitation is to discover, at the centre, both energy and power, and in silence, in stillness, to discover in that power the peace that is beyond all understanding.

We have to use certain words to talk about this. We use words like 'enlightenment' or 'vitalization'. But they are terms that we use to describe what can only be *known*. And the wonder of the experience of prayer, of deep meditation, is that in the experience of the power of God we awaken to reality – a reality that is everywhere. What we discover is that we cannot know that reality from outside, and this for the very simple reason that there is no reality outside of God. That is why we must enter within. We must leave the world of illusion and enter the world of reality. The energy released in meditation is not an energy that is released and received from some outside force. It is the very life-force that each of us possesses, coming to fulfilment, coming to actualization when we turn our whole attention beyond ourselves to the Other. This is the experience of transcendence. This is the expansion of spirit that brings each of us wholly into the gift of our own being.

What we have to discover in meditation is that we *are*, that we are alive, that we are real and that we are rooted in reality. Talking about prayer or about meditation or talking about God serves only one purpose – not to teach us anything 'new' but to reveal to us what is present, what is actual, what is real. To sit down to meditate, to sit down to be still, we need simplicity. We need to become childlike. We must understand that the peace within us is beyond all understanding. We are invited to enter wholly into the experience of it. Meditation, we might describe, as accepting fully the gift of our own continuous creation.

But above all we must beware of becoming intoxicated by the words. Let me end by repeating for you the process that leads us to simplicity, to silence, to awareness and to transcendence which is leaving ourselves behind, leaving our own thoughts behind, leaving our imagination and our own ideas behind. The way is the way of the mantra, of *the* word. When you sit down, sit still and comfortably, begin to say your word and say it from the beginning to the end – 'Ma-ra-na-tha'.

St Paul wrote this to the Corinthians:

For the same God who said, 'Out of darkness let light shine', has caused his light to shine within us, to give the light of revelation – the revelation of the glory of God in the face of Jesus Christ.[1]

The power of this light is to be found within our own hearts, within each one of us. What each of us must learn to do is to be open to that power and to live our lives out of it. What I

1. 2 Cor. 4:6

suggest to you is that you try to build into the structure of your life a time each morning and evening to be still, to be silent, to be humble, to be simple, to be *in* God.

Leaving Distractions Behind

Learning to meditate is the most practical thing in the world. You require only one quality when you begin. That is seriously to want to learn to meditate. The process is absolute simplicity. In general, we are obsessed with the idea of techniques, methods, methodologies, and so on, but in meditation the Way is simplicity itself. Let me describe it to you again.

You need to find a quiet place, as quiet as you can and, having found it, you sit down. I recommend you to close your eyes gently and then to begin to say your word. The word I have suggested that you say is the word *maranatha*. It is an Aramaic word and its importance is both that it is one of the most ancient Christian prayers there is and that it possesses the right sound to bring us to the silence and stillness necessary for meditation. That's all there is. Sit upright, and remain sitting upright. Then in a growing stillness of body and spirit say your word, 'Ma-ra-na-tha'.

I want now to address a particular question that we all encounter. It is the question of distractions. What should you do when you begin to meditate and distracting thoughts come into your mind? The advice that the tradition has to give us is to ignore the distractions and to say your word and to keep on saying your word. Don't waste any energy in trying to furrow your brow and say, 'I will not think of what I'm going to have for dinner', or 'who I'm going to see today', or 'where I'm going tomorrow', or whatever the distraction may be. Don't try to use any energy to dispel the distraction. Simply ignore it and the way to ignore it is to say your word.

In other words, when you meditate your energy must be channelled in a single course, and the way of that course is your word. You can't fully appreciate this advice outside of the experience of meditation. Meditation is, as I have suggested to you, about stillness. It is like the stillness of a pool of water. The distractions that we have when we begin to meditate are only ripples and currents and eddies that disturb the water. But as you begin to meditate, and stillness comes over you, the depth of the water becomes clearer and clearer in the stillness. The experience of meditation, the experience to which each of us is summoned and which all of us are capable of, is to discover that depth within us which is like a deep pool of water, water of an infinite depth. The marvellous thing about such a pool of water is that when it is still and the sun strikes it, every drop of the water in its infinite depth is like a drop of crystal alive with the light of the sun. That is exactly what we are called to in meditation – to discover the depth of our own spirit and the capacity of our own spirit to be in complete harmony with the God who tells us that he is light. 'I am the light of the world.'

Don't misunderstand this. As I have told you with absolute truth, meditation *is* simplicity itself. But you do have to be serious in your own commitment to this deep harmony within your own spirit – a harmony that reveals to you the spirit of God within you. You have to be serious.

Consider the problem of distraction again. One of the things that all of us find as we tread our path of meditation with simplicity and with humility is that there will be certain things in our lives that have to change. For example, I should think it would be very difficult to meditate if you spend three or four hours a day watching television. A great enemy of all prayer and of all recollection is a plethora of images in our minds. You will all discover, and I am sure you are already discovering it from your own experience, that it is foolishness to add indiscriminately to this plethora of images.

Listen to the words of St Paul writing to the Corinthians, 'Remember: sparse sowing, sparse reaping; sow bountifully, and you will reap bountifully.'[1] There is a marvellous harvest for all of us in our own spirit. But the call to this openness to the spirit of Jesus does ask for real generosity from each of us. Firstly we need generosity in putting aside the half-hour for

1. 2 Cor. 9:6

meditation every morning and every evening. And I understand very well that that does ask for a very generous response and a very creative response, given the tasks and responsibilities of your own lives. Secondly, a great generosity is called for in the actual time of your meditation to say your word, *maranatha*, from the beginning to the end. So often we want to follow our own thoughts, our own insights, our own religious feeling. But we must learn to leave everything behind and to seek the spirit in our own hearts.

Thirdly, there is the generosity needed to put our whole life into harmony with the spirit in our heart – to see to it that we don't add to the distractions. All of us have distractions arising from our very life. We all have things we are concerned about, things we are worried about, things we are responsible for. So what we must do is put our whole life into harmony with this search, this pilgrimage, which is a pilgrimage to our own heart. It is a pilgrimage that leads us to a freshness of spirit, a clarity of heart and a vitality of spirit. Meditation is not turning our back on our life or on our responsibilities. Quite the contrary, in meditation we seek to be open fully to the gift of the life that is given us. This is nothing less than the gift of eternal life, eternal life that we are invited to be open to *now*. We need to be responsible people, to be *responsive* people, responsive to the gift of eternal life. As Jesus tells us, eternal life is to know our heavenly Father. In meditation we turn aside from everything that is passing away in order to know what is eternal.

Now let me remind you. Sit down when you go to meditate. Sit comfortably with your spine upright. Close your eyes and very peacefully and serenely begin to say your word in your heart – silently – 'Ma-ra-na-tha'. Forget the time. We will meditate for about twenty-five minutes. You have to *be* during that time. To be at peace, to be still, still in body and still in spirit and to be open to life and to the Lord of life.

Listen again to St Paul writing to the Corinthians:

For the love of Christ leaves us no choice, when once we have reached the conclusion that one man died for all and therefore all mankind has died. His purpose in dying for all was that men, while still in life, should cease to live for

111

themselves, and should live for him who for their sake died and was raised to life.[2]

2. 2 Cor. 5:14–15

A Call to Fullness of Life

One of the great difficulties about learning to meditate is that it is so simple. In our society most people think that only very complex things are worthwhile. To meditate you have to learn to be simple, and that provides a real challenge for all of us.

The simplicity that is involved in learning to meditate is turning away from multiplicity and from all the options that are before us and concentrating in utter simplicity of being. Think of learning to ride a bike. To learn how to ride it you have first of all to learn to balance yourself on the bike. And later you have to concentrate both on keeping your balance and steering a straight course. The extraordinary thing is that as you do devote all your energies to being balanced and steady you discover unexpected harmony and a new freedom. The same is true with meditation. Like learning to ride a bike you have to be willing to learn. You have to be willing to concentrate. You have to learn to direct all your energies to the simple task of being balanced and travelling steadily in one direction.

To be *on the way* in meditation you have to be simple enough to turn aside from everything else so that you can really be harmonious and free. Meditation is openness to a reality that we can only discover and only encounter in the depths of our own being. So we have to learn to be silent and to be profoundly silent. The extraordinary thing is that, in spite of all the distractions of the modern world, this silence is perfectly possible for all of us. To descend into this silence we have to devote time, energy and love. The first thing you have to understand about meditating is that you have to devote the time to it. It is necessary to meditate every morning and every evening. The minimum amount of time is twenty minutes. I recommend you, as gently as you can, to extend that to about half an hour.

Now let me just repeat to you what is to be done in that time. Sit down and spend a couple of moments in sitting comfortably so you can stay still in the same position for the whole time. Then close your eyes and begin to recite your mantra interiorly, in silence. The art of meditating is to learn to recite your word from the beginning of your meditation to the end, 'Maranatha'. I cannot over-emphasize to you how important that is. What I would suggest to you is never be deflected from the path of saying your word, your mantra, from the beginning to the end of your meditation time. You should sound it silently in your heart. It's the sounding of the word interiorly that opens up for us levels of awareness that are not possible outside this depth of silence. I said that meditation is a learning process. But most learning processes that we are familiar with are learning processes in which we are learning to do something. Meditation is not learning to do, it is learning to *be*. It's learning to *be yourself*, to enter into the gift of your own being. We have come to understand this very clearly and confidently. Another way of putting the same thing would be to say that meditation is learning to accept the gift of your own being, of your own creation. To be in harmony with your own being and with your own continuous creation is also to be in harmony with all of the creation around us, it is being in harmony with the Creator.

One thing we learn in meditation is the priority of being over action. Indeed, no action has any meaning, or at least any lasting depth of meaning, unless it springs from being, from the depths of your own being. That is why meditation is a way that leads us away from shallowness to depth, to profundity. Learning to be is learning to begin to live out of the fullness of life. That is our invitation. It is learning to begin to be a full person. The mysterious thing about the Christian revelation is that as we live our lives fully, we live out the eternal consequences of our own creation. We are no longer living as if we were exhausting a limited supply of life that we received at our birth. What we know from the teaching of Jesus is that we become infinitely filled with life when we are at one with the

114

source of our being and enter fully into union with our Creator, the One who *is*, a God who describes himself as 'I Am'.

The art of living, living our lives as fully human beings, is the art of living out of the eternal newness of our origin and living fully from our centre, which is to say from our spirit as it springs from the creative hand of God. The terrible thing about so much modern, materialistic living is that it can be so shallow, without a serious recognition of the depths and the possibilities that are there for each of us if only we will take the time and undertake the discipline to meditate. The discipline is to sit down to meditate and during meditation to say our word from the beginning to the end, every morning and every evening.

In the Christian vision we are led to this source of our being by a guide, and our guide is Jesus, the fully realized man, the man wholly open to God. As we meditate each day we may not recognize our guide. That is why the Christian journey is always a journey of faith. But as we approach the centre of our being, as we enter our heart, we find that we are greeted by our guide, greeted by the one who has led us. We are welcomed by the person who calls each one of us into personal fullness of being. The consequences or results of meditation, are just this fullness of life – harmony, oneness and energy, a divine energy that we find in our own heart, in our own spirit. That energy is the energy of all creation. As Jesus tells us, it is the energy that is love.

The vision is a staggering vision and we have to learn, as I am saying, to be simple and humble as we approach it. The simplicity and the humility we learn by saying our word from beginning to end, with patience and with faithfulness, with courage and with love. Listen to the words of St Paul writing to the Philippians:

I count everything sheer loss, because all is far outweighed by the gain of knowing Christ Jesus my Lord, for whose sake I did in fact lose everything. I count it so much garbage, for the sake of gaining Christ and finding myself incorporate in him. . . . All I care for is to know Christ, to experience the power of his resurrection, and to share his sufferings, in

115

growing conformity with his death, if only I may finally arrive at the resurrection from the dead. . . . He will transfigure the body belonging to our humble state, and give it a form like that of his own resplendent body, by the very power which enables him to make all things subject to himself. Therefore, my friends, beloved friends whom I long for, my joy, my crown, stand firm in the Lord.[1]

That is what meditation summons us to – to experience in our own spirit the power of the resurrection with Jesus.

1. Phil. 3:8, 10–11, 21—4:1

Infinite Expansion of Love

These words of Jesus are reported in the Gospel of St John:

> In very truth, anyone who gives heed to what I say and puts his trust in him who sent me has hold of eternal life, and does not come up for judgement, but has already passed from death to life.[1]

Meditation is focused right in the heart, right in the centre of the Christian mystery. And the Christian mystery can only be penetrated if we enter into the mystery of death and resurrection. That is the essential message of Jesus. No one can be a follower of Jesus unless he leaves self behind. The person who would find his life must be ready to lose it.[2] And in all the parables drawn from nature which Jesus gives, the seed must fall into the ground and die, or it remains alone.

What we do in meditation and in the life-long process of meditation is to refine our perception down to the single focal point which is Christ. Christ is our way, our goal, our guide. But he is our goal only in the sense that once we are wholly with him, wholly at one with him, we pass with him to the Father. In meditation we come to that necessary single-point-edness and find it is Christ.

It is impossible to talk about meditation as it is impossible to talk about the Christian experience in any adequate terms. As one philosopher put it, 'As soon as we begin to speak of the mysteries of Christ, we hear the gates of heaven closing.' Yet we have to try to speak, though we speak only to bring people to silence. The silence of our meditation is our way into

1. John 5:24   2. cf. Mark 8:35

117

the indescribable mystery to be found within the heart of each one of us, if only we will undertake this pilgrimage to one-pointedness, to single-mindedness. We have to find some way of trying to explain what the journey is and why the journey is so worthwhile and why it requires courage.

The modern consciousness is not very keen on the idea of narrowness. Yet meditation is a way by which we focus our attention. We *narrow* our attention down to one point. It seems to me that it might help you to understand what meditation is about if you can see it as a great double triangle.

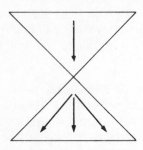

Here you have the triangle on the top, pointing down and then the triangle underneath it, opening out. The triangle on the top is learning to concentrate, learning to focus our attention entirely upon and within Christ. In that sense it is narrowing our attention to a single point. But as soon as we do, the way is opened to infinite expansion on the other side. A single point thus leads us into infinite expansion. It is through Jesus that we pass over from everything that is dead, from everything that is restricted, mortal and finite, into the infinite expansion of God which is infinite expansion of love.

As we come to that one-pointedness we need courage. We need the courage to persevere, not to be afraid of the narrowness and not to be afraid of the demand that is being made on us. The demand *is* an absolute demand, the demand of faith, to believe that what Jesus says is true when he says that if we lose our life, then and only then, will we be able to find it.

Meditation is like breaking through the sound barrier. When you come to that point there can be a lot of turbulence. It is

118

at this moment that the discipline you have learned by saying your mantra and by faithfully continuing to say it, will enable you to be entirely open to the love of Jesus which takes you through it. We need discipline to love and to be open to love because we need discipline to be free. As we approach that point it seems that we require great courage. It seems that we require great perseverance. What we come to know is that all the courage and all the capacity to persevere are freely ours in Jesus.

This is the intoxicating foundation of the whole Christian mystery – that the passover is accomplished. It is achieved in Jesus and it is his courage, his faithfulness and his love that take us into the infinite expansion that is God. So there is no essential ground for our fear, for our postponement, for our holding back. Everything *is* ours in the love of Jesus. Our task is a very humble one. It is the task of acknowledging and entering into our own poverty. We do that by saying our word, by faithful commitment to our mantra. It is a very humble task but it is a task that leads us into the infinite love of God.

We have to remember that the axis of Christian life is death and resurrection. The resurrection is to new life, limitless life, eternal life. Jesus tells us that if we are open to him, if we have the courage to listen to him, to hear what he says, then eternal life, infinite life and the infinite expansion of life is ours. That is the mystery. That is what we are invited to be open to. That is what we are invited to proclaim to the world.

The Way is the way of daily fidelity, a daily aligning and re-aligning of our lives on the mystery that is simplicity, that is love, that is unity. Listen to Jesus again, 'In very truth, anyone who gives heed to what I say and puts his trust in him who sent me has hold of eternal life and does not come up for judgement but has already passed from death to life.'

Discipline and Liberty

One of the things that I suppose everybody strives for in their life is to discover a real liberty of spirit. We are constrained by so many things – by fear and by trying to project the image of ourselves that we feel others expect. I think people suffer a great deal of frustration because they cannot be themselves and cannot make contact with themselves. James Joyce once described one of his characters as 'always living at a certain distance from himself'. Now what Jesus came to proclaim was precisely this liberty. The liberty to be ourselves and the liberty to find ourselves in him, through him and with him. Meditation is simply the way to that liberty. It is the way to your own heart. It is the way to the depth of your own being where you can simply *be* – not having to justify yourself or to apologize for yourself but simply rejoicing in the gift of your own being. Freedom is not just freedom *from* things. Christian liberty is not just freedom from desire, from sin. We are free *for* intimate union with God, which is another way of saying we are free for infinite expansion of Spirit in God.

Meditation is entering into that experience of being free for God, transcending desire, sin, leaving it behind; transcending ego, leaving it behind, so that the whole of our being is utterly available to God. It is in that profound availability that we become ourselves. Consider these words of Jesus:

Turning to the Jews who had believed in him, Jesus said, 'If you dwell within the revelation I have brought, you are indeed my disciples; you shall know the truth, and the truth will set you free.[1]

1. John 8:31–2

Meditation is simply dwelling within the revelation, dwelling within the vision of God.

To meditate each of us must learn to be wholly still and that is a discipline. When you meditate you should spend a few moments just getting into a comfortable sitting posture. But then all of us at some time during our meditation feel like moving and by not moving, by staying still, we will undergo what may perhaps be our first lesson in transcending desires and overcoming that fixation that we so often have with ourselves. So I want you to understand that meditation does involve this real discipline and the first discipline we probably have to learn is to sit quite still. That is why it is important to take care of the practical details like wearing loose clothing, and finding a comfortable chair or cushion to sit on, so that you can be comfortable and so enter in fully and generously to the discipline.

Then you close your eyes gently and begin to repeat your word – 'Maranatha'. The purpose of repeating the word is to gently lead you away from your own thoughts, your own ideas, your own desire, your own sin and to lead you into the presence of God, by turning you around, by turning you away from yourself towards God. Say the word gently but deliberately, say the word in a relaxed way but articulate it silently in your mind, 'Ma-ra-na-tha'. Gradually, as you continue to meditate, the word will sink down into your heart. And this experience of liberty of spirit is the uniting of mind and heart in God.

As you begin to meditate all sorts of questions will arise in your mind. Is this for me? What does it mean? Should I be doing this? Am I getting anything out of it? and so forth. All these questions you must leave behind. You must transcend all self-questioning, and you must come to your meditation with childlike simplicity. Unless you become like little children, you *cannot* enter the Kingdom of Heaven.

So my advice to you is, say your word, be content to say your word and allow the gift to be given by God. Don't demand it. We should come to our meditation with no demands and no expectations, but with just that generosity of spirit that allows us to be as present as we can to ourselves and to God. Meditating is very, very simple. Don't complicate it. As you meditate you should become more and more simple, not more and more complicated. As you know, nothing in this life that is really worth having, can be had without a considerable amount of self-transcendence. It is the real loss of self that brings us the joy. And meditating is having the nerve to take the attention off yourself and to put it forward, to put it forward on God, to look ahead.

We are used to dwelling in a world with thousands of mirrors, seeing ourselves, seeing how others see us, constantly. Meditating is a definitive smashing of all the mirrors. It is looking, not at reflections of things, not at reflections of yourself. It is looking into the reality that is God. And, in that experience, being expanded into infinity. That is liberty of spirit. The liberty is the fruit of the discipline and so if you want to learn to meditate it is absolutely necessary to meditate every day. Every day of your life, every morning and every evening. There are no short-cuts. There are no crash courses. There is no instant mysticism. It is simply the gentle and gradual change of direction. The change of heart that comes is to stop thinking of yourself and to be open to God, to the wonder of him, to the glory of him and to the love of him.

Silent Communion

In our Community we are trying to share, as widely as we can, the tradition of Christian meditation. We hold the conviction in our Community here that all the spiritual riches of the New Testament, the full riches of what Christ came to proclaim, are available for each of us if only we can enter into his experience. Look simply and clearly at the New Testament and you will see that the central thrust of the Gospel is this proclamation of fullness of life, fullness of being. And the fullness of life it speaks of comes from living out of the depths of our being. This conviction of the New Testament grew out of the experience of the men who made the proclamation that all of us are invited to live our lives out of the power of God, the power of his love. To 'enter the kingdom of God' is simply to live our life out of this power and to have our lives transformed by it.

What we have to share, out of the tradition of monastic prayer, is that this power is to be discovered in all of us when we commit ourselves to *depth* of living and when we commit ourselves with all seriousness. The language of the New Testament described this commitment as being 'rooted and founded in Christ'. I think we might describe this in more modern language as the full acceptance by each one of us of the challenge to *be*. The New Testament also used the word 'maturity'. That is what we are called to by this challenge. An adult acceptance of all the challenges and the responsibilities of life leads to 'fullness of being'. What is abundantly clear from reading the New Testament is that the call of Christians is a call to 'growth', to 'depth', and equally clear is that this depth and maturity take place 'in Christ'. Here we enter the heart of the Christian mystery. To 'be a Christian' is to be one with Christ. Putting this another way, it means that to be a Christian is to live your life out of the resources of your union with Christ. This is precisely what Christian prayer is about.

This union of course clarifies our perception. We must be very clear of what it is about or we are in danger of missing the whole point of Christianity. The call of Jesus is to oneness with him, so that with him we may be one with the Father. So what we have to try to remember and be always mindful of is that the essence of Christian prayer is not dialogue but union, oneness. I think most of us know this in our heart of hearts. We know from our own experience that if we see prayer as dialogue, 'dialoguing with God', it frequently ends up as a monologue.

The tradition that we follow as Benedictine monks calls us both to understand and to experience our prayer as silent communion within our own heart. Union brings us to communion, that is to a oneness discovered within ourselves but which leads us to oneness with God and to oneness with all. It is a communion that is indescribably enriching, because it takes us right out of ourselves, beyond ourselves into union with all, with the All, with God. Unity, union, communion is the threefold growth of a Christian.

The experience of prayer is the experience of coming into full union with the energy that created the universe. What Christianity has to proclaim to the world is that that energy is love and it is the well-spring out of which all creation flows. It is the well-spring that gives each one of us the creative power to be the person we are called to be – a person rooted and founded in love.

Our tradition tells us all that, but it tells us still more. It tells us too that this is not just poetry. Our practice of meditation tells us that this is the *experience* to which each of us is summoned. The way to it is the way of simplicity and of faithfulness. What our tradition teaches is that to enter this mystery we must learn to be silent. Meditation is entry into profound silence. To meditate means to live out of the centre of our being,that profound centre we find when we determine not to be shallow, not to be content to rest on the surface but to live out of the depths of our being. We must opt for this, because it is in the depths of our being that the union with Christ is continuously taking place. The path to follow is a path of almost incredible simplicity and this is perhaps a good part of the difficulty for us as men and women of the twentieth century. To enter into the simplicity of it demands courage. To meditate, each of us must learn to be very simple, to be very quiet, to learn to say our word.

When we meditate the first thing to do, after sitting down, is to spend a couple of moments getting comfortable, knowing that during your meditation you are going to sit as still as you can. Close your eyes. Then you begin to say your word. The word I recommend you to say is the word, *maranatha* (an ancient Christian prayer, in Aramaic, the language of Jesus, which means, 'Come, Lord'). The art of meditation, and what we have to learn, is to say the word from the beginning to the end of our meditation and to say it effortlessly, peacefully, serenely: 'Maranatha', four syllables – ma-ra-na-tha. It is the recitation of the word that gradually, over a period of weeks and months and years, brings you to that depth, to that silence.

Now when you begin, you have to take this on faith. You have to learn to accept it as part of a tradition. To learn to be faithful to it you have to try, as best you can in the circumstances of your own life, to meditate every morning and every evening. As I said, meditation is a commitment to depth and a turning aside from shallow, surface approaches to living and to understanding life. It is certainly my own experience that the minimum that is required if you are serious about learning to meditate, is to take that half-an-hour slot in the morning and again in the evening every day. During your half-hour each morning and each evening follow the same routine. But it is never the same. Choose a quiet place, sit comfortably. The only essential rule of posture is that your spine is upright. You can either sit on the floor on a cushion or on a chair, whichever is more comfortable for you and then, with every muscle in your body relaxed, including the muscles of your face, begin to recite your word, gently, peacefully, serenely but continuously.

If you are patient and if you are faithful (and meditation will teach you to be both patient and faithful), then meditation will bring you into deeper and deeper realms of silence. It is in the silence that we are led into the mystery of the eternal silence of God. This is what St Paul says when writing to the Ephesians and telling the ordinary people of Ephesus, people who are not that different from us – what is the promise of the Christian life:

So he came and proclaimed the good news; peace to you who were far off and peace to those who were nearby; for through him, we both alike have access to the Father in the one Spirit.[1]

That is what meditation is about – access to the Father in the one Spirit, the Spirit who dwells in your heart and in mine, the Spirit who is the Spirit of God. Christian meditation is simply openness to that Spirit, in the depth of our being, in all simplicity, in all humility, in all love.

1. Eph. 2:17

The Peace of Christ

There is an aspect of meditation that experience makes us all familiar with. It is an aspect that is deeply inserted into the Christian tradition. The Christian knows that Jesus is the Way, the Truth and the Life. And as he himself told us, he came to give us his peace and to leave us peace. St Luke begins his gospel saying that Christ came 'to guide our feet into the way of peace'.[1] Christian peace is something unique and we can only encounter it in Christ.

As St Paul puts it in the Letter to the Romans, 'Let us continue at peace with God through our Lord Jesus Christ'.[2] Meditation is our way into the peace of Christ because he dwells in our heart, and in meditation we seek him in our heart because 'he himself is our peace'.[3] In his letter to the Ephesians Paul speaks of Christ as having broken down all the barriers symbolized by the dividing wall in the Temple, which separated the outer from the inner court, the outer from the inner reality. In Christ reality is one again.

Meditation does just that in our own lives. It breaks down all the barriers set up within us, between our outer and inner life and brings the whole of us into harmony. The peace of Christ, which is beyond all understanding, beyond all analysis, arises from this unity. The choice proposed by Paul, the challenge in Paul, is to live according to the Spirit which creates this unity. In other words we are invited to live out of the fullness of power that is there in the heart of each of us, if only we will turn to it and if only we will be open to it.

What Paul is saying is that the invitation is to live out of the depth of our being, not according to the surface or to 'the flesh'

1. Luke 1:79   2. Rom. 5:1   3. Eph. 2:14

or to 'the world'. What Paul sees so clearly is that the world and the flesh divorced from the Spirit can only lead to death. But the Spirit enlivens everything, fills everything with life, including the world and the flesh. It enlivens by calling all into unity with Christ. All things, the whole of creation are brought into unity in Christ. This is the source of our peace.

In the Christian vision of the New Testament peace arises from harmony, communion with God. 'Peace is my gift to you,' said Jesus.[4] In his farewell discourse at the Last Supper, as reported by John, Jesus speaks of his return to the Father, and then he adds, 'I have told you all this so that in me you may find peace.'[5]

Now meditation is our way to peace. A commitment to silence is the first step into finding this peace of Christ. We discover in the practice of meditation, returning to it day after day, morning and evening, that the silence which is the peace of Christ enables us to be fully awake, fully alive. It is a silence of wakefulness and vitality because it is a silence filled with God's presence. Christian prayer is a commitment to a silence in which we find our own roots in the eternal silence of God, a silence in which we enter into profound harmony and find ourselves in communion.

The way of prayer is the way of union, of oneness. No Greek, no Jew, no male, no female – but eternal harmony and eternal fulfilment in God. This was the message of Paul writing to the Ephesians:

Your world was a world without hope and without God. But now, in union with Christ Jesus, you who once were far off have been brought near through the shedding of Christ's blood. For he is himself our peace. Gentiles and Jews, he has made the two one, and in his own body of flesh and blood he has broken down the enmity which stood like a dividing wall between them; for he annulled the law with its rules and regulations, so as to create out of the two, a single new humanity in himself, thereby making peace.[6]

Meditation is a commitment to unity, and so it involves a

4. John 14:27   5. John 16:33   6. Eph. 2:12–15

turning away from alienation, from external divisions and from internal dividedness. The spiritual man or woman is one who is 'in love' – in love within themselves beyond dividedness, and loving towards all the brethren beyond division. And most miraculously we are in love with God beyond all alienation, in Jesus. St Paul ends that section 'for through him we both alike have access to the Father in the one Spirit'. If you leave it at the level of words Christianity is unbelievable. We couldn't believe that it is our destiny to have such perfect access to the Father and the Spirit. It is beyond what the human mind could think of or comprehend. It is only in the experience of prayer that the truth of the Christian revelation engulfs us. That is the invitation of Christian prayer, to lose ourselves and to be absorbed in God.

Commitment to Simplicity

The more we talk about meditation the more we need to remind
ourselves of it as a way of simplicity. Simplicity is the condition
of goodness, happiness, blessedness and we learn simplicity
through poverty. Jesus taught, 'How blessed [how happy] are
those who know that they are poor; the kingdom of heaven is
theirs.'[1]

As a goal simplicity is something very unfamiliar to us. Most
of us are carefully trained to see that only complexity is really
worthy of respect. To understand simplicity we have to enter
into it ourselves. We have to enter the simplicity of God and
be simplified ourselves in the process.

You have heard it said, I am sure, that meditation is 'the
way to reality'. It is firstly the way to the reality of our own
being. By meditating, we learn to *be*. Not to be any particular
role or particular thing but just to *be*. The best way of describ-
ing that being is to say that we are in a state of utter simplicity.
We are not trying to act. We are not trying to apologize for
being who we are or as we are. We are, simply, living out of
the depths of our own being, secure and affirmed in our own
rootedness in reality. As I say, this is an ideal unfamiliar to
most of us because we are trained to think that we find truth
only amid complexity. Yet I think we all know at a deeper level
of our being that truth can only be found in utter simplicity, in
openness. Remembering the sharpness of our vision in childhood should teach us this. What we all require is the child's
sense of wonder, the simple childlikeness to worship before the
magnificence of creation.

Simplicity is not necessarily easy. One of the difficulties for

1. Mat. 5:3

130

people who want to learn to meditate is just this. They ask, 'What do you have to do to meditate?' When they are told that you have to sit still and you have to learn just to say one word or one short phrase, people are often scandalized. I have had people say to me, 'Well, I've got a Ph.D. in Advanced Physics or Comparative Religion. That might be all right for the common people but for me, there must be something a little more demanding than that.' But that is the essence of meditation, to learn to be silent, to learn to be still and to learn that revelation comes in penetrating to the roots of things, to the silent roots.

Meditation is a way of breaking through from a world of illusion into the pure light of reality. The experience of meditation is that of becoming anchored in Truth, in the Way and in Life. In the Christian vision that anchor is Jesus. He reveals to us that God is the ground of our being, that none of us have any existence outside of him, that he is the Way, the Truth and Life. The great illusion that most of us are caught in is that we are the centre of the world and that everything and everyone revolves around us. Getting our Ph.D.s can serve to confirm us in that illusion. But in meditation we learn that this is not the truth. The truth is that God is the centre and everyone of us has being from his gift, from his power and from his love. Now this doesn't happen over night and, as I have suggested to you, to learn to meditate you must return to it every day, every morning and every evening, and during your meditation you must learn to recite your word from beginning to end.

The experience of meditation is that we are gradually made free. Meditation is the great way of liberation. For example, we are liberated from the past because in our meditation, we let it go when we say our word. We become open to the present through the discipline of saying the word. Thus we learn to be more and more open to our life in the present moment. The fears and regrets of the past lose their power to dominate us. We are no longer dominated by them because we are securely inserted in Being. In meditation we learn that we are because God is. We learn that simply being is our greatest gift. By being open to it, we become rooted in the ground of our being. Similarly, we are liberated from the future, from worry or from fear. Indeed what we learn in meditation is that in the power of Christ we are liberated from all fear. Fear itself is the greatest obstacle between us and reality. The Christian vision has this to show each of us – that the great power that dispels all fear is love. The heart of the Christian message is that God is love and that Jesus has delivered us from the slavery of fear and has brought each of us into the light and love of God.

What each of us is invited to be open to is the capacity to enter into the very experience of Jesus himself. In the Christian revelation he has broken through the veil of fear and limitation. His risen life has opened up the way for us to enter into the pure light of reality, the pure light of love. What we learn in meditation is that this isn't just theology or theological poetry but that this is the present, living reality that is at the centre of our being. But to enter the Way as a way of Light, a way of Love, a way of limitless Life requires openness, generosity and simplicity on our part. Above all, it requires commitment. Not commitment to a cause or to an ideology but commitment in our own lives to the simplicity of the daily return to the roots of our own existence, a commitment to respond to life with attention, to create the space in our own lives to live fully. What we learn in meditation, in the silence of it and the simplicity of it, is that we have nothing to fear from the commitment to creating this space.

I think all of us fear commitment because it seems to be a reducing of our options. We say to ourselves, 'Well, if I commit myself to meditating, then I'll not be able to do other things.' But I think what all of us find is that this fear dissolves in the actual commitment to be serious, to be open, to live not out of the shallows of our being, but out of its depths. What we all find in the experience of meditation is that our horizons are expanding not contracting and we find not constraint but liberty.

How does this happen? I think it happens as a result of our commitment, not to an abstract ideal or to an ideology but to simplicity, the simplicity that is required to sit down every morning, to close our eyes and to recite the one word from beginning to end. Begin your day like this, out of the essence of your own nature. Prepare for your day by being. Then in the evening return and give meaning to everything you have done during the day by similarly being open to your own root-edness in God and open to the ground of your own being.

The mantra will lead you into a greater silence. The silence leads you to greater depth. In the depth you find not ideals or ideologies but a person who is God, who is Love. The Way is the way of simplicity. What we have to learn in meditation is to accept to be more and more simple every day of our lives. Listen to the words of Jesus again:

How blessed are those who know that they are poor; the kingdom of heaven is theirs. . . . How blessed are those whose hearts are pure; they shall see God.[2]

Meditation is the way to purity of heart, leaving behind all fear and all limitation and entering – simply – into God's presence.

2. Mat. 5:3, 8

The Way of Liberation

Some of you will have been meditating for long enough now for me to try to say something about the way that meditation leads us. I want to say a few words about meditation as a commitment to reality. I am sure you know from your own experience so far that meditation doesn't allow us to play any games. If we are committed to saying the mantra from the beginning to the end, and if we are committed to it absolutely on a daily basis in our life, every morning and every evening, then as we continue we are more and more profoundly committed to, and open to, reality: the reality of our own being, the reality of all creation and the reality of God. The truly religious man or woman is the one who lives their life responding to reality. Not to goals, not to ambitions, not to secondary things, not to material things, not to what is trivial. We know only too well that if we respond to what is trivial we ourselves are trivialized.

Let me give you an example. The great illusion that we all start with is that we are at the centre of reality. This is a very easy illusion to fall into because in the opening consciousness of life it seems that we are understanding the external world from our own centre. And we seem to be monitoring the outside world from an interior control centre. And so it seems as though the world is revolving around us. Then logically we begin to try to control that world, to dominate it and to put it at our service. This is the way to alienation, to loneliness, to anxiety because it is fundamentally unreal.

What we find in meditation, from our own experience, is that God is the Centre. God is the Source of all reality. What we discover, from our own experience, is that there is nothing real outside God. Only illusion exists outside the real centre.

In meditation we find the courage to live in the clear light of that centre and of the reality that is God. The reality that is his creation and the reality that is my being created by God emerges from this. The result is that in meditation and through our commitment to it we become anchored in Truth. We become anchored firstly in the Way, the pilgrimage of meditation. Most importantly of all, we become anchored in Life. Our lifeline is clear. We are anchored in God. We begin to know, from our own experience that he is the ground of our being. In him we live. Through him we live. And with him we live.

What is required is commitment, perseverance. The result is that our meditation becomes the way of liberation. We are made free to *be* in the present moment, to accept fully the gift of our creation, to be fully in the eternal NOW of God. As I am sure you know from your own experience this commitment to being and to living fully in the present moment becomes a commitment to live fully every moment of your life. The reason is not hard to understand. The reason is that in meditation we are open to the Life Source within us. Once we are open to it the Life Source flows in our inmost being at every moment of our lives. In essence this is what Christianity is about. This is what Jesus came to proclaim – 'that men may have life and have it in all its fullness'.[1] In other words, we don't need to apologize for being, to make excuses for being. We don't need to spend our lives making ourselves acceptable to others. We need only to be rooted in reality and then to stand still in the ground of our own being, to live out of the power of the reality of our own being.

Meditation is a way of liberation from all fear. Fear is the greatest impediment to fullness of life. The wonder of the vision proclaimed by Jesus is that the great power of love which dispels fear is the power that we make contact with in the depths of our own being. The power of love is the energy that sweeps all before it. What we need to understand and what we need to proclaim if we are going to proclaim the Christian message to the world is that in prayer we begin to live fully

1. John 10:10

135

from the life force that is set free in our inmost being and that life force is love because it is God.

This requires commitment to life and to love. This is the commitment that Jesus proclaimed with his own life and with his own love. We must understand from our own experience that this life and love are a present reality to be found and contacted within each of us, within the heart of each one of us. This is something we must learn from our own experience. It is not enough to know from other people's experience that the Spirit of Christ dwells in our hearts and that in our hearts the living Christ summons each of us to fullness of life. That is what we must be, committed to knowing ourselves and committed to living in the power of Christ.

There are no half measures. You can't decide to do a bit of meditation. The option is to meditate and to root your life in reality. The reality is the reality of liberty – that you are freed to be, and to be fully, every moment of your life. As far as I can understand it, that is what the Gospel is about. That is what Christian prayer is about. A commitment to life, a commitment to *eternal* life. Jesus taught that the kingdom of heaven is here and now. What we have to do is to be open to it, which is to be committed to it. Listen to Jesus' words in the Gospel of Matthew:

The kingdom of heaven is like treasure lying buried in a field. The man who found it, buried it again; and for sheer joy went and sold everything he had, and bought that field.

Here is another picture of the kingdom of heaven: A merchant, looking out for fine pearls, found one of very special value, so he went and sold everything he had and bought it.[2]

This is the sort of commitment that we need – the commitment to meditate every day and in our meditation, to say the mantra from the beginning to the end.

2. Mat. 13:44–6

136

Beyond Illusion

To understand anything about meditation you have to find your way to a certain simplicity. In the world we live in we are so used to placing our hope and our faith in complexity. But I think all of us know, at a deeper level of our being, that real peace is to be found in a profound simplicity of spirit. These words of St Paul writing to the Ephesians need to sink into our hearts;

> Your world was a world without hope and without God. But now, in union with Christ Jesus, you who were once far off have been brought near through the shedding of Christ's blood. For he is himself our peace.[1]

One of the things that we are all invited to know from our own experience is that we *have* been brought near, through the life and death and resurrection of Jesus, to this profound peace. Aristotle defined peace as the 'tranquillity of order'. Peace and order are necessary for all growth. They are necessary for the depth of being, necessary for all of us to realize our full potential. So peace could be described as 'the harmony of directed energy'. That is what meditation is about. It isn't about passive stillness. It is about the realization of the nearness of each of us to the source of creation, the source of our own creation and of all creation. It is realizing that the power of creation, the energy of creation flows in our hearts.

The enemy of peace is distraction. We are distracted when we lose sight of the harmonizing goal of our life, the harmonizing power within which we have our being. We can lose sight

1. Eph. 2:12–14

of it. And we can regain it. Distraction is caused by desire, by the wish to possess. The loss of the goal leads us away from what is real into unreality.

Remember again the way of meditating. We sit down, we sit with our spine upright, we breathe calmly and regularly and we begin to say our word, *maranatha*. Four equally stressed syllables, 'Ma-ra-na-tha'. We say our mantra from the beginning to the end of our meditation. The purpose of the word is to keep us on the path, to take us away from illusion, from desire, into the reality that is God. As long as we are on the way, as long as we are saying our mantra, we are turning aside from distraction and we are on the way to make contact with the root from which we are sprung.

Once we lose sight of our goal we become confused. We become frightened. That is when we tend to seek solace in more and more distraction and illusion. What the way of meditation invites all of us to do is to confront the unreality, fear, fantasy and distraction and to pass through it. On the other side of all this illusion and fear and unreality is peace, the tranquillity of order. Energy directed to its ultimate end. What each of us is called to know in meditation is that that energy is love. What each of us is invited to discover from our own experience, is that God is love.

As I have suggested to you, meditation has nothing to do with quiet reverie. It is to do with wakefulness. We awaken to our nearness to God. All our power and all our potential is then directed towards their true end. That end is God, the end who is our beginning. In the experience of the peace of meditation it is revealed to us where we are. It is revealed to us that we are on the journey away from fear, away from unreality, away from illusion into the only reality there is. That Reality is God. That Reality is Love.

Each of us has to learn to say our word, our mantra. We have to learn to say it from the beginning of our meditation until the end, to root it in our hearts so that we can listen to it sounding there, in the depth of our being. Learning to root the mantra takes time. If you ask yourselves, 'How much time will it take?' you can answer by saying that 'it takes only that amount of time to realize that it takes no time at all'. We are already there. Listen to St Paul again: 'But now, in union with Christ Jesus, you who once were far off have been brought near through the shedding of Christ's blood, for he himself is our peace.' This is what we have to come to understand, to *know* in meditation. To know it as a personal experience. Our redemption *is* accomplished. The power of the Spirit *is* set free in our hearts. What prevents us from realizing this is that we are distracted. Our minds are cluttered and we must free them. This is what meditation is about. That is the importance of returning to it every morning and every evening.

Sit down and, in saying your mantra, loosen the chains, the bonds that bind you to unreality, to illusion and to fear. Understand that those bonds have no power over you, if only you are open to the experience of Jesus. His experience is that he is the beloved Son of God. What he has achieved for us is that we can be open to the self-same experience of knowing that we are sons and daughters of a loving, compassionate and understanding Father. In that experience we discover that our meaning is to be fully open to his love, wholly open to the nearness of his mysterious being which is wholly open to our own hearts, to our own centre. For in our centre he is to be found. Meditation, saying the mantra from beginning to end, saying the mantra every morning and every evening, is simply our pilgrimage to that centre where he is and where we are in him.

We Have Meaning for God

These are some remarkable words from the letter to the Colossians:

> Therefore, since Jesus was delivered to you as Christ and Lord, live your lives in union with him. Be rooted in him; be built in him; be consolidated in the faith you were taught; let your hearts overflow with thankfulness . . . For it is in Christ that the complete Being of the Godhead dwells embodied, and in him you have been brought to completion.[1]

These are words addressed to each one of us. 'Live your lives in union with him' is the Christian invitation. Not to admire from a distance, not even to worship from afar but to live 'in union'. That is the redemptive invitation that the Gospel addresses directly to each one of us.

We all come to know from our own experience that union requires selflessness, a real loss of self because in union we surrender ourselves into the greater reality of the union. In that reality each finds the other and, in finding the other, discovers his own essential personhood. We discover ourselves because in union we experience ourselves as known, loved, cherished, cared for. The Christian gospel reveals to each of us that this is precisely what we have been created for. We are made for union, for the perfection that comes to us from knowing ourselves known, from discovering ourselves 'in love'. 'Live your lives in union with him.' This is the invitation we respond to in our meditation. We respond to it, just as St Paul described it, by being 'rooted' in him, by being 'built' in him.

1. Col. 2:6–7, 9–10

What we each have to discover for ourselves is that God is the root from which we are sprung. He is the ground of our being. The most elementary sanity requires that we live out of this rootedness. Living our lives rooted in Christ, *knowing* ourselves rooted in him, as a daily experience in our daily return to our meditation means that we enter into a radical stability that is impervious to change, to passing, ephemeral contingency. In the silence of our meditation, we gain an experience of ourselves as beyond contingency. We know that we are and that we are in God and that in him we discover our own essential identity and unique meaning. The wonder of Christian prayer is that what we discover is that we have meaning for God. The astonishingly, barely believable thing about the Christian revelation is that our meaning is not less than *to bring perfection to God*. That is, to be so in harmony with him that we reflect back to him all the brilliance of his own glory, all the fullness of his own self-communication.

St Paul tells us that 'in him you have been brought to completion'. The Christian mystery summons each of us to enter into the divine milieu and to take our own appointed place within it. The fullness of the Godhead dwells in Christ and Christ dwells in us. In his indwelling we find our own completion. To be complete as human beings we must live this mystery not just intellectually, not just emotionally but with our full being. What the New Testament cries out to us is that the fullness of being we are summoned to dwells within our being as it is now and is realized when our being and the being of God come into full resonant harmony. Meditation invites us to enter the resonant harmony of God.

Beyond a certain point language always fails us. But we have to try to use language to direct our attention towards the mystery and its depths. The mantra takes up where language fails. It is like God's harmonic. By rooting it in our heart, every corner of our heart, every fibre of our being is open to him and every ounce of his power is channelled into us. That is why we must learn to say the mantra faithfully, continually and in ever-deepening poverty. Sainthood, wisdom, are simply names for reality. God is Real. We discover by that daily fidelity in our meditation that godliness is full sanity. Full sanity flowing from the full power of God's love. Each of us is summoned to discover that this godliness flows freely in the depths of our own heart.

The Reality that is Love

I have suggested to you that to meditate you have to learn to become really simple. This is quite a challenge to all of us who have been brought up with a modern consciousness in a scientific age. It may help to try and focus in on one particular aspect of this simplicity.

Let me stress for you again always to remember the importance of actually saying the mantra during the whole time of your meditation. This is what every modern person finds most difficult to understand and remember. When you start to meditate you find it difficult to believe that just in the process of taking the word *maranatha* and repeating it over and over again you can be on the way. When you begin you have to take that on faith. Nothing is more important if you want to come to a depth of perception and if you want to come to understand fully what the Christian vision of life is about. Nothing is more important for that than coming to the silence, stillness and discipline that the mantra leads you to. We have to begin by understanding that as clearly as we can. The necessity of meditating every morning and every evening and the necessity of saying your word, your mantra, from beginning to end.

Having understood that, you will come to understand from your own experience that meditation is not concerned with analysis. You are not analysing your own experience. You are not analysing your own feelings. Far from having anything to do with analysis meditation is concerned with synthesis, that is with coming to a full understanding and experience of the wholeness of creation, of your own wholeness and of your own integral part in the whole system of creation. In the Christian vision far from being concerned with analysis, which is the breaking down of reality into its component parts, the experience of meditation leads us to unity, to the building up into oneness of everything we are. Listen to St Paul:

> Therein lies the richness of God's free grace lavished upon us, imparting full wisdom and insight. He has made known to us his hidden purpose – such was his will and pleasure determined beforehand in Christ – to be put into effect when the time was ripe: namely, that the universe, all in heaven and all on earth, might be brought into a unity in Christ.[1]

That sounds inspiring when you listen to it but it is only words, verbal inspiration, unless you enter into the experience of it – unless you enter into a way of prayer, the meditation that can leave analysis behind and open your heart and mind to the great synthesis that happens in Christ, with Christ and through Christ.

In the monastic tradition meditation doesn't have us analyse differences in the various parts of the reality that we inhabit. Much more, we become aware of the correspondence between every part of creation as it is aligned upon Christ. So we are not analysing, we are not dividing, we are synthesising, we are unifying. It is the mantra that leads us to that by gradually calming down all our own self-important fixations, all our own self-regarding analysis. Once you begin that process, the invitation of the good news of the Gospel becomes a real possibility to live our lives out of an integral wholeness. I think you will discover, if you can persevere in saying the mantra, that your experience in meditation gradually becomes the experience throughout your life. Instead of approaching your life analysing, noticing the differences, you approach your life wholeheartedly, responding to the correspondences.

The way the early Christians described this was that you come to approach your life with love because what you encounter in your heart is the living principle of love. St Paul here is suggesting how we should be aligned on this principle in our relationships with one another:

> Be forbearing with one another, and forgiving, where any of

1. Eph. 1:7–10

you has cause for complaint: you must forgive as the Lord forgave you. To crown all, there must be love to bind all together and complete the whole.[2]

That is the new vision of life that we enter into through our meditation – completion, wholeness, unity, 'in love'. We come to know then that the greatest theological statement was made by St John when he said, 'God is love'. The great mystery of the Christian faith is that this love is to be found in your own heart if only you can be silent and still and if only you can make this love the supreme centre of all your being and action. That means turning to it wholeheartedly, paying full attention to it. It means going beyond yourself into the reality that is infinitely greater than you are and yet which contains you. And in which each of us has an essential and unique place.

In the Christian tradition the experience of prayer, the experience of meditation, is of unity, of oneness. It is an experience that changes the whole of our perception of reality. We see reality as a whole unified by the basic energy of the cosmos which is the energy of love. This is the message of the truth that sets us free.

And you too, when you had heard the message of the truth, the good news of your salvation, and had believed it, became incorporate in Christ and received the seal of the promised Holy Spirit; and that Spirit is the pledge that we shall enter upon our heritage, when God has redeemed what is his own, to his praise and glory.[3]

The most important thing that Christians have to proclaim to the world, to whoever has ears to hear, is that this Spirit does indeed dwell in our hearts and that, by turning to it with full attention, we too can live out of the fullness of love. We too can live out of this power that is the kingdom of God.

We can only proclaim what we know. The daily return to meditation is essential to knowing; this and the discipline of the mantra from beginning to end is essential. But never become

2. Col. 3:13–15   3. Eph. 1:13–14

discouraged or down-hearted. If unity is our goal, we all have to begin from a fairly fractured beginning. Learning to say the mantra requires great patience and demands great perseverance. Don't give up too easily. When you find that you have strayed from it, return to it immediately. Stillness of body and stillness of Spirit, this is the aim. To be totally open to the only reality that is ultimately real, the reality that is love.

The Temple of Your Heart

It is important to be aware of the danger of using the imagination when you come to think about prayer or meditation. I don't think it is any exaggeration to say that the imagination is the great enemy of prayer. This idea has been impressed on me by people I have met recently who seem to me to miss the whole point of prayer and the richness of the Christian understanding of prayer by an over-active imagination. The imaginative stories I have heard people tell of praying in a church at night, when suddenly Christ walks down the aisle to speak to them. When I ask them, 'What did he look like?' they say, 'Tall, Jewish, with flowing hair, piercing eyes . . .' and so forth . . . Now I don't question for a moment the sincerity of people who see visions of this kind, even though these visions are often caused by badly digested meals. What I want to suggest is the more important conviction of the early Church concerning the reality of the presence of Jesus within us. This is the reality of the presence of his indwelling Spirit. The real wonder of the Christian life is that each one of us is called to live out of this reality, to live out of the eternal part of our own being. The two great Christian words that refer to this living out of the eternal are meditation and contemplation.

Meditation means remaining in the centre, being rooted in the centre of your own being, and *contemplation* is being in the temple with him. The temple is your own heart, your own centre. The essence of being with him in the vision of the early Church is an absolute oneness, a oneness with the Absolute. We have to try to proclaim to the world that it is our destiny to be thus divinized by becoming one with the Spirit of God. Divinization is something utterly beyond our imagination and beyond our own powers of understanding to comprehend. But, and here is the mystery that the New Testament speaks of, it is not beyond our capacity to experience it in love. It is our capacity to love and to be rooted in love that is the essence of our divinization.

When St Paul speaks about the reality of this, he emphasizes the presentness of it. For him it was Jesus who has already brought us salvation. 'Salvation' is deliverance from all our own limitations. It is the Hebrew word for deliverance from bondage and slavery into the 'glorious liberty and splendour of the children of God'.[1]

> It is he who brought us salvation and called us to a dedicated life, not for any merit of ours but of his own purpose and of his own grace, which was granted to us in Christ Jesus from all eternity, but has now, at length, been brought fully into view by the appearance on earth of our Saviour Jesus Christ. For he has broken the power of death and brought life and immortality to light through the Gospel.[2]

The Gospel is just that 'good news' of our deliverance from slavery. If we wanted to put that into language for our own time, it is a deliverance from our own egoism, from everything in us that isolates us, limits us; all these limitations are exchanged for the limitless love of God. It is the reality of this that we must be open to in our prayer – the presentness of it. This Spirit of Christ which is pure gift, the gift of his Spirit, is the very basis of all reality. And the art of living, of all fully human living, is not to live at the surface or at the level of trivia but to live out of what Jesus called that 'inner spring' of eternal life always welling up within us.

This is the message of St Paul:

> I want them to continue in good heart and in the unity of love, and to come to the full wealth of conviction which understanding brings, and grasp God's secret. That secret is Christ himself; in him lie hidden all God's treasures of wisdom and knowledge.[3]

1. Rom. 8:21   2. 2 Tim. 1:9–10   3. Col. 2:2–3

This is possible for us because 'it is in Christ that the complete Being of the Godhead dwells embodied, and in him you have been brought to completion'.[4] That is why in our prayer, as we meditate as faithfully as we can each morning and evening, we must go beyond all imagination, beyond all thought, even holy thought and holy imagination. It is why we must be utterly still and reverent in the presence of the mystery of God, this 'inner spring', because it is out of that mystery that we are invited to live. 'Be rooted in him; be built in him; be consolidated in the faith you were taught; let your hearts overflow with thankfulness'.[5]

Let us see this clearly. Wonderful as this message is, intoxicating though it is, we must approach it with simplicity and humility. That is why we must learn to say our word and to say it with a deepening faithfulness morning and evening. We must say it without expectation, without thinking that we are going to put pressure on God or that we are going to twist his arm and make him reveal himself to us in some way. We are simply doing the most direct thing we can do if we genuinely want to live our lives to the full and to live them out of the infinite depth they possess, their infinite potentiality.

We live them in union with Christ. That is the real wonder of meditation, that we do lose ourselves because we are in the temple with him. It is in that loss of self that we find ourselves in Christ. And in him we are infinitely expanded in heart by love. We are each called to the experience that inspired St Paul to write these words to the Colossians,

Therefore, since Jesus was delivered to you as Christ and Lord, live your lives in union with him. Be rooted in him; be built in him; be consolidated in the faith you were taught; let your hearts overflow with thankfulness . . . For it is in Christ that the complete being of the Godhead dwells embodied, and in him you have been brought to completion.[6]

4. Col. 2:9–10   5. Col. 2:7   6. Col. 2:6–7, 9

Rooted in the Centre

The other day I was reading of a Buddhist monk from Vietnam who was giving a talk in an American university and at the end of his talk, one of the students asked, 'Would you tell us what method of meditation you teach to the novices who come to your monastery?' His reply was, 'For the first three years the novices make the tea for the senior monks.' You can understand the wisdom of that, particularly in a society that is not dominated by time and by speed. But in our own society I think all of us have a more acute sense of urgency, that we have to do something *now* to understand the mystery of our own existence. Whereas it might well be wiser to spend three years just making tea, most of us feel that we haven't the time and we have to begin right away. That sense of urgency we have in the West can be a very great strength to us; if we act on it. In this talk I want to try to put before you something of the wisdom that is involved in coming to terms with that fundamental question of the purpose of our own existence.

A point in mathematics has position but no magnitude; it has no size. It has its place and that is all it has. What *we* have to do is to arrive at the central point of our own being. This is the purpose of meditation. The mathematical idea of the point having position but no magnitude is very descriptive of our meditation. In meditation we find our point, our position in the cosmos. And in the Christian tradition and vision of meditation each of us has our own unique place. We can describe that place in various ways. Now, I just want to suggest that that place is found when each of us is rooted in God, rooted in the centre of all creation, of all energy and of all power.

Meditation makes demands on us. It is a discipline. It isn't good enough just to read books about it or follow courses on it. You have to practise it. In the practice, you find your place. But to find your place you have to reduce yourself constantly until you become just a point. We all know that there is nothing worse than self-importance. There is nothing worse than selfishness. The purpose of meditation is to enter into our central point which is the experience of self-transcendence, a going forward. We leave self utterly behind and our ego is reduced and reduced and reduced until we have our place but no magnitude.

Coming to that point at the centre of our own being is like adjusting the aperture of a camera. When we have reduced ourself to that one-pointedness and when we are still, the light shines into us, into our hearts. That is the light of God, the light that enlightens and illuminates our entire being. Once we have achieved that pointedness and stillness the light shines in our heart for all eternity. Don't misunderstand me. To tread this path you do not require any special characteristics or special talents except the ordinary talent of knowing that we must go beyond self-importance and self-centredness. And it does not take much ingenuity to realize that. We must root ourselves not in self-love but in universal love. We become persons, not for ourselves, but for others, for all, for *the* all.

The light coming in that aperture is like a long exposure, the camera must be completely still and we must learn to be still. Before you meditate it is sometimes good to listen to a little music. The music helps you to forget the words, ideas and images that we have just been using. When the music is finished try to be as still as possible. Sit as upright as possible, close your eyes gently, and then begin to say your word, your mantra, 'Maranatha', four equally-stressed syllables. That is all we have to do for the twenty-five to thirty minutes of our meditation. Don't think about God, don't try to imagine God but simply be, be in his presence. We can be inspired to do this by what the prophet Isaiah says, 'I was there to be sought by a people who did not ask, to be found by men who did not seek me.'[1] That is the way of meditation – to be still, to be one-pointed, to be rooted in God. As St Paul, writing to the Romans, put

1. Isa. 65:1

it, 'Remember that it is not you who sustain the root: the root sustains you.'[2] That too is the way of meditation – to be utterly still, humble and reverent in the presence of God.

Don't worry about how the time is passing. Do not be disappointed if you find that you follow your thoughts instead of saying your mantra. Return to it, return to it gently, return to it constantly. If you want to learn to meditate, if you want to set out on this road of transcendence and one-pointedness, it is essential that you learn the practice of meditating every day of your life, every morning and every evening. The optimum time is half an hour, the minimum time is about twenty minutes. You will find that in the time of your meditation nothing happens. Say your word and be content to say your word. But in the perseverance along the way of meditation you will begin to understand the truth about one-pointedness, about centredness and from your own experience you will begin to understand what St Paul meant when he said, 'Remember that it is not you who sustain the root: the root sustains you.'

2. Rom. 11:18

Smashing the Mirror

These are some words of St Paul from the Letter to the Colossians:

> May he strengthen you, in his glorious might, with ample power to meet whatever comes with fortitude, patience and joy; and to give thanks to the Father who has made you fit to share the heritage of God's people in the realm of light.[1]

We should notice the extraordinarily positive and confident quality of those words, 'ample power'. This is exactly what Christianity is about. It is living our lives to the full out of that ample power of God and living them, as St Paul put it, with fortitude. That means living with courage, not afraid of difficulties or of ourselves or of others. Above all, not afraid of God because we are united to him as our supreme power source.

One of the misunderstandings people have about meditation arises from seeing it as something passive. They see it often in terms of surrender. This is because the words of the traditional religious vocabulary have been words like surrender, abandonment and self-forgetfulness. They have real meaning but we have to understand them in the light of the experience of the power and the joy that St Paul speaks of. I would like to suggest to you that a way for us to understand what this Christian experience is about and the way to enter it in meditation is not so much surrender or abandonment but *empathy* with God. To use a contemporary analogy, it is like getting on to the same wavelength. All the essential ideas of St Paul have this sense of resonating on the same frequency with Christ. He calls it

1. Col. 1:11–12

union with the power source. What prevents that union, that co-resonance?

The only thing that can prevent it is what we might describe as self-consciousness, the hyper-self-consciousness of egoism. I do not think it is any exaggeration to say that original sin is self-consciousness, because self-consciousness gives rise to the divided consciousness. This is like having a mirror between God and ourselves. Every time we look into the mirror we see ourselves. The purpose of meditation is to smash that mirror so that we no longer look at reflections of things and consequently see everything backwards, including yourself. The essence of meditation is taking the kingdom of heaven by storm. The mirror must be smashed. And Jesus is talking about overcoming self-consciousness, the mirroring self, when he says no one can be a follower of his unless he leaves self behind.

Now it does not take very much knowledge of life to perceive that this self-consciousness deludes us into seeing the whole universe revolve around us; or to conclude that this self-consciousness is an appalling state to be in. Perhaps that is what brings most of us to meditation. We don't want to look into that mirror and see everything backwards for the rest of our lives. We want to look through it, beyond it, and beyond ourselves. We want to look with courage into the infinite mystery of God. But when we begin to feel that first loss of self-consciousness and when we begin to enter into the deep silence of meditation we can become disturbed and take fright. This is where we need the support of brethren. That is why our regular meetings are so important. We need to realize that faith is a gift – given to us, as St Paul tells us, in abundance if only we will be open to it and continue hammering at that mirror until it shatters utterly. We hammer at it with our mantra.

There is nothing passive whatsoever about meditation. It is a state of growing and deepening openness with the power source of all reality which we can only adequately describe in words as God-who-is-love. The aim of our life and the invitation of our life is nothing less than complete union, full resonance with that power source. What are the fruits of un-self-consciousness? Joy, love, peace, self-control, patience, fidelity

154

– all the things that St Paul speaks about as the fruits of the spirit. This is the state of being where we are free to be ourselves, free to receive the gift of our life without fear, in the state of grace, of love.

St Paul mentions patience in that list of spiritual gifts. Each one of us must learn patience and there is no greater school of patience than the willingness faithfully to recite your mantra day after day, unconcerned with progress, unconcerned with results, aware that there is only the pilgrimage. If we are not on the pilgrimage, we are nowhere. Our call and our destiny is to be in Christ.

Meditation is about openness to that 'ample power' of God. It brings us to the confidence of knowing that we can meet whatever comes, not out of our own resources or our own self-consciousness but out of *the* consciousness of Christ, his consciousness of his Father and our Father. That consciousness is to be found in our hearts beyond all mirrors, beyond all images. That consciousness is not threatening. That consciousness is the gentle power of Jesus Christ.

The Way to the Eternal

One of the questions all meditators have to face is, 'Why do we meditate?' I suppose none of us would meditate unless it had occurred to us that there was more to life than just being producers or consumers. All of us know that we can't find any enduring or ultimate meaning in just producing and consuming. So we seek that ultimate meaning. We come to meditation because an unerring instinct tells us that if we can't find any ultimate satisfaction in consuming or producing nor can we find ultimate meaning outside of ourselves. We have to *begin with* ourselves.

In our society a lot of people, faced with the problem of being, living and meaning, seek refuge in oblivion. It is summed up in the expression, 'being stoned out of your mind'. And Marx, one of the most formative influences on the society in which we live, saw religion as the opium of the people. There is a real sense in which we can turn to religion as an anaesthetic, to be comforted or to be put into a state of unconsciousness. But Christian meditation has nothing to do with anaesthesia. Meditation is the way to illumination, to light and to life. Christ's message is one of vitalization and illumination, complete enlightenment. The way to this is the way of single-mindedness, not being distracted by things that are passing away but ever more deeply committed to what is enduring, to what is eternal.

Our own spirit is enduring. Our own spirit is eternal in God.

That is all right as an intellectual insight, as a religious insight or even a religious conviction. But the call of Christianity is the authenticating call of every truly spiritual doctrine – to be open yourself to your own eternal spirit, open to your own rootedness in the Eternal. Start to tread the way, the pilgrimage to fullness of light and fullness of meaning. Now what is the way?

It is the way of poverty and simplicity, because the way to fullness of knowledge is the way of unlearning. Let me remind you again of the way of meditation. Sit down and sit still, close your eyes and begin to say your word, 'Maranatha'. Say the word deliberately yet relaxedly, say it faithfully and yet serenely – four syllables all equally stressed, 'Ma-ra-na-tha'.

We say the word because the pilgrimage is a pilgrimage beyond ourselves, beyond our own limitations. To go beyond ourselves we must transcend thought and imagination, and the word is the way, the vehicle that carries us forward. The challenge of meditation is to undertake the discipline of saying the word and continuing to say it while learning to be patient, learning how to wait and learning that the way forward is the way to our own centre. The way to enduring riches is the way of poverty. The way to enlightenment is the way of darkness. We have to go through with ever greater discipline, with ever greater faithfulness.

But we must understand this – the way is simple. It is wholly uncomplicated. The way is sure. All that is required is the daily return to it – not with demands or any materialistic measuring of success. Just simple faithfulness, simple poverty of spirit. Every morning and every evening devoting your time not to what is passing but to what is enduring: your own spirit alive and full of light in God. We have an amazing call. Listen to it described in the second letter to the Thessalonians:

We are bound to thank God for you, brothers [and sisters] beloved by the Lord, because from the beginning of time God chose you to find salvation in the Spirit that consecrates you, and in the truth that you believe. It was for this that he called you through the gospel we brought, so that you might possess for your own the splendour of our Lord Jesus Christ.[1]

1. 2 Thess. 2:13–14

Original Innocence

When we have just celebrated one of the great feasts of the Church I think we have a good opportunity to reassess our own commitment. None of us can be unmoved when, for example, we enter into the liturgy of Good Friday and are confronted with the faithfulness and dedication of Christ. None of us can experience the joy of Easter morning, the universal promise of the new life of the Resurrection without again understanding in the centre of our being that there *is* new life, a re-creation around us at all times. This is a good moment for us to understand our own commitment to meditation, our own commitment to prayer as giving quality to our whole life by finding meaning and purpose in living in our prayer, by discovering Christ in our own heart.

I would like to try to redefine for you or to reclarify what meditation is about. When we sit down to meditate and turn our minds away from thinking and imagining, away from thinking about ourselves or about God, what we are doing is entering into the centre of our own being. The purpose of saying the one word during meditation, the one phrase, the mantra, is that each of us can become wholly still at the centre of our being.

The call of Jesus is to maturity. The whole thrust of St Paul is that we become mature in Christ. In all nature, growth is from the centre outwards. The centre is where we begin. This is the experience of meditation as we return to it day after day. There is no short-cut, we must meditate every morning and every evening of our lives precisely because this is the most central of all activities in our life. The experience of growth is of returning to our origin, to our centre, to God. St John of the Cross described it most beautifully when he said, 'God is the centre of my soul'.

As modern men and women we are much influenced by the concept of progress. But I think we must understand that progress does not consist so much in leaving our origin but much more in realizing all the potential in our origin, which we do by returning to our origin. All growth that endures in nature must be thoroughly rooted, and it is the summons of each one of us to be thoroughly rooted in Christ. I think there is a real sense in which meditation is a return to our original innocence. The Fathers describe this way as 'purity of heart'. The call of each one of us from Jesus is to find our own heart and to find it unclouded by egoism, unclouded by images, unclouded by desire. Meditation leads us to the clarity that comes from original and eternal simplicity. So we are content simply to be with him, content simply and in a childlike way to say our word, our one word, from the beginning to the end of our meditation.

To begin to meditate requires nothing more than the determination to begin. To begin to discover our roots, to begin to discover our potential, to begin to return to our source. And God is our source. In the simplicity of meditation beyond all thought and imagination we begin to discover in utter simplicity that we are in God; we begin to understand that we are in God in whom we live and move and have our being. We try to describe this growing awareness that we discover in the silence and daily commitment as 'undivided consciousness'. Meditation is just this state of simplicity that is the fully mature development of our original innocence. As St Catherine of Genoa expressed it, 'My me is God. Nor do I know myself save in him.' The wonder of the proclamation of Christianity is that everyone of us is invited into this same state of simple, loving union with God. This is what Jesus came both to proclaim and to achieve. This is what each of us is invited to be open to. 'My me is God. Nor do I know myself save in him.'

And how do we know this? We know it because, as St Paul expresses it, 'We possess the mind of Christ'.[1] This sentence of

1. 1 Cor. 2:16

St Paul is one of the most extraordinary sentences in Christian revelation. As I have said before, if we Christians have a fault, it is that we are so blind to the extraordinary riches that are already ours, achieved for us, given to us by Jesus. We possess the mind of Christ – Christ who knows the Father and who knows us. This is what each of us is invited to discover from our own experience – that we know because we are known and that we love because we are loved. St John writes, 'The love I speak of is not our love for God, but the love he showed to us in sending his Son'.[2] All great truths are simplicity itself. We can only know them when we become simple. When we sit down to meditate and begin to say our word, our mantra, we are on our way to that simplicity. We are on our way to the foundation on which our whole being rests. We are on our way to union, union with Jesus. We are on our way with him to the Father.

This was and is the inspiration of the words of St Paul:

> Among men, who knows what a man is but that man's own spirit within him? In the same way, only the Spirit of God knows what God is. This is the Spirit that we have received from God, and not the spirit of the world, so that we may know all that God of his own grace has given us.[3]

That is the invitation given to every one of us so that we may know personally from our own experience all that God of his own grace gives us. The way to that knowledge is the way of faithfulness, a daily faithfulness to our meditation. Faithfully every morning and every evening of our lives to turn aside from everything that is passing away and to be open to the eternal Spirit of God. It is also the way of faithfulness during our meditation, faithfully to say our word, our mantra, from beginning to end, no following of thoughts, no spinning of phrases or words; in growing simplicity. The power by which we do all this is given to us. It is the power of the love of Jesus. As St Paul calls each of us to know: 'Surely you know that you are God's temple, where the Spirit of God dwells.'[4] In our

2. 1 John 4:10   3. 1 Cor. 2:11–12   4. 1 Cor. 3:16

meditation we seek to be as fully open as we can be in this life to the Spirit of God dwelling within us.

Simplicity is Oneness

We can always find new ways to describe what meditation is really about. But remember always to keep clear in your minds how you meditate. That is, you take your word, your mantra, and you begin to recite it at the beginning of your meditation and you keep it going through the meditation. You must never lose contact with the fundamental simplicity of that. There is always a danger that in thinking or talking about meditation we can use so many superlatives that we lose contact with its essential simplicity which is, of course, the essential simplicity of simply saying the mantra. In that is the purification of our whole being.

I want to try to describe to you what this purification is that we are undertaking when we meditate. I want to suggest that meditation is simply a way of coming to your own centre and remaining in your centre awake, alive and still. The great problem with the lives of so many of us is that we live at an incredibly shallow level. By meditating we seek to find our way to the depths of our own being. The word 'meditation' comes from the Latin *meditare* which breaks down into the roots *stare in medio* – to remain in the centre. The word 'contemplation' suggests the same. The word contemplation does not mean looking at anything – God or anyone else. Contemplation is 'being in the temple' with God. The temple is your own heart, the depths of your own being.

By meditating we leave the shallow levels of our life behind and enter into something that is profound. By meditating we leave behind the passing, ephemeral things of life and enter into what is eternal. The ultimate goal of all religion is a *re-linking* and it is essentially the re-linking with our own deep centre. To be re-linked to our own centre is the purpose of all religion. We know from the Christian revelation that the Spirit of God dwells in our own centre, in the depths of our own spirit. The truth we discover from our own experience, if only we will tread the pilgrimage to that place of holiness, is that there is only one centre and that that centre is everywhere.

What I think each one of us has to discover from our own experience in order to come alive is that this pilgrimage is the first responsibility of our lives. It is the first responsibility of every life that would be fully human – to return to our own centre and to live out of the depths of our own profound capacity for life. We then discover that being reconnected with our own centre reconnects us with every centre. The truly spiritual man or woman learns first of all to live in harmony with themselves and then to live in harmony with the whole of creation. What we can say is, 'To be in one's own centre is to be in God.' Or in the words of Jesus, 'The kingdom of heaven is within you.'[1] We must remember that this kingdom is not a place but an experience. It is the wholly integrated and inte-grating experience of the reality of the power of God. And in the Christian vision it is knowing that that power is the power of love.

When St John of the Cross said, 'God is the centre of my soul,' it was because at the centre we experience silence, utter stillness and the peace that is beyond all understanding. The way to this is the way of the mantra. We should be very practical. In meditating we seek to enter into an ever more profound simplicity. As I said in the first of these talks, the way is the way of unlearning. The way is the way of disposses-sion. The way is the way of simplicity. We unlearn and we dispossess ourselves by turning aside from all our own words and thoughts and staying solely with the mantra. That is what takes us to the depths. What all of us must understand is that you can't just do a bit of meditation. If you want to meditate then you have to place it in a central position in your life and you have to make sure that everything in your life is in harmony with the harmony you come to find in your own spirit. You cannot live, as it were, a double life and only in one half be

1. Luke 17:21

163

a harmonious, integrated person, on your way to depth, to enlightenment and to profound vitalization. You have to be a simple person. You have to be a person who is living the oneness in your own life. Simplicity is oneness.

These words of St Peter say something that all of us have to listen to carefully, because the problem for people in our own time in learning to meditate is to have a sufficient grasp of their own potentiality as well as a firm enough belief that they really can live out of depths profounder than the shallowness of every day. These words of St Peter are a call to us to recognize who we are, to recognize our own dignity, to recognize the wonder of our own being and to recognize above all our own lovableness.

So come to him, our living Stone – the stone rejected by men but choice and precious in the sight of God. Come, and let yourselves be built, as living stones, into a spiritual temple; become a holy priesthood, to offer spiritual sacrifices acceptable to God through Jesus Christ . . . you are a chosen race, a royal priesthood, a dedicated nation, and a people claimed by God for his own, to proclaim the triumphs of him who has called you out of darkness into his marvellous light.[2]

2. 1 Pet. 2:4–5, 9

Beyond Technique

One of the great problems about learning to meditate is that it is so simple. In the sort of society that we live in we are not used to putting our total trust and faith in something that is very, very simple. We have all been brought up to trust only complex things. So when we approach something like meditation, we tend to get interested in the techniques that are involved. The techniques have their place. But they are not the first thing to turn your mind to when you are learning to meditate. The most important thing when you are beginning is to understand the absolute simplicity of it. Then, remain faithful to the simplicity of the practice.

When we begin to meditate we take our place in a great tradition. We are not just starting on something new to which we are bringing all the elements of new-found knowledge. We are entering a tradition of hundreds, indeed of thousands of years. When we begin we have to be humble enough to accept the tradition. We have to accept it on faith. This is our tradition as Benedictine monks – to meditate you must learn to *be* still. You must learn to sit absolutely still in your bodily presence and you must move towards an interior stillness in your spirit. The way into this that we have from the tradition passed on from our great monastic teacher, John Cassian, is to take a very simple word or phrase and just repeat it over and over again. The word I suggest that you take is the word *maranatha*. Say the mantra as gently as you can. Use no force but move towards absolute fidelity. To learn to meditate it is necessary to meditate every morning and every evening every day of your life; and it is necessary to repeat the mantra from the beginning to the end.

Meditation is the way of becoming wholly present to God by

coming to understand the fullness of the mystery of life. Most of us in our sort of society think of God, indeed think of ourselves as a sort of problem. God is a problem that we have to solve. Our life is a problem we have to solve. And to solve the problem you need an adequate technique. But what the tradition of meditation has to tell us is that God is not a problem, nor is our life a problem. God is a mystery and our own life is a mystery. In the presence of mystery what we must do is let the mystery be. Allow the mystery the fullness of its own being. Allow it to reveal itself. When we meditate that is exactly what we do. We allow God to be God. We allow ourselves to *be* in his presence. That is the extraordinary power of it.

Chronologically, the first thing we have to do is to become fully present to ourselves. That is why absolute stillness of mind and spirit is necessary. For many of us, it will be the first experience we have had of the totality of our being. What we do when we meditate is enter fully into the present moment and each time you recite your mantra, you are wholly present to that moment. You are not thinking of the past, you are not planning for the future. You are there, totally in that moment. Jesus is always calling on us to wake up. 'Can't you wake up? Be awake.' In meditation we learn to wake up to the reality of our existence and the reality of God.

There is nothing more maddening than talking to a person who is only half listening to you. Someone was telling me the other day that they were talking to someone about the terrible problem of starvation in part of East Africa. The conversation took place over some coffee and when the first person who was talking about the starvation was half way through and paused the person she was talking to said, 'How many eggs have you put into this cake? It's delicious.' That is an example of the maddening frustration of being with someone who is only half present to you. The gospels show how exasperated Jesus became with such people.

What Jesus tells us is that there is nothing worse than being half awake (or half asleep). When you sleep, sleep fully and when you are awake, come to full wakefulness. And that is what our meditation leads us to. By becoming wholly present in *this* moment, in the moment when we say our mantra, we enter into the Eternal Now of God. The principal criticism one might have of contemporary Christians is that we are and have been so slow to understand the full, present magnificence of the invitation that we have to be wholly open to Christ. St Paul writing to the Corinthians of this invitation to life says, 'It is God himself who has called you to share in the life of his Son Jesus Christ Our Lord; and God keeps faith.'[1] The tradition tells us that the life, the power of God, the power of his love is to be found in our own hearts. Finding that power requires that we be totally present to it. The tradition also tells us that our call is to become wholly awake to this mystery and to awaken to it as a mystery of wholeness. We discover ourselves by losing ourselves in the Other, and only then can we discover our essential place in the total mystery of Reality.

Most modern people, as a result of the philosophies of the last two or three hundred years, have thought of this as an invitation to come merely to the knowledge of their own limited or individual being. But what the Christian tradition reminds us is that our invitation is something much greater than that. It is to find our place, our insertion point in a Reality that is infinitely greater not only than each of us but of the sum total of all of us. The invitation is to find ourselves wholly alive within the mystery of God. The task we face is to become simple enough, humble enough simply to say our word, simply to return to saying our word and leaving behind all thought and imagination at the time of meditation. Remember, of course, that there are other times for reflection, for analysis, but those times are not the times of meditation. During the time of meditation we must learn to be like little children, to be spiritually childlike, which is to be content with saying our word and letting go of all thought, imagination and analysis.

When we meditate we are like the eye that looks forward into the mystery of Being and, like the eye, we cannot see ourselves. But we can *see* and our invitation *is* to see. The way is the way of meditation as a way of silence, a way of simplicity, of humility and above all, the way of the mantra. Learning to

1. 1 Cor. 1:9

167

say the mantra to the exclusion of everything else. Say it, recite it, listen to it. This is how we respond to the call addressed to each of us by 'God himself': thank God for all the enrichment that has come to you in Christ. In him you possess full knowledge and you can give full expression to it. There is no single gift you lack. 'It is God himself who called you to share in the life of his Son Jesus Christ Our Lord; and God keeps faith.'

Death

A question that all societies in every time and place have exercised their minds about is the question of death. All people who have a serious approach to life see death as a moment of supreme importance for all of us. Yet, in the Christian vision, death is not the all-important moment in our life. That is, not if we have listened to what Jesus has to say to us or if we have listened to what the revelations of the early Christians have to say to us – and if we have acted upon these. This is what I want to reflect on now.

For St Paul, the supreme all-important moment in any life is the moment of full openness to Jesus. Openness to his power, openness to his glory. That moment is an eternal moment. Nothing subsequent to it can fundamentally shake us from what he describes as the rootedness in Christ which grows out of this moment. For Paul, Jesus is the revelation of God and he is the revelation of his glory in our own heart. The call of the Christian life is simply to be open to that glory. The whole purpose of our life is a pilgrimage to that moment. As I have often said to you, the only ultimate thing of significance for each of us is that we *are* on the pilgrimage. The moment of revelation is given in God's time. What we have to do is to tread the way of poverty, of obedience and of simplicity. To be ready. The danger of Christian life is that we can become so easily intoxicated by the sheer wonder of the proclamation that we don't take the practical steps necessary to put ourselves into readiness.

All my life I have met with people who are intoxicated by the sheer beauty of the Christian vision but who undergo that intoxication from a distance. Entering into the eternal life of that moment seems to them impossible. Yet, the whole proclamation of the early Church is that everyone of us is invited to this. We are invited to it as the supreme opportunity of our life. We needn't think about our 'obligation' to worship God if we can understand something of the pure gift of his communication of this life to us. Even if we can understand in only the most elementary way that Jesus is this vital principle within each of us, then we are already opening our minds to the wonder of what St Paul calls the 'glory', the 'splendour' of God.

What is equally clear from the New Testament is that Jesus achieved his mission by total abandonment of self, by handing over his life to the Father: 'Not my will but thy will be done.' That is exactly the way for all of us. And it is the precise purpose of all meditation. To lose our lives, to lose ourselves and to become totally absorbed in God through the human consciousness of Jesus is what gives meaning to death, because it gives ultimate meaning to life. Meditation is a powerful way if you can learn to say the mantra continually, ceaselessly, because that is the way in prayer to leave self behind, to lay down our life so as to be absorbed in the infinite mystery of God. People ask, 'What is the experience of prayer?' The experience of prayer is of going utterly beyond ourselves, going beyond any words that we could possibly use to describe the experience. St Paul describes it as the entry into the glory of God. But in saying our mantra we leave behind all the words, because they limit the experience. They make the experience self-reflective. The experience is one of infinity, and no finite word can possibly encompass the experience. But again let me stress for you the way is the way of simplicity and childlikeness. 'Unless you become like children . . .' means unless you find again in your own heart the capacity for wonder, for innocent wonder, an innocence we all lose so easily and so carelessly. But we must find it again. The way we find it is to enter into silence, to be, to be open to God's glory, to the wonder of his being. That is why our mantra is of such supreme importance. That is why day-dreaming is such a dreadful loss of opportunity, such a dreadful encapsulation in time. Whereas all of us are called into that eternal moment when we lose ourselves in God.

Listen to St Paul again,

We are bound to thank God always for you, brothers beloved by the Lord, because from the beginning of time God chose you to find salvation in the Spirit that consecrates you, and in the truth that you believe. It was for this that he called you through the gospel which we brought, so that you might possess for your own the splendour of our Lord Jesus Christ.[1]

Those words give us some idea of what the invitation is – salvation in the Spirit. Salvation in the Spirit means being taken utterly beyond ourselves into supreme liberty of being in the Spirit of God. We are called to that now. 'The kingdom of heaven is among you.' We are called to it in the most practical way – to take our day and to put eternal life in the first place of our day. It is in eternal life that we turn definitively from death and dying. The only ultimate tragedy is a life that has not opened to eternal life. The only ultimate tragedy is a life that is dying.

1. 2 Thess. 2:13–14

Death and Resurrection

St Benedict told his monks, 'Always keep death before your eyes.'[1] We don't talk much about death in the modern world. But what the whole Christian tradition tells us is that if we would become wise we must learn the lesson that we have here 'no abiding city'. Our life begins, develops, matures and then we must prepare for the end of this mortal life. What the wise men of ages past and present say to us is that to have life in focus we must have death in our field of vision. Death is important because it reminds us of the fragility of the human condition. Our awareness of it is the constant reminder of the mortality of life. This knowledge of death is the source of compassion, of forgiveness, of gentleness, because death makes each one of us aware of our own weakness and mortality. We can be noble in the face of death but it is hard to be proud. So death is important because it teaches us compassion and humility. It is in the compassionate and humble heart that the power of God reaches us. 'When I am weak, then I am strong.'[2]

Talking about death is hard for the worldly to understand. Indeed the principal fantasy of much worldliness operates out of completely the opposite point of view: not the wisdom of our own mortality but the pure fantasy that we are immortal, beyond physical weakness. But the wisdom of the tradition of which St Benedict is the spokesman, is that awareness of our physical weakness enables us to see our own spiritual fragility too. There is a profound awareness in all of us, so profound indeed that it is often buried for much of the time, that we must make contact with the fullness of life and the source of life. We must make contact with the power of God and

1. Rule of St Benedict, ch. 4   2. 2 Cor. 12:10

somehow, open our own fragile 'earthen vessels' to the eternal love of God, the love that cannot be quenched. All of us know, if only dimly at this deep level, that our mortal bodies do need this new life of love. Indeed, we know that this is what we were created for. Meditation is our way to full awakening on this level of profoundity when we meet the basic truth about the human condition, that each of us was created for infinite expansion of mind and heart.

Meditation is a way of power because it is the way to understand our own mortality. It is the way to get our own death into focus. It can do so because it is the way beyond our own mortality. It is the way beyond our own death to the resurrection, to a new and eternal life, the life that arises from our union with God. The essence of the Christian gospel is that we are invited to this experience now, today. All of us are invited to death, to die to our own self-importance, our own selfishness, our own limitations. We are invited to die to our own exclusiveness. We are invited to all this because Jesus has died before us and has risen from the dead. Our invitation to die is also one to rise to new life, to community, to communion, to a full life without fear. I suppose it would be difficult to estimate what it is people fear most – death or resurrection. But in meditation we lose all our fear because we realize that death is death to fear and resurrection is rising to new life.

Every time we sit down to meditate we enter this axis of death and resurrection. We do so because in our meditation we go beyond our own life and all the limitations of our own life into the mystery of God. We discover, each of us from our own experience, that the mystery of God is the mystery of love, infinite love – love that casts out all fear. This is our resurrection, our rising to the full liberty that dawns on us once our own life and death and resurrection are in focus. Meditation is the great way of focusing our life on the eternal reality that is God, the eternal reality that is to be found in our own hearts. The discipline of saying the mantra, the discipline of the daily return morning and evening to meditation has this one supreme aim – to focus us totally on Christ with an acuity of vision that sees ourselves, all reality as it is.

Listen to St Paul writing to the Romans:

No one of us lives, and equally no one of us dies, for himself alone. If we live we live for the Lord; and if we die, we die for the Lord. Whether, therefore, we live or die, we belong to the Lord. This is why Christ died and came to life again, to establish his lordship over dead and living.[3]

We meditate in order to enter into the meaning of those words.

3. Rom. 14:7

The Spirit of Lent

On rereading Paul's first letter to the Thessalonians, which is one of the oldest pieces of Christian writing we have, I was struck once more by the challenge of finding expressions for the ineffable. The great problem for us as Christians is that we use a vocabulary that, just like a currency, can become devalued. We trip off the phrases from our lips – faith, hope, charity – without really understanding the depth of meaning that is involved. The real meaning of faith is vital for a clear understanding of meditation. There is an enormous need for us as persons and as Christians to really develop a faith dimension in our lives if we are to become fully human, fully real, fully rooted in the gift of our own being. And, as I have suggested before, the way of prayer is a way that calls each of us to deepen this faith dimension by deepening our faith in what is.

Consider these words of St Paul writing to the Thessalonians:

> We call to mind, before our God and Father, how your faith has shown itself in action, your love in labour and your hope of our Lord Jesus Christ in fortitude.[1]

Christian hope is above all a supreme confidence that comes to us once we begin to suspect the limitless dimension to the glory of Christ, his splendour and wonder – the words that St Paul constantly uses to express the ineffable. As I have often suggested to you, faith must be a personal response. Each one of us must accept the responsibility to tread this way ourselves and that is what our daily commitment to meditation is about.

So it is with hope. It is a supreme confidence that comes

1. 1 Thess. 1:3

175

from our conviction that total goodness, complete love, is to be found in our own hearts. So often we can become discouraged. So often we think of ourselves as unworthy, but in the experience of prayer we must not think of ourselves at all. We must not think of our own unworthiness, but what we must *know*, and know with utter clarity, is that the life of God is poured out into our hearts. Just reflect for a moment what an influence for good we could be, as a small meditation group meeting weekly and within the Church as a whole, if each of us could realize our own goodness and if we could realize what the Lord Jesus has achieved for us personally. That is the task of meditation and that is the special task of Lent. Lent is not a time for self-important beating of our breasts and lamenting over our sinfulness. Lent is a time to prepare for the glory of Christ, the glory of Easter, the Paschal glory. We do so, not by concentrating on our own sinfulness, but by forgetting ourselves and by opening our hearts to the Lord Christ.

Our daily meditation is an entry into the supreme conviction that God has revealed himself in Jesus and that Jesus reveals himself to us in our hearts. If only we will pay attention, if only we will be silent, if only we will be simple, humble, obedient. In order to learn that obedience, simplicity and humility, we say our word. Our hope is rooted in the supreme goodness of God. And the hope is made personally real in the supreme goodness he has given to each one of us in Jesus. Listen to how St Paul goes on:

> We are certain, brothers beloved by God, that he has chosen you and that when we brought you the Gospel we brought it, not in mere words, but in the power of the Holy Spirit, and with strong conviction, as you know well.[2]

These words point up the need that our contemporaries have. It is a need for men and women who are not religious bigots, not intolerant of other religious men and women, but who are strong with the power of the Spirit and who know that it is a universal spirit of love. We need Christian people who realize

2. 1 Thess. 1:4

that we have nothing whatever to fear from the Buddhist tradition or the Hindu tradition or any tradition that is truly spiritual. We have only to learn to see one another in the light of Christ. But that we can only do if we allow his light to burn, not just brightly but brilliantly, in our own hearts by standing back, getting out of the way, so that the light of love, compassion and forgiveness may become supreme in our own spirit.

St Paul goes on to say:

And you, in your turn, followed the example set by us and by the Lord; the welcome you gave the message meant great suffering for you, yet you rejoiced in the Holy Spirit.[3]

Meditation is a time of profound joy. It is the peace beyond all understanding, beyond all words, concepts or analysis. Let me remind you again what is involved.

Firstly, a daily commitment and a commitment that goes totally beyond what we feel. We do not meditate when we feel like it or not meditate when we do not feel like it. We accept the discipline of the daily meditation and the daily return to it. Then we accept the discipline of the word of the mantra, the recitation of it from beginning to end. And all because of the glory of God revealed in Jesus. All because of the supreme conviction that Jesus is Lord and that we are able to say that he is Lord because he has given us the Holy Spirit.

3. 1 Thess. 1:6

The Meaning of Silence

There is a great feeling among our contemporaries, I think, of the need, perhaps even the extremely urgent need, to recover the spiritual dimension in our lives. There is a feeling that unless we do recover that spiritual dimension we are going to lose our grip on life altogether. In meeting that feeling we must be perfectly clear that a commitment to spiritual values is by no means a rejection of the ordinary things of life. Indeed the exact opposite is true. Commitment to the spiritual reality is simply commitment to reality and it is the way to really appreciate the wonder of all life. It is the way to come to understand the extraordinary fact of the mystery of life itself, the inner hidden secret of life that gives it its real excitement. Entering on the spiritual path is coming to appreciate our life as a voyage of discovery. It is certainly my experience that, if you set out on the path of meditation with this commitment to enter deeply into your own interior hidden life, then every day for you will become a revelation of new dimensions to that life and a deeper understanding of it.

Now to tread the spiritual path we must learn to be silent. What is required of us is a journey into profound silence. Part of the problem of the weakening of religion in our times is that religion uses words for its prayers and rituals, but those words have to be charged with meaning and they must be charged with sufficient meaning to move our hearts, to set us out in new directions and to change our lives. They can only be charged with this degree of meaning if they spring from spirit, and spirit requires silence. We all need to use words, but to use them with power we all need to be silent. We all need religion, we all need the Spirit. Meditation is the way to silence because it is the way *of* silence. It is the way of the mantra, the word that leads us to such a silence that it ultimately charges all words with meaning. Now we don't need to be too abstract about this. We all know that we can often come to know another person most profoundly in silence. To be silent with another person is a deep expression of trust and confidence and it is only when we are unconfident that we feel compelled to talk. To be silent with another person is truly to *be* with that other person. Nothing is so powerful in building mutual confidence between people than a silence which is easeful and creative. Nothing reveals inauthenticity more dramatically than silence that is not creative but fearful.

I think what all of us have to learn is that we do not have to create silence. The silence is there within us. What we have to do is to enter into it, to become silent, to become the silence. The purpose of meditation and the challenge of meditation is to allow ourselves to become silent enough to allow this interior silence to emerge. Silence is the language of the Spirit.

These words of St Paul writing to the Ephesians, are charged with the power of silence:

> With this in mind, then, I kneel in prayer to the Father, from whom every family in heaven and on earth takes its name, that out of the treasures of his glory he may grant you strength and power through his Spirit in your inner being, that through faith Christ may dwell in your hearts in love.[1]

The words we use in trying to communicate the Christian message in the Christian experience have to be charged with strength and power, but they can only be charged with strength and power if they spring from the silence of the Spirit in our inner being. Learning to say your mantra, leaving behind all other words, ideas, imaginations and fantasies, is learning to enter into the presence of the Spirit who dwells in your inner heart, who dwells there in love. The Spirit of God dwells in our hearts in silence, and it is in humility and in faith that we must enter into that silent presence. St Paul ends that passage in Ephesians with the words, 'So may you attain to fullness of being, the fullness of God himself'. That is our destiny.

1. Eph. 3:14–16

The Life Source

It is important to learn to see meditation as a way of growth, a way of deepening our own commitment to life, and so as a way leading to our own maturity. To see this, it is a most important priority for every one of us to allow our spirit two things: first, the deepest possible contact with the Life Source and then, as a result of that contact, to allow our spirit space within which to expand. Now when we listen to that as a theory it sounds like just so many words. What does it mean for us when we say that a high priority in every life that would be truly human should be this contact with the Life Source?

Every great spiritual tradition has known that in profound stillness the human spirit begins to be aware of its own Source. In the Hindu tradition, for example, the Upanishads speak of the spirit of the One who created the universe as dwelling in our heart. The same spirit is described as the One who in silence is loving to all. In our own Christian tradition Jesus tells us of the Spirit who dwells in our heart and of the Spirit as the Spirit of love. This interior contact with the Life Source is vital for us, because without it we can hardly begin to suspect the potential that our life has for us. The potential is that we should grow, that we should mature, that we should come to fullness of life, fullness of love, fullness of wisdom. The knowledge of that potential is of supreme importance for each of us. In other words, what each of us has to do and what each of us is invited to do is to begin to understand the mystery of our own being as the mystery of life itself.

In the vision proclaimed by Jesus each one of us is invited to understand the sacredness of our own being and life. That is why the second priority is of such great importance: namely, that we should allow our spirit the space within which to expand. In the tradition of meditation this space for expansion of spirit is to be found in silence, and meditation is both a *way* of silence and a *commitment* to silence which grows in every part of our lives. It becomes a silence that we can only describe as the infinite silence of God, the eternal silence. And, as I am sure you will find from your own experience, it is in this silence that we begin to find the humility, the compassion, the understanding that we need for our expansion of spirit. Thoughtful men and women everywhere in the world today are beginning to see that spiritual growth, spiritual awareness, is the highest priority for our time. But the question is – how do we do it? How do we enter on this path?

That is where the tradition of meditation is of supreme importance for us, as a tradition of spiritual commitment by men and women down through the ages and yet a tradition available for you and for me. The only thing that is necessary is that we enter into it by beginning the practice. The practice is very simple and very obvious. We have to put time by, we have to spend some time each morning and each evening of our life to make ourselves available for this work of making contact with the Source of all life and for the work of making space available in our lives for the expansion of spirit. The deepening of faith and the actual practice of meditation are both very simple. Simply take your word, your mantra, and repeat it.

That simplicity is one of the great problems for men and women of our time. We are so used to complexity that the simplicity of meditation, just being content to say your word, to sound your word in your heart, is a major challenge. That is why, when we meditate together or alone, each of us must try to say our word as faithfully as possible, as continually as possible.

The word I recommend you to say, the Aramaic word *mara-natha*, should be said without moving your lips, that is, said interiorly in your heart, and you should continue to sound it from the beginning to the end of your time of meditation. Meditation is a process of growing, of growing more spiritually aware and, like all processes of growth it has its own speed, its own pace. It is an organic process. You have as it were to root the mantra in your heart. Jesus so often spoke of the Word of the Gospel taking root in the hearts of men and women and he tells us it has to fall into receptive soil. In other words, the whole of your being has to be involved in this process. You sound the mantra and by your fidelity in returning to it day after day, you root it in your heart and once rooted, it flourishes. Indeed it flowers. And the flower of meditation is peace, a profound peace. It is a peace that arises from harmony, from the dynamic harmony that you encounter when you make contact with the ground of your being, because what you discover is that the mantra is rooted in your heart, the centre of your being, and your being is rooted in God, the centre of all being.

The way of meditation is a way of great simplicity, and so you must take it a day at a time. You don't demand results. You don't look for progress. You simply repeat your mantra every morning and every evening for the entire time of your meditation, and *in the process itself*, which is a process of forgetting yourself, of taking the searchlight of consciousness off yourself, you find yourself in God. Finding yourself in God, you come to an understanding which is the understanding of the *Is*-ness of life. You come to see that your life is a gift, that you offer it back to God and the gift that was a finite gift when it was given to you becomes in the offering back an infinite gift.

Reflect on this in the light of these words from the letter to the Hebrews:

The kingdom we are given is unshakable; let us therefore give thanks to God, and so worship him as he would be worshipped, with reverence and awe.[1]

The awesomeness of God's closeness to us leads us into profound reverence. We have only to learn to be still, to be silent.

1. Heb. 12:28

182

The Reality of Faith

This is a Christian understanding of the real nature of faith from the letter to the Hebrews:

> And what is faith? Faith gives substance to our hopes, and makes us certain of realities we do not see. It is for their faith that the men of old stand on record. By faith we perceive that the universe was fashioned by the word of God, so that the visible came forth from the invisible.[1]

The great problem that Christians face in this moment in history is that so many of the words we use to express our belief have failed us. They no longer have power to move our hearts, to change our lives. One of the key words is the word 'faith'. And I think that meditation is of supreme importance for us because it takes us into the experience of faith. Faith is simply openness to, and commitment to, the spiritual reality which is beyond ourselves and yet in which we have our being. St Peter, writing to the early Christians, advised them, 'Hold the Lord Christ in reverence in your hearts,' and the Pauline authors of the letter to the Hebrews tell us that by faith we go beyond what is visible to the invisible, the spiritual reality. Both these insights are rooted in the experience of prayer.

That is why the discipline of our daily commitment to meditation is of such importance. As you know, when you start to meditate and to build prayer into your life, it can be 'kinda fun' to follow up our first burst of spiritual enthusiasm. But when you have to return to your sitting, day by day, and learn to sit in deepening silence and openness, then you soon discover

1. Heb. 11:1–3

183

that this calls for more and more love on your part, not just enthusiasm. People seeing you will say, 'What are you doing, sitting in silence, doing nothing?' Almost all the values of our society militate against that act of faith whereby you sit down and you close your eyes to the visible and open them to the invisible reality. Later on in the letter to the Hebrews the authors say:

> We must . . . run with resolution the race for which we are entered, our eyes fixed on Jesus, on whom faith depends from start to finish.[2]

That is what faith is about. It is opening our eyes to the larger reality that is revealed in Jesus who reveals to us the Father. Our eyes are taken off ourselves. When we meditate we are not concerned with ourselves, with our own perfection or our own wisdom or even our own happiness. Our eyes are fixed on Jesus and we receive from him everything, literally everything, we need to run the race and everything that we need to make light of the difficulties we have, whatever they are. Jesus – who, for the sake of the joy that lay ahead of him, endured the cross, making light of its disgrace, and has now taken his seat at the right hand of the throne of God.

Meditation does make us 'light of heart', because we know that there is only one thing essential to life and that is that we ourselves are fully open to and fully in harmony with the author of life, the Word through whom we have our being, the incarnate Son of God, our Lord Jesus. Our faith is faith in what the synoptic gospels call 'the Kingdom of God' and the Kingdom of God is simply God's power enthroned in our hearts.This is what makes us light of heart and it is what Christian joy is about.

That power of God is rooted in our heart unshakably. Nothing, no powers, no dominations, no trials can loosen that rootedness of faith. The Kingdom we are given is unshakable. As Christians we have to be able to communicate that Kingdom and that faith. But we can only do so if the reality of that

2. Heb. 12:1–2

184

Kingdom is not just known to us but embedded in the bedrock of our being. As you know, to meditate is to learn to be profoundly still and profoundly attentive to the spiritual reality. In meditating we learn to distinguish between what is passing away and what endures. We learn to distinguish between time and eternity; and the marvellously liberating experience of prayer is to be liberated from time, to be so profoundly inserted into the present moment of the Kingdom that we glimpse the eternal *now* of God.

> The kingdom we are given is unshakable; let us, therefore, give thanks to God, and so worship him as he would be worshipped, with reverence and awe; for our God is a devouring fire.[3]

Again the authors of the letter to the Hebrews wonderfully proclaim what the Christian invitation is about: to worship, which means to bow and to bend low in spirit before the eternal, the spiritual, the reality that is God. All of us need to find and experience that reverence and that awe, deep in our own heart, deep in our own spirit. The simple exercise of our repeated word brings us to that simplicity, the necessary poverty of spirit. The author of *The Cloud of Unknowing* speaks of meditation as the exercise that loosens the root of sin within us. Saying your word, meditating every morning and every evening, loosens the root of the ego within you, and all of us need that root to be loosened so that we may be rooted and founded in Christ.

Listen again to the letter to the Hebrews:

> Remember where you stand: not before the palpable, blazing fire of Sinai. . . . you stand before Mount Zion and the city of the living God, . . . and Jesus, the mediator of a new covenant.[4]

To prepare to meditate simply listen to this call to faith from the letter to the Hebrews, and let us by our profound stillness

3. Heb. 12:28–9   4. Heb. 12:18, 22, 24

and silence, be led into that reverence and awe, led to know that we are in the presence of the Lord Jesus, the mediator of the New Covenant, the Covenant of Love.

The Wholeness of God

In these talks we are always starting again. It is not that in each talk anything new is said, but our aim in each talk is to come, surely and gradually, nearer the centre of the mystery. Meditation is always a return to our beginning, which is our centre and our source. Each time we sit down to meditate, every morning and every evening, our aim is to clear the ground so that the energy at the centre may radiate freely and penetrate universally. We have only one ultimate hazard, and that hazard is distraction.

As we all know from our own sad experience we are so easily distracted. God's love is given to each of us freely and generously and universally. God's love flows in our hearts in a mighty stream. But, like Martha in the gospel story, we are all of us so busy about so many things. We have to learn, and it is absolutely necessary that we do learn it, that only one thing is necessary, because only one thing *is*. All of us must therefore address our own lack of discipline. We must bring our restless wandering minds to stillness. It is one of the first great lessons in humility we learn, when we realize that we come to wisdom and stillness, and we pass beyond distraction, only through the gift of God. His prayer is his gift to us and all we have to do is to dispose ourselves, and this we can do by becoming silent. Silence is the essential human response to the mystery of God, to the infinity of God. We learn to be silent by being content to say our mantra in humble fidelity.

It is as though the mystery of God is a wonderful multi-faceted diamond. When we talk or think about God it is as though we are responding to one or another of his facets, but when we are silent – which is to say, in his presence – we respond to the mystery which we call God *as a whole* and do so omni-dimensionally. The wonder of it is that it is the whole of us that responds to the entirety of the mystery of God. It is not just our intellect, not just our emotions, not just the 'religious' side of us or the 'secular' side of us. Everything that we are responds to everything that he is, in absolute harmony, in absolute love. That is what the experience of Christian prayer is. A wholeness. The essence of the wholeness is to be found in our union with him who is One.

How is this possible? It is possible through the Incarnate Reality which is Jesus. God is fully revealed in Jesus, fully present in Jesus. The love of Jesus has made us one with him. By becoming open through silence to his reality we become open in wonder to the reality of God. That is why the way of prayer is a way of ever deeper, ever more generous silence. It is not enough just to think about silence or to talk about silence – we must embrace it! To learn this silence, to be open to the gift of it, we must learn to say our mantra. Our regular times of meditation immerse us in this silence and we emerge from the silence refreshed, renewed and re-baptized in the power of the Spirit. As I have so often said to you before, what each of us discovers in our prayer is that simply to *be* in his presence is all sufficing. In that presence we are healed. In that presence we find the courage to live our lives through him, with him, in him and for him. Once we begin to be open to this power, everything in our lives is charged with meaning. The meaning comes out of the silence. All our talking, all our living, all our loving find meaning from this silence and flow back into it.

People often ask, 'What is the experience of prayer like? What is it really like?' By that they mean, 'What happens?' What is it like? It is like silence. And what happens? In the silence – peace. In the silence – presence. And deeper silence. The way into that silence requires great patience, great fidelity and it requires in our tradition of meditation that we learn to say our mantra. As John Cassian said, the mantra contains all the human mind can express and all the human heart can feel. That one little word conveys and leads us into the silence which is the silence of creative energy. How long this takes us is of no concern to us. 'To the Lord a thousand years are as a day.' The only thing that matters is that we are on the way and that

188

means the simplicity of our daily meditations, every morning, every evening.

The wonder of the way is caught in these words of St Paul writing to the Romans:

Therefore, my brothers, I implore you by God's mercy to offer your very selves to him: a living sacrifice, dedicated and fit for his acceptance, the worship offered by mind and heart. Adapt yourselves no longer to the pattern of this present world, but let your minds be remade and your whole nature thus transformed. Then you will be able to discern the will of God, and to know what is good, acceptable, and perfect.[1]

1. Rom. 12:1–2

Being Yourself

The two big questions about meditation we have to consider are, firstly – Why should we meditate? and secondly – How do you meditate? In our Introductory Night talks to our groups what we try to look at is not so much – 'Why should you meditate?' but the question – 'How do you meditate?' If you genuinely look at the first question, it is my personal conviction that meditation can add a dimension of incredible richness to your life. I wish that I had the persuasive powers or the eloquence to convince everyone that I meet of the importance of meditating.

The importance of it is that you can be yourself. When you are meditating you do not have to apologize for being, you do not have to try to make yourself acceptable to anyone else, you do not have to play any role. One of the roles you have to beware of playing is any sort of spiritual role ('I am now getting into my holy act'). You just sit still and it is in that stillness that you gain the wisdom to see that you can only be yourself, you can only become yourself who is the person you are created to be, if you are willing to lose yourself. The truth that you can discover from your own experience is this – that any one of us can only find ourselves in the other. No amount of self-analysis or self-examination, will ever reveal to you who you are. But if you can take the focus of your attention off yourself and project it forward then you will discover the other and in discovering *your other*, you will discover *your self*.

The *other* is the Ground of All Being, the other we call God, Supreme Wisdom, Supreme Being, Supreme Love. The name is not important. Indeed, in meditation and in the silence of it, the complete silence of it, we go beyond all names, beyond all words, to the Reality.

But now I want to repeat *how* we meditate. It is necessary to repeat this over and over again just because meditating is so simple. For us, as self-consciously complex Westerners, it is difficult to believe and to accept that anything so simple could be so powerful. So once again, to meditate, what you have to learn to do is to sit still and recite, interiorly, in your heart, in your mind, a word or phrase. The word I have recommended you to recite is the Aramaic word *maranatha* to be recited as four equally-stressed syllables 'Ma-ra-na-tha'. That is all there is to meditating. I first learnt to meditate some thirty years or so ago, and my teacher used to say to me – in answer to whatever the question I put to him about meditation – 'Say your mantra, say your word'. The longer I have meditated over the years, the more I have realized the absolute wisdom of what he taught me. If you can learn just to say your word and keep saying it, keep repeating it throughout the twenty or twenty-five minutes or half-an-hour of your meditation, keep repeating it from the beginning to the end, you will eventually be unhooked from your ideas, your concepts, your words, your thoughts, all that amalgam of distraction that is going on in your mind most of the time, and you will come, with patience and with fidelity, to clarity of consciousness.

Now let's look at some practical questions. What should you do if, when you sit down to meditate you feel very nervous or you begin to see colours or hear noises or whatever? – all of these probably symptoms of tension. A very simple relaxation exercise is to lie on the flat of your back, spend a couple of moments allowing the floor to take the weight of your body and then breathe in very deeply into the diaphragm. Don't move the chest, but hold the breath in your diaphragm for about five or seven seconds or so and then exhale through the mouth. Do that about ten times, then sit up and then, or later, meditate. You will find that it is a very relaxing exercise and, to begin with, it might be very useful for you to precede your meditation with a little relaxing exercise of that kind. Because for most of the day we are fairly tense. We are having to deal with driving through traffic or dealing with our job or family problems, and this all leaves us fairly tense. But as you progress in your meditation, the meditation times themselves will bring you to a much deeper relaxation and you will probably be able to come straight from your work or other activity into your meditation and become quite relaxed straight away.

The other point to notice when you are beginning is that whatever phenomena present themselves to you – whether you see colours or hear sounds or see visions, whatever it is – take it as the general principle that it is all utterly unimportant. It has no real significance of any kind, except perhaps that you may need to be a bit more relaxed before you start. One of the things you have to learn in approaching your meditation is to approach it by not expecting anything. A lot of us in the West, when we begin meditating hope it will bring us to see visions or to understand life with deeper insight, teach us wisdom or knowledge. But you must come to it absolutely generous and absolutely poor in spirit, that is, without demands or any sort of expectations other than this – a conviction that you will come to in the meditation itself – that this is what we were created for. This is what everyone reading this book was created for – to be, and to be in relationship with our Creator.

That is the fundamental relationship of our existence – creature and Creator. In meditating you enter into the harmony of that relationship. You put yourself into harmony with the Creator and so one of the fruits of meditation is that the harmony which you discover in yourself you also begin to discover everywhere. So, the truly spiritual man or woman is someone who is in harmony with everyone they meet. You meet others not on the basis of competition or of projecting any image to them of who you might be or would like to be or think you ought to be. But you begin to meet everyone as you are, the person you are, comfortable, accepting of your own being. And you accept it because, in the silence of your meditation, you come to the knowledge that you are accepted. It is not just that you are acceptable because you have done all the right things. What you discover as you begin to explore that basic relationship of creature–Creator is that you are accepted. In the Christian vision of meditation you discover something even more. You discover in the silence that you are loved, that you are lovable. It is the discovery that everyone must make in their lives if they are going to become fully themselves, fully human.

In the vision proclaimed by Jesus you begin to know what St John meant when he said, 'God is love'. The extraordinary thing is (and this is again what I personally would like to be able to convey, to communicate to everyone I meet) that that love is to be found in your own heart. Each of you, if only you can come to this silence, will find it. If only you can come to the space within yourselves where you can discover that you can breathe this pure air of love.

Going back to this first question, 'Why should you meditate?', this is really why we meditate. To come to what perhaps we can describe best as a pure liberty of spirit. In meditation you are utterly un-constrained. You are not in any way enslaved to any image or idea, because you are beyond all images and ideas and you are in that state where you have the perfect liberty to be yourself. You have that liberty because you are one with the One who is. If you want to ask yourself when you put this book down, 'What is meditation really about?' just say to yourself, 'It is about being. It is about *is*-ness. He is. I am.' You can say either of those, but ultimately the experience of meditation is concerned with *being*.

Now let me just remind you again. We meditate at first for about twenty-five minutes and I should repeat the importance of being as still as you can. It is not a hard task. If you feel that you really must move, then don't feel that you will ruin everything by moving. But learn in time to sit as still as you possibly can because meditation is about a unity of body and spirit and a stillness of body and spirit. So when you start, take a moment to get really comfortable in your sitting posture and then begin to say your mantra. Don't think about anything. Don't think, 'Why am I doing this? Am I getting anything out of this?' Don't encourage any thoughts. Just say the word and listen to the word. My heartfelt advice to you is that if you do want to learn to meditate it is necessary to meditate every day in your life for a minimum of twenty minutes in the morning and twenty minutes in the evening. The ideal time is probably about half an hour. If you find that too long to begin with, start with twenty and gradually increase it to thirty minutes.

193

The ideal time to meditate is before your breakfast and before your evening meal. The place should be quiet and if possible always the same place.

Turn from your own thoughts now by attending to this reading from St Paul's letter to the Colossians. He is speaking about what Jesus will do for each of us if we are truly open to him:

> May he strengthen you, in his glorious might, with ample power to meet whatever comes with fortitude, patience and joy; and to give thanks to the Father who has made you fit to share the heritage of God's people in the realm of light.[1]

Meditation is about enlightenment because it is about coming into the light of God. That is the basic relationship, Creator and creature. And the Creator gives each of us the light to be ourselves.

1. Col. 1:11–12

Space to Be

St Paul writes this to the Thessalonians:

> We are bound to thank God always for you, brothers beloved
> by the Lord, because from the beginning of time God chose
> you to find salvation in the Spirit that consecrates you, and
> in the truth that you believe.[1]

I think it is a major concern of everyone to come to know
themselves, to understand themselves, and one of the great
ways put forward for this in our own society is experience.
People are encouraged to experiment with their experience.
But I think experience is only useful and only instructive for
us if we are able to evaluate it adequately. So often, as we all
know from our past, we have the experience but we missed the
meaning.

Our monastic tradition tells us that, if we want to understand
ourselves and to know who we are, then we have to make
contact with our own centre. We have to make contact with
the Ground of our being where this centre is, and unless that
process is underway all our experience will leave us in the
shallows. More and more people in our society are coming to
understand that both our personal problems and the problems
that we face as a society are basically spiritual ones. What more
and more of us are understanding in this world is that the
human spirit cannot find fulfilment in mere material success or
material prosperity. It isn't that material success or prosperity
are bad in themselves but they are simply not adequate as a
final, ultimate answer to the human situation.

1. 2 Thess. 2:13

So many men and women are discovering that their spirit is stifled as a result of the materialism in which we live, and much of the frustration in our time is due to the feeling that we were created for something better than this, something more serious than just a day-to-day survival. To know ourselves, to understand ourselves and to be able to start solving our problems, to get ourselves and our problems into perspective, we simply must make contact with our spirit. All self-understanding arises from understanding ourselves as spiritual beings, and it is only contact with the universal Holy Spirit that can give us the depth and the breadth to understand our own experience. The way to this is not difficult. It is very simple. But it does require serious commitment and serious involvement in our own existence.

The wonderful revelation that is there for all of us to discover, if only we will set out on the path with discipline, is that our spirit is rooted in God and that each of us has an eternal destiny and an eternal significance and importance. That is a primary discovery for each of us to make, that the nature we possess has this infinite potential for development and that development can only come if we undertake this pilgrimage to our own centre. Our centre is our own heart because it is only there, in the depths of our own being, that we can discover ourselves rooted in God. Meditation is just this way of making contact with our own spirit and in that contact finding the way of integration, of finding everything in our experience coming into harmony, everything in our experience judged and aligned on God.

The way of meditation is very simple. All each of us has to do is to be as still as possible in body and in spirit. The stillness of body we achieve by sitting still. So each time you begin to meditate take a couple of moments to assume a comfortable posture. The only essential rule is to have your spine as upright as possible. Then the way to the stillness of spirit that we have in our monastic tradition is to learn to say silently, in the depth of our spirit, a word or a short phrase. The art of meditation is simply learning to repeat that word over and over again – the word I have recommended you to use is the Aramaic word, *maranatha*. Don't move your lips, but recite it interiorly. What is important and you must understand from the beginning, is to recite your word from the beginning to the end of your time of meditation. Learning to meditate is learning to let go of your thoughts, ideas and imagination and to rest in the depths of your own being. Always remember that. Don't think, don't use any words other than your one word, don't imagine anything. Just sound, say the word in the depths of your spirit and listen to it. Concentrate upon it with all your attention.

Why is this so powerful? Basically, because it gives us the space that our spirit needs to breathe. It gives each of us the space to be ourselves. When you are meditating you don't need to apologize for yourself and you don't need to justify yourself. All you need to do is to *be* yourself, to accept from the hands of God the gift of your own being, and in that acceptance of yourself and your creation you come into harmony with the Creator, with *the* Spirit. Meditation is about our spirit coming totally into harmony with the Spirit of God. But if you want to learn to meditate and to live your life from the depth of your being, then you must build this into your every day and make a space in your life every morning and every evening. The minimum time is about twenty minutes, the optimum time about thirty minutes. Once you do learn that discipline you will begin to live your life in harmony, harmony within yourself, because everything in your life will come into harmony with God, and harmony with all creation, because you will have found your place, your place in creation. The astonishing thing about the Christian revelation is that your place is nothing less than to be rooted and founded in God.

From the pilgrimage of meditation we hear St Paul with new ears:

We are bound to thank God always for you, brothers beloved by the Lord, because from the beginning of time God chose you to find salvation in the Spirit that consecrates you, and in the truth that you believe. It was for this that he called you through the gospel we brought, so that you might possess for your own the splendour of our Lord Jesus Christ.[2]

2. 2 Thess. 2:13–14

That is what the path of meditation is about. To come into full harmony, to full union with the Spirit of Jesus who dwells in our hearts.

The One Centre

It is always important to try to put before ourselves a general idea of what meditation is about. For those of you who have been meditating for a while this will be like a little revision. For those who are about to start it can serve as an introduction.

Basically, meditation is a way of coming to your own centre, the foundation of your own being, and remaining there – still, silent, attentive. Meditation is in essence a way of learning to become awake, fully alive and yet still. It is the stillness of meditation that leads you forward to that state of wakefulness and the sense of being completely alive that dawns in you because you are in harmony with yourself and, gradually, in harmony with the whole of creation. The experience of meditation puts you in resonance with all life. But the way to that resonance, the way to that wakefulness is silence and stillness.

This is quite a challenge for people of our time, because most of us have very little experience of silence, and silence can be terribly threatening to people in the transistorized culture that we live in. You have to get used to that silence. That is why the way of meditation is a way of learning to say the word interiorly, in your heart. The purpose of repeating the word is to launch you into the silence. So, lay aside all kinds of materialistic ideas about how long this will take. It might take twenty years. But that doesn't matter at all. It might take twenty minutes. That doesn't matter either. The only important thing if you want to re-establish contact with your centre is to be on the way. The wonderful thing we discover when we do get underway is that there is only one centre, that that centre is everywhere and that meditation is the way of being linked to it in our own centre. Because we are then rooted in ourselves we find our place in the universe and so we find the centre of the universe. We find God.

The truly spiritual man or woman is the person who is so rooted in themselves that they are able to be in harmony with anyone and everyone. The whole purpose of the spiritual journey is to enter into a profound harmony with yourself, your neighbour, the universe and with God. Let me remind you again. The way to do this, the way of meditation is a way of utter simplicity. You have to learn to say your word, 'Maranatha'. It is difficult, just because this is not the conventional wisdom. Most people in our society think that wisdom is about growing in complexity and the more abstruse and rarefied the ideas that you can examine and master, the wiser you will become. If you say to someone, 'I am going just to sit down every morning and every evening and I am going to learn to say this word,' many people will say to you, 'Well you must be a fool. Surely life is too precious, and time too precious for you to waste time, for half an hour in the morning and half an hour in the evening, just saying a word like this. Weren't you given your mind for something more worthy, something better than that?'

So it takes a good deal of courage for each of us, as men and women of the twentieth century, actually to sit down and to meditate, every morning and every evening. But that is what is required. If you want to learn to meditate, you must try to make that time available each morning and each evening, and you must learn the discipline and be prepared for it as a real discipline. It is a discipline that will bring you to great stability, to great unity, to great harmony. The discipline is the discipline of saying the word.

A friend of mine recently sent me a cartoon from the *New Yorker*. It was of two Buddhist-like monks sitting in a meditation posture and one was saying under his breath to the one sitting beside him, 'What do you mean what happens next? This is it.' That is how a lot of people in our society see meditation. Another cartoon someone sent me a little while ago was a picture of a long-haired youth sitting in a meditation posture and his father, evidently an executive of some sort, was talking to some friends of his saying, 'It is absolutely marvellous, you know. Before he took up this meditation, he just sat around all day doing nothing.' That would give you an idea, if you just consider the humour of the *New Yorker*, as to how people in our society view meditation.

We ourselves should approach it, I think, with a certain humour too and not get too solemn about it. But that is the deal. That is what is required. If you want to learn to meditate, you must learn to sit still and to say your word from beginning to end. Now what you will find, if you can persevere, is that after a little while of saying the word you will feel a certain peacefulness and relaxation and you will be tempted to say to yourself, 'This is rather good. I'd like just to experience this now and to know what I am feeling now, I'll give up saying the word. I'll just go with the experience.' That is the high road to disaster. You meditate not to experience the experience. You meditate to enter into the experience. Meditation is a coming to consciousness and a going beyond self-reflective consciousness. Meditation is learning to look out beyond yourself, breaking out of the closed system of self-consciousness, that prison of the ego, and we do so by that discipline of saying the word. When you are saying the word you are not thinking your own thoughts. You are not analysing what is happening to you. You are letting go. Meditation, in the Christian vision of it, is simply launching out into the infinity of God through the Spirit who dwells in our hearts. It is a letting go, a launching out into the deep. And people, in all ages throughout history, have found that it requires an act of faith to leave yourself behind.

So, do not complicate your meditation. In my humble opinion, the less you read about meditation the better. The less you talk about meditation, the better. The real thing is to meditate. The simple rule to remember is this – find a quiet place in your home or wherever you are at the time. Sit down and sit upright. Don't bother when you begin with too much of technique. It is not necessary to sit in the lotus position. It may be very helpful if you can. It might be worth learning. But sit upright. The essential rule of posture is that your spine is as upright as possible. Breathing – the simple rule is breathe. Do not get too het up about whether you should breathe in or

201

breathe out. Do both! Then, the rule that is the most important of all – say your mantra, say your word. And that is the art of meditation, to learn to say it from the beginning to the end.

Simple Enjoyment of the Truth

St Thomas Aquinas says that 'contemplation consists in the simple enjoyment of the truth'. Simple enjoyment! Now it is true that thinking, analysing, comparing and contrasting, all have their place in all the various disciplines, including theology. But contemplation, as St Thomas calls it, meditation as we would call it, is not the time for activity, for the activity of thinking, analysing, comparing or contrasting. Meditation is the time for being. Simple enjoyment. And the simplicity that St Thomas speaks of is oneness, union.

The challenge to us as men and women of the twentieth century is that we live in an age that stresses activity, and it seems that if we are to come to terms with our problems and difficulties then surely we must *do* something about it. I was talking to a man yesterday who met someone in a hotel and they started to talk about the problems of life. The man he was talking to said, 'You know you could solve all this if only you would follow a course that I am going to.' And my friend said to him, 'How long will it take?' The fellow thought for a moment and he said, 'About ten days'. And then he described the course, all the various techniques that are required for activating personal fulfilment and so forth. Our society is full of this sort of thing – how to win friends and influence people. All these courses are full of exercises, procedures, questionnaires to be filled out, profiles to be elaborated and so forth. Many of them even consist of the technique of exhausting the participants, keeping them short of food, announcing that there will be a food-break shortly which never comes. (Indeed, the course that was described to my friend went on until four o'clock in the morning!)

So all these courses (and they are rife in our society) have a lot of content in them, much input and they demand intense activity. No doubt there is a place for some of them. But there is an ancient Islamic story which we should listen to before taking one of these courses. It tells of a man in a town at night looking for his key that he has dropped. He is looking under a street lamp, searching everywhere for the key. A passer-by sees him searching and says, 'What are you looking for?' 'My key,' he said, 'I've dropped it.' And so the passer-by searches too, everywhere. There is not a sign of the key. The passer-by says to him, 'Where did you drop it?' And he said, 'Down the road there about fifty yards.' The passer-by asked, 'Well, why are you looking here?' He said, 'Well, there is more light here.'

Now I think that we are very much like that man looking for our key where there is more light. Everyone in our society, I suppose to some extent, is searching for the key to the mystery of life, through all sorts of techniques and procedures. No doubt, each of them has a certain validity. But the search that we are talking about is beyond all activity. It is not a matter of assimilating more knowledge. It is really a matter of letting go, a running off. In fact, it is not a search, strictly speaking at all. We are not, as it were, looking for God who is lost. We know that he is here, that he is now. We know that he is present in this space, in this time, and the path of meditation we are following is simply to be open to what is, to the *is*-ness of God and to the *is*-ness of our own creation. This openness requires of each of us that we become present to the *now*, the here, and that we pay attention at the core of our being. That is the challenge of Christian meditation. In a way, we have to leave the street lamp that is familiar to us in our own society and we have to go off where there is no such clear light. We have to go into the dark. Learning to say our mantra is just that commitment to finding the light within ourselves.

St Thomas speaks of simple enjoyment of the truth. The mantra is the key to that simplicity. The mantra is indeed a principle of pure simplicity. It is the definitive leaving of complexity behind. Only one word. Childlike faith to say the one word. The truth that St Thomas speaks is the only truth there is. The Truth who is also the Way, the Truth who is also Life.

Meditation is equally simple enjoyment of the Way. Simple enjoyment of life. When we meditate we become as it were reduced to our essential being. In that reduction we become small enough to enter through the eye of the needle. Meditation teaches us humility, and in coming to that smallness, undergoing that reduction, we enter out into life, unlimited life. Apply this to the teaching of St John's Gospel:

> The time approaches, indeed it is already here, when those who are real worshippers will worship the Father in spirit and in truth. Such are the worshippers whom the Father wants. God is spirit and those who worship him must worship in spirit and in truth.[1]

Meditation is the way of making full contact with your own spirit, of making full contact with truth. Remember the Way. Say your mantra from the beginning to the end. Meditate every morning and every evening, faithfully, simply and humbly. Contemplation consists in the simple enjoyment of the truth.

---

1. John 4:23–4

The Light of Christ

These words are from the Gospel of John:

> If you dwell within the revelation I have brought, you are
> indeed my disciples; you shall know the truth, and the truth
> will set you free.[1]

Meditation could be described as a way of truth. The Greek
word for truth *aletheia* comes from 'a–lethes' which means
something that is not hidden. So, *aletheia* suggests that the
truth is a revelation for us. It is a revelation of the essential
structure of things. I want to talk a little about meditation as
a *way* of revelation.

As we all know we begin to meditate with all our confusion
around us. We do not even quite understand why we are meditating. I think a lot of us start as very reluctant meditators. We
hear about it and we begin in a half-hearted sort of way. But
gradually a glimmer of light comes. We suspect that there might
be something in it. The darkness is still all around us but there
is just the faintest glimmer of light. When that happens the first
step to take is to start meditating seriously, not with half your
heart but whole-heartedly. That means to put the time aside
for this way of revelation every morning and every evening.
That is the first thing to do. The second step is to begin to
commit yourself (and it takes time because you have to be
patient) to saying your mantra for the entire time of your
meditation. You should not be discouraged if you are a slow
starter. It takes some of us four or five years to come to that
stage. But what you will discover from your own perseverance

1. John 8:31–2

is that saying the mantra is like a very gentle and very gradual dispelling of the dark.

Just imagine for a moment a vast, dark, empty hall. Each time you say your mantra it is like lighting a small weak candle. And I think so often it seems to us that just as we light one, the previous one gets blown out. But very gradually the dawn comes and you begin to realize that the whole hall is flooded with light. The wonder of meditation is that this revelation that the light has conquered the darkness and that Jesus is the light becomes universal in your experience. Everything and everyone is now flooded, illuminated with this light.

This is very different from the pagan conception of things. You may know of the story in *Beowulf* when the banqueters and revellers are in the hall and suddenly a bird flies in through a window, briefly through the hall and out again into the dark. The revellers look at the bird flying in one window and out of the other, and they say, 'This is what human life is like. Out of darkness, a brief moment of revelry and back into the darkness again.' Now in the vision proclaimed by Jesus the understanding of the human condition is totally different. For us the banqueting hall is the heart, and that is where the darkness is when we begin. But by the discipline of our daily commitment, which is our commitment to the light in spite of our own weakness and in spite of our own half-hearted starts and false starts, we can find in our hearts the light that is also outside our hearts. The marvel of the proclamation of the Gospel by Jesus is that everyone and everything, inner and outer, is enlightened in a universal dawn of grace. This is what the power of the cross is about. This is what the power of the resurrection of Jesus is about. The universal dawn has occurred, and our commitment is to that enlightenment, that truth and that revelation. We have been using the metaphor of the light. What is the light for us who accept the revelation of Jesus?

The light is nothing less than the consciousness of Jesus himself. I do not think it is wrong to say that while we are looking for him we are always looking for the wrong thing because so often as Christians we are looking for an object of knowledge distinct from ourselves, but the truth is that we have already found Christ. We have found him when we realize –

207

that is, when we know fully – that what he has achieved for us is that we see with his vision. We see with his consciousness. We understand with his understanding because his invitation to us is that we should be united with him, one with him. It is not true to say that he is just within us or just beyond us. He is both within us and beyond us, and the enlightenment of Jesus enlightens us and enlightens the whole of creation. The challenge to us, and the great challenge to our belief, is that such an elusive mystery is not beyond our experience. It is not too difficult for us, but we can know it intimately and power-fully only when we forget ourselves. What we have to learn in our meditation is that the loss of self-consciousness enables us to come to full consciousness both with him and in him, with his own self-knowledge.

How do we lose our self-consciousness? It is very simple. It is very practical. The simple tool we use is that we must stop thinking about ourselves. That is why we have to learn to say the mantra. When we learn to say it with our total attention, with an undivided heart, we are on our way to being what Jesus invites us to be, one with him as he is one with the Father. In that oneness we are made free and we have been freed by the revelation of Jesus himself, because what he reveals to us is the glory, the wonder and the love of the Father. In this con-sciousness let us listen to St John again:

He who sent me is present with me, and has not left me alone; for I always do what is acceptable to him. . . . If you dwell within the revelation I have brought, you are indeed my disciples; you shall know the truth, and the truth will set you free. . . . If then the Son sets you free, you will indeed be free.[2]

2. John 8:29, 31–2, 36

The Inner Christ

Who is going to do you wrong if you are devoted to what is good? And yet if you should suffer for your virtues, you may count yourself happy. Have no fear of them; do not be perturbed, but hold the Lord Christ in reverence in your hearts.[1]

'Hold the Lord Christ in reverence . . . in your hearts.' The world in which we live is passing away. As we all know, empires arise. They have great periods of power and then they crumble. The lesson of history is that when they crumble they crumble very quickly. Wisdom in this situation is the ability to identify what endures, to understand what lasts and what is truly important. The early Christian community understood very clearly that each of us possesses and possesses right now, in this life, an eternal principle within us, something in our hearts that endures for all eternity – the Lord Christ. And so we are to 'hold the Lord Christ in reverence in our hearts'.

To live our lives well we don't need to be depressed by the fact that the world is passing away, that civilizations do crumble. Nor do we need to be disturbed by the fact that the world is often a largely chaotic world. As we all know, there is so much confusion. There are so many people who are confused, and all of us know that from time to time in our lives we experience that chaos and confusion in ourselves. But the challenge for each of us, and one that every human person must ultimately face, is to find in the real world, that is, a world that is chaotic and passing away, true peace, adequate order and a harmony that will make sense of all the voices competing

1. 1 Pet. 3:13–15

for our attention. Again, the early Christian community saw clearly, because they knew from their own experience, that Jesus himself is the way to order, harmony and peace. They know that he is the way because he leads us into the resonant harmony of the Trinity itself, the order, the supreme order, that is based on the supreme love of the Father, the Son and Holy Spirit.

The way of meditation is not a way of escape. Above all, it is not a way of illusion. We neither try to escape the real world of untidy ends and chaotic beginnings and nor do we try to construct an alternative, illusory reality of our own. What Jesus promises us is that if we do hold him in reverence in our hearts, if we believe in him and believe in the one who sent him, his Father and our Father, then all the chaos and all the confusion in the world can have no ultimate power over us. The stresses, the strains, the challenges, all remain but they are powerless to defeat us when we have founded our lives on the rock who is Christ. This is the real task. This is the real challenge that each of us must face, to enter into the reality that is Christ, the rock on whom we can build our lives with the absolute assurance that he will love us through all our mistakes, through all our changes of heart and mind and through every moment of our lives until the last moment of our life, because he is supreme love.

That is why St Peter tells us of the importance of holding the Lord Christ in reverence in our hearts. Rooted in him we are rooted in the principle of all life, in reality itself and, founded in him, nothing else has ultimate power over us, not even death itself. The challenge is to find our way to him by finding the way to our own heart so that we can hold him in reverence there. The way of meditation is consequently a way of learning to die to illusion, to all unreality, and so it is the way of learning to rise with Christ, to rise beyond ourselves and our limitations to eternal life. It is learning to do this now, today, and not to postpone eternal life to a time when we may get to heaven. The Kingdom of Heaven is among us now and we must be open to it now because, as St Peter says, we must be alive in the Spirit and become fully alive with the life of God. As Christians we must never settle for less. Our Christian life is not just a question of finding a way of getting through our lives. Every word of the New Testament suggests to us that it is of supreme importance that we live our lives in a state of continuous expansion, expansion of heart and expansion of Spirit, growing in love and becoming more firmly rooted in God. Each of us has to understand our potential, that we *are* an expanding universe, and so each of us possesses the potential for an energy-expansion that is not less than infinite.

St Peter tells us in the same letter 'to live an ordered life, founded on prayer' and he tells us 'to keep our love for one another at full strength'. This is the way of meditation – to tap that life source, that source of energy and power so that we can live our lives to the full. And we do so holding the Lord Christ in reverence in our hearts. Listen to St Peter again:

Who is going to do you wrong if you are devoted to what is good? And yet if you should suffer for your virtues, you may count yourselves happy. Have no fear of them: do not be perturbed, but hold the Lord Christ in reverence in your hearts. . . . Why was the Gospel preached to those who are dead? In order that, although in the body they received the sentence common to men, they might in the spirit be alive with the life of God. . . . you must lead an ordered and sober life, given to prayer. Above all, keep your love for one another at full strength, because love cancels innumerable sins.[2]

2. 1 Pet. 3:13–15; 4:6, 7–8

211

Free to be True

These are words spoken by Jesus and recorded in the Gospel of John:

> If you dwell within the revelation I have brought, you are indeed my disciples; you shall know the truth, and the truth will set you free.[1]

All of us, I think, feel within ourselves the primary necessity to come to grips with the truth. It is a need to find something, some principle in our lives that is absolutely reliable and worthy of our confidence. All of us feel this impulse to somehow or other make contact with rock-like reality. In the Old Testament truth was seen as an attribute of God and it was felt as God's trustworthiness. In him you could have complete confidence because he was true – as the Old Testament expressed it, 'Yahweh will not depart from his word'.

Now this is what the path of meditation is about. When we set out on the path of meditation we set out on the path of truth. 'His word is true.' Of course none of us can be just content with other people's experience of the truth, and so all of us have to come to know the truth from our own experience. If you want to follow this path, you have to commit yourself to meditating every day, to meditating every morning and every evening. The way is simplicity itself. All you have to do is to sit down and say your word, 'Maranatha'. When we meditate alone or in a group each of us has to accept the responsibility of saying the mantra from beginning to end. The saying of the word is itself an experience of liberty. We let go of all our

1. John 8:31–2

212

immediate concerns – everything that troubles us today, everything that makes us happy today. We turn aside from everything that is passing away in order to be open to absolute and ultimate Truth.

Wisdom teaches us that arriving at the Truth is experiencing the graciousness and loving kindness of God. And in the Christian vision of meditation the whole purpose of meditation is simply to be open to this presence of God in our hearts. People often ask, 'Why should I meditate? Why do *you* meditate?' I think part of the answer is that in the experience of meditation we come to know ourselves as true, as real, not ourselves as acting a role, not ourselves fulfilling other people's expectations of us, but the experience of being who we are. Meditation is important for us because each of us has to learn how to be true, how to be faithful to the truth of our own being. The one who is true is the one who is faithful. And the power of meditation is that in the personal experience of it, in the silence to which our word leads us, we learn to live out of the goodness of God when we have made contact with his goodness in our hearts. God is true, and anyone who discovers their own oneness with God has entered into the fundamental relationship of life, and as a result of this relationship all our relationships are filled with the kindliness and the truth of God. Jesus says, 'The truth will set you free.' The freedom is the freedom to be ourselves and the freedom to let others be themselves. The freedom to love ourselves, to love others and to love God. But that freedom depends upon a total commitment to truth.

People ask, 'How long will this take?' or they say, 'I have been meditating every morning and every evening for six months and I'm not sure if it has made any difference yet.' The answer to that is that it doesn't matter how long it takes. All that matters is that we are truthfully on the way, on the pilgrimage, and that each day – although perhaps only by one centimetre at a time – our commitment to truth and to freedom grows. The growth is often imperceptible, but that does not matter. All that matters is that we are growing, that we have not settled for half and that we have not betrayed the gift of our own being but that we are committed to growth and to maturity.

213

The opposite of the truth is falsehood or illusion, and meditation is a single-minded, clear-sighted commitment to the truth. It is a commitment to turn away from trying to make our own reality towards living in the light of God and by the light of God. The daily commitment to it, and the powerful gentleness of it as we meditate day by day, is a way of learning to accustom our eyes to seeing what is really before us rather than trying to imagine what is before us and then taking that for reality. What is real? What is truth?

God is real and the reality of God is the truth revealed in Jesus. The greatest part of the Christian proclamation of the Gospel is that Jesus in all his reality is to be found in our own hearts. In his light we see light. And in that light we know ourselves to be free. Now when you begin you have to begin in faith, and you have to continue in faith because the only way of arriving at that light, at the truth and the freedom, is by faith. Every time you sit down to meditate, your faith will be tested and so your faith will be strengthened. The time of meditation, when you say your mantra from beginning to end, might often seem to you to be a complete waste of time, but only remember that Jesus dwells in your heart. He is the revelation of God. Only in God and only from God do we have our reality. Saying the mantra is turning from all illusion, from all imagination, from all falsehood to ultimate Truth. Remind yourself of the way continuously. Sit comfortably, upright and as still as you can. Meditation is a way of total stillness, body and spirit. Then say your word as faithfully as you can.

There is a great power in meditating together. Your pilgrimage will be greatly helped by finding a group to meditate with regularly. We share that faith that is necessary for the inner journey and we share the presence of the God who is in our midst and in our hearts. That sharing takes place in silence and in stillness. Now consider these words of Jesus again:

He who sent me is present with me, and has not left me alone. . . . If you dwell within the revelation I have brought, you are indeed my disciples; you shall know the truth, and

the truth will set you free. . . . If then the Son sets you free,
you will indeed be free.[2]

2. John 8:29, 31–2, 36

The Accuracy of Sacrifice

In a previous incarnation – that is, before I became a monk – I served in the Counter Intelligence Service and one of the jobs that I had to do was to locate radio stations operated by the enemy. And so we would tune in our receivers to them, but the enemy were very clever and if they were operating say on a frequency of ninety metres, at eighty-nine metres they would send out a jamming wave, a jamming signal, and at ninety-one they would send out another. So, in order to tune in exactly on their station you had to have an extremely fine tuning on your own radio. But we liked to think that we were just as clever as the enemy and so, when we found out the frequencies that they were broadcasting on, we took quartz crystals and then we would plug in the crystal to our receiver. Our receiver would then pick up their signal absolutely spot on, and none of the jamming devices interfered with it.

I was just thinking about this the other day when it struck me that the mantra is very like a quartz crystal. The enemy that we all face, our ego, is sending out all sorts of contrary signals around the wavelength of God, and what we have to do is to get on the 'God frequency' exactly, or as exactly as we can. As you all know from your own experience, the mantra is not magic. It is not an incantation, and learning to say your mantra means learning to follow a way of life in which *everything* in your life is attuned to God. And so, in a sense, everything in your life is attuned to the mantra.

The essence of the Christian message is that God is a present reality, and this is to say that God is a reality who is present to us. If you consider for a moment that 'God is present' you begin to understand that he is present in every moment of our life and is so because of the extravagant generosity of Jesus.

The Presence is communicated through Jesus. The call to each one of us is to respond to his presence and to live in it. To respond to his generosity we become present to him ourselves. That means our hearts are open to him at all times. The generosity of Jesus demands of us that we seek that Presence selflessly, not so that we will become wiser or holier, not so that we will possess God, but simply because it is right and fitting that we respond to his generous self-giving, his generous self-sacrifice by our own self-giving and our own self-sacrifice.

The challenge of meditation is that it does make each of us face the basic redemptive question. The basic question is, 'Do we seek God or do we seek ourselves?' Another way of phrasing that would be to say, 'Do we seek our destiny within our own confined limits, do we seek to define ourselves merely within our own resources, or do we seek our destiny beyond ourselves, in God?' That is what our meditation is about – seeking to burst the limits imposed on us by our own egoism. The tragedy of Faust, for example, was that he threw away his eternal destiny for the perishable, limited crown of mere worldly fulfilment. Faust is such a tragedy because he knew that that was what he had done. It is knowledge that underlies so much of the anxiety and fear of our society.

Now the challenge for us is not to reject the world nor to reject ourselves. The challenge is to learn to sacrifice. To sacrifice we offer something to God, and in the Jewish law it is the whole thing that was offered. It was called a holocaust. Nothing was kept back. Everything was given to God. That is what our meditation does to our life. The mantra, our medita-tion, enables us to lose ourselves entirely, to offer ourselves entirely, in our wholeness, to God. It helps us to become a holocaust in which everything we are is offered to God uncondi-tionally. That is why we keep only the mantra sounding. When the time comes, we are prepared to surrender that too, because in our meditation we are entirely at his disposition. We exist only in his presence and we are in his presence because of his generosity. The wonderful thing about meditation is that in this self-sacrifice and loss of self, his Presence becomes our presence and his generosity becomes our generosity. As we persevere in meditation the loss of self becomes more and more complete, the sacrifice becomes more and more perfect and so the generosity is constantly increasing. That is why I stress to you so often the importance of saying your mantra from the beginning to the end of your time of meditation. No thought, no words, no imagination, no ideas. Remember the holocaust, the sacrifice. Now perhaps this is the greatest thing that we can do as conscious human beings – to offer our consciousness to God. In offering it we become fully conscious.

This is the experience of St Paul when he is speaking about the nearness of God:

> The peace of God, which is beyond our utmost understanding, will keep guard over your hearts and your thoughts, in Christ Jesus.[1]

What we have to learn is to seek that peace absolutely. Some people would think that it is unwise to speak of the absolute commitment that Jesus calls us to. Some people would think that even to hear about it is only for experts. But as far as I can understand it, the invitation of Jesus is given to each of us to take up our cross, to follow him to Calvary and to join him in his sacrifice and to go through with him, into the infinite love of the Father.

1. Phil. 4:7

The Present Christ

Further Steps in Meditation

Contents

Key to Letters

Introduction

An experiential theology

Not long ago I received a letter from a Carthusian monastery asking for more of the books of John Main to pursue the interest excited there by reading *Word into Silence*. A few weeks later they wrote again to express their great sense of discovery. It reminded me of an incident Father John related about the response to his talk on prayer to a Trappist community in Ireland. The abbot had surprised him with a request for an hour's conference on contemplative prayer and he had been led into a gaunt church filled with two rows of silent, hooded monks. He spoke, as increasingly he did in his last years, without notes and from the heart. At the end of his conference the monks filed out silently, without any indication of their response. But just before he left he was approached by an old monk, in his eighties, who whispered his question, 'What was the mantra you gave?' Father John told him, 'Maranatha'. The old man absorbed it for a few moments. Then, as he moved away, he looked at Father John and said, 'You know, I have been waiting for this for forty years.'

To those who heard him pass on the tradition of Christian meditation, John Main's personal presence and authority were powerful reinforcements of the ancient teaching. To Father John himself, an incident such as the awakening of the old monk testified only to the authority of the teaching itself. The medium of communication or persuasion was not his human personality but the Spirit of Christ equally present in speaker and hearer and in the living word that connected them. He spoke and wrote, of course, with the authority of one who had himself been led into the tradition and who had appropriated it within his personal experience. But it was not his own experience *per se* he was trying to communicate. 'In your own experi-

223

ence' was a Pauline phrase he used emphatically in his oral and written teaching. He had supreme confidence in the teaching itself to do the work of persuasion. Cassian's *experientia magistra* (experience is the teacher) expressed a profoundly Christian truth: that Christ is the teaching and the teacher, and that if we can faithfully meet the time-tested spiritual conditions – silence, stillness and simplicity – we will be led into the experience of this unity. 'The first task of the human teacher', John Main would say, 'is to phase himself out as quickly as possible and to lead people to see Christ as the teacher.'

There is then a strong emphasis on experience in John Main's teaching. He restrained the temptation to develop a speculative theology or a teaching that would always be trying to find something new to say. His imaginative intelligence would have allowed him to follow this path. But his own experience – based on his daily meditation – was too real to allow him to forget his personal discovery that Christian prayer is about participatory knowledge, not thought. Seeking only experience, however, could not be the way. In much of the confusion and eclecticism of modern 'spirituality' he saw the dangers of hunting for experience and so of making prayer an experience of inflated self-consciousness. 'If anything happens during your meditation, ignore it. Say your mantra.' This uncompromisingly pure rendering of the teaching would lead to the experience of the Kingdom that cannot be observed. His emphasis on experience carried no dangers of the new gnosticism or the old dualistic pietism, precisely because of this demand of faith. Experience by itself could indeed lead to spiritual anarchy, but experience attended in faith active in love manifests us as citizens of the Kingdom.

John Main, as one of his recent theological commentators has remarked, was not a systematic theologian.* But he was a theologian in the sense of Evagrius' definition: one who truly prays is a theologian; a theologian is one who truly prays. And theology implies some form or system by which both our experience and our understanding of its meaning can be expressed in a way useful and comprehensible to others. To

---

* F. Gérard, 'John Main: A Trinitarian Mystic,' in *Monastic Studies*, No. 15, Montreal 1984.

read John Main's writings, like listening to his tape-recorded talks, impresses one with the inner coherence of his teaching. What is this coherence? The experience of discovering the answer will be the inspiration intended by John Main to lead you into the experience of the pilgrimage. Being given the answer is not the same as finding it for yourself.

However, having said this it is difficult not to suggest my own perception of the pattern, in the hope that it may encourage another person's encounter with the teaching. Certain themes inevitably recur and recombine throughout John Main's writings, from *Word into Silence* to this, the second collection of his 'newsletters'. The coherence of these themes is better sensed when you remember that the context of his writing was always an attempt to communicate experience more directly than we usually associate with the book form. Often his books took shape from talks he gave, and so they deliberately retain as much of the flavour of the spoken word as the medium allows. In the letters sent from the Montreal monastery to a growing number of recipients around the world between 1977 and his death in 1982, there is *teaching*, it is true, but there is also *news* of the community in which this teaching first found expression and which was the human family in which the experience behind the teaching unfolded. Each of these twenty-four letters, the last twelve of which form this volume, represent in modern form an ancient tradition among Christians of writing to each other about their interior experience of Christ and their communal experience of discipleship. St Paul's letters are the pattern for this tradition, but most Christian theology in the early centuries saw the light through the same medium. Where faith and experience are strongest, the highest theology is the least academic. Letters are the most personal form of written communication.

So, the form of these letters itself carries a teaching: the experience *can* be shared, *must* be shared, and the sharing of it creates the community which is, both in its widest and most immediate sense, the Church. John Main loved and respected the Church in its institutional form. But he still saw the Church essentially as an event both personal and organic, and this event was for him the *tradition*, the passing on of the Good News, the transmission of the timeless Spirit which will continue until the end of time. Everything that advances this primary purpose of the Church is therefore traditional. However novel something may seem at first, if it is 'of God', time will show it as being a contemporary restatement of an ancient form, or rather, as being another form of a perennial Christian reality.

As the Montreal community developed we sensed the emergence of this traditional identity. As our own community traditions and customs developed we sensed a rediscovery of an energy which is both form and spirit. Curiously, given our urban setting and small numbers, it became clearer that the traditional model on which we were being formed was not medieval but primitive monasticism. This reinforced John Main's own perception that the most purely traditional is the most radically innovative, because it has restored conscious contact with its roots. It was in John Cassian (a fifth-century monk whose *Conferences* had a formative influence on Western spirituality) that he had found the clearest expression of what we, as twentieth-century monks, were doing. Tradition, in this perspective, becomes not a brake on progress but the rails on which we run the straightest course in the evolution of Christian life and teaching.

John Main's letters began to form a tradition of their own within the larger tradition of epistolary theology. From the first two-page letter written at Christmas 1977, to his last teaching on death before his own death in December 1982, Father John developed a simple format of news and teaching. The teaching section usually followed the news and often was related to one of the news items: a meeting he had had, a development in the community, a new member joining or one leaving. He resisted a proposal to make the format more like that of a conventional community newsletter. To the last the letter was typed on ordinary paper, and he personally wrote the salutation 'My dearest Friends' and signed it. Circulation was about three thousand at the time of his last letter, and, as we sent them out, we were encouraged by the thought that everyone of that number had asked to be on the mailing list.

Tradition and personal experience, Church and society, meditation and prayer: these are the themes you will find weaving in and out of these letters. At the centre is the experience of awakening, of spiritual vision. But it is not just one experience among others in the theological system; it is the controlling experience which encompasses and unifies all the rest. John Main does not try to describe 'what it is like'. For him the experience of the Kingdom, like leaven in the dough, permeates every dimension of living, solitary and relational. One senses this pervasive presence in these letters, written from a vision of the 'new creation' of Christ, full of hope and prophetic encouragement. These twelve letters convey the development of his later theology while his vision of 'Christ in all' was becoming sharper and purer. Anyone who reads them in conjunction with *Letters from the Heart* will sense this growth and feel swept along with it.

The rest of this introduction is meant only to give some pointers to the way into this movement and some of the background from which the letters were written.

A monastic chronicle

Monastic communities like other kinds of families are aware of themselves as passing through time. They also possess the human instinct to record their growth and development and to protect their most significant experiences from distortion or oblivion. The early experiences of a young family, though perhaps the most mundane of its life, are also the most precious and memorable. Meaning always seems most lucid at the beginning.

It may appear conceited or naive of us to feel that the daily life of our new monastic community and its points of growth should be of more interest to people than any other community history. One family photograph album is much like another. Yet hundreds of people who received these newsletters wrote back expressing their interest in the 'news-items' and often asked for more. Perhaps it was the fact that the demand made by the spiritual teaching seemed more humanly possible in the context of the realities of redecoration, individual comings and goings, talks and visitors, guests and additions to the community. This was not just trivia; it was a sign of Christian realism – a sign, too, that what was being passed on in the teaching was not just thought, but experience. The combination of news and teaching made the letters part of a tradition.

In his Introduction to *Letters from the Heart* John Main

describes the genesis of the community. After five years as Headmaster of an American monastic high school he had returned to his own monastery in London to start a lay community based on meditation. He took this step because of a growing sense of failure in monastic schools (most monasteries in Britain and America run schools as their principal work) to provide a truly Christian preparation for life. They sent out well-educated and sophisticated young men who would have a better chance than most of being successful in business or the professions, but 'would they know life in the dimension of Spirit, as a mystery rooted in the joy of being? Or would their contact with life be restricted to the sense of a struggle for success to which the fading memory of their monastic schooling would become increasingly irrelevant' (p. 7).

In writing this he had in the back of his mind the integral spiritual–social role played by Buddhist monasticism in the East. In Malaya he had seen how the young would naturally spend an often prolonged period of spiritual training in a monastery before starting their careers in the world. It is significant that right at the beginning of his experiment in the 'new monasticism' John Main was thinking of the young – the focal point of hope in any society. He sensed a great potential for monasticism in contemporary society and urged this extension, though with little success, on his fellow monks. At first he tried to draw the new, vigorous monasticism he sensed out of the old and tired forms. The lay-community he started in the monastery in London was exceptionally observant of the monastic spirit and daily horarium. Its members lived in a house where silence was practised, television was renounced and they meditated three times daily before walking over to the church to sing the Divine Office with the monks who were coming back from classrooms or parish visiting.

Out of this small community of six laymen living together for six months came the meditation groups that started to meet weekly at the house. These drew in people from outside and generated a need for teaching material in book and tape form.

When news of these developments reached Montreal it evoked an invitation to start a similar venture there. This was an attractive prospect, offering an opportunity for unrestricted development of John Main's monastic vision of a contemplative community forming an intense and revitalizing element in the spiritual life of the local church.

The stages by which this eventually came about are described in *Letters from the Heart*. The passage of time since then has given us a clearer perspective on the conjunction of themes as well as circumstances that led John Main to Montreal: contemplative teaching, monastic tradition, ecclesial need.

In April 1976 John Main was at Gethsemani, Thomas Merton's monastery in Kentucky. He had been invited to give three conferences to the community on 'Prayer in the Tradition of John Cassian'. The transcripts of these talks became his first published teaching on meditation, *Christian Meditation: The Gethsemani Talks* (2nd edn, Montreal, 1983). While at Gethsemani he spent time in Merton's hermitage and wrote from there to a friend: 'I have just celebrated the most loving mass of my life in Merton's little chapel. My purpose in coming here was to talk to the community about prayer, but in fact I have learnt so much myself while I have been here.'*

It was a turning point in his own life; his first major public teaching on the tradition of Christian meditation brought to him an awareness of the purpose for which his life had been a preparation. From there he went straight to Montreal, at the invitation of Bishop Leonard Crowley – for whom he was to develop the highest regard as one who served the Kingdom before all else – and he decided that here was the place to begin afresh. It was also, as we are seeing in hindsight, a turning point or new unfolding of the tradition of Christian meditation. He began his own teaching at the point where another monastic prophet, Thomas Merton, had been cut short, and he would address a great part of the audience whose spiritual attention Merton had gained. He wrote less than Merton, and his teaching was more specific.

In September 1977 John Main and I flew to Montreal to establish its first monastic community. A small meditation group was already meeting weekly at a church in the city, and was using tapes of John Main's talks. So, although we were otherwise unknown there at least Father John's voice had already been heard. After some delay we moved into a house

* Cf. My article 'John Main's Monastic Adventure', in *Monastic Studies*, No. 15, Montreal 1984.

on Avenue de Vendôme, which Bishop Crowley had acquired for us, just before Christmas. By then, two of the London lay community had come over to join us. The groups started to meet at the house almost immediately, and they developed rapidly.

Many people asked us why we had come to French-speaking Quebec when so many anglophone Canadians were leaving. That social context was a challenge to our faith in the venture. It never deterred us, and in fact the anomaly of the situation may have actually strengthened our sense of calling to that particular place. However, guests came from way beyond Quebec, many of them coming from the extended community of oblates and meditation groups that has grown up over the years in many cities around the world. Again, seen in retrospect, the choice of this particular city has increased in significance. It is a vital and culturally conscious city, large enough to be international, small enough, in its two cultural groupings, to be human. It is French and English, European and Anglo-Saxon, and is influenced but not overwhelmed by its American neighbour. As a meeting-point of the old and new world it makes an ideal place to renew an old tradition.

The events of the community's growth from 1977 to 1980 are told in *Letters from the Heart*. The present book picks up the story and carries it through to John Main's death.

Almost from the time of our arrival in Montreal we had felt the need for a larger house. The lay community rented an apartment near our monastery, and women guests had to stay in a neighbouring convent. We were receiving an increasing number of long-term guests, including monks and monastic candidates. As yet no novices had been received, although three young men had asked about coming to join us in the autumn of 1980. Every new site we looked at turned out to be either unavailable or too expensive. Then, out of the blue, one of our regular meditators, who had heard of our search, told us of a house his family owned in the centre of the city which might suit us. We were doubtful of this because we needed space and silence and were looking at places outside the city. However, when he showed us the house we realized that Providence was guiding our steps. It was an eighteen-bedroom house with a coachhouse, set in three acres of garden on the slopes of Mount Royal Park, a few minutes from the city centre and yet secluded and silent. By the time of my ordination in June 1980, the house, along with its contents, had been offered to us as a gift by the McConnell family whose home it had been.

My ordination took place in the motherhouse of the Congregation of Notre Dame, who had been very helpful to us in our early days. Their large chapel was filled with oblates and friends of the community, priests of the diocese, and Benedictine and Trappist monks from neighbouring monasteries. It was a symbol of the roots we had sunk and a sign of growth for the future.

Shortly before we left Vendôme on 3 November, we received His Holiness the Dalai Lama at the monastery for the midday Office and meditation, and to lunch afterward. Father John had earlier welcomed him as a fellow-monk at an inter-faith service in the cathedral presided over by the Archbishop of Montreal. In the simpler surroundings of the Vendôme house we shared a deep silence and sense of unity. There is, seen in retrospect, a fitting kind of symmetry to the visit of this Buddhist spiritual leader. Thirty years earlier, John (then Douglas) Main had learned to meditate, as a Christian, with a Hindu teacher, Swami Satyananda, in Malaya. When he became a monk he was told to give up what seemed to his novice master an 'eastern' practice. But then some years later, after enduring the 'spiritual desert' that had ensued, he had rediscovered the mantra in the *Conferences* of John Cassian as being entirely within the Western tradition. Because of the transparent sanctity of his first teacher John Main had never felt threatened by the great spiritual traditions of the East. His own rootedness in the Christian faith was unshakeable and could only be deepened by encountering the self-revelation of God in other religions. So often when Eastern religious leaders come to meditate with Westerners the method followed is taught from the Hindu or Buddhist faith. Now a Buddhist leader had come to share in the depth and silence of a Christian contemplative path, and the unity thus experienced was the more inspiring for all precisely because of that.

Our contact with missionary orders was increasing during this time. John Main had been to Ireland in the summer of 1980 to give retreats to missionaries, Benedictines and Dominicans, and later to monks in the United States. His retreats were always an introduction to meditation in practice as well as theory: the retreatants would meditate together for two or three half-hour periods. These retreats altered the course of many lives.

The larger capacity of our new house saw the expansion of the regular Monday (introductory) and Tuesday (ongoing) evening groups.* There were always guests with us, and many returned home to start small meditation groups on the model of those they had participated in while at the Priory. The simple format of the meeting – talk, meditation, discussion – lends itself to a meditation group in any parish, college, community or home. Every meditator comes, in time, to sense the need for the personal support and encouragement of others on this faith-demanding pilgrimage. It is from this spiritual need that groups have come into being in many parts of the world, and in their development have provided an inspiring model of the Church. These groups have not been initiated from the Priory, but they look back to it as a focal point of the spiritual family of which they now sense themselves to be a part. As they grow, through their experience of the faith-filled presence of their silence, they become not self-serving but other-centred communities of the gospel. The monks who came to form the Priory have, in recent years, also discovered that community is created in the silence of their prayer together. Such a community becomes a hologram of the Church: a part of it, but in that part containing the whole Presence of Christ. They thus revitalize its members' sense of what it means to be a member of the Church as well as what it means to be sharers of the Word. Each group is a cell of Christian teaching; it enters into the presence of the teacher, it consolidates, and its members develop each other's faith.

In Montreal the community integrates its four daily periods of meditation with the Divine Office and Mass. In preparing for meditation – St Benedict's 'pure prayer' – with and by the Office, we feel we have recovered a more traditional sense of the Office as a communal *Lectio* (spiritual reading) rather than as an obligatory act of worship. When we have young people staying with us who have little or no religious formation, it often impresses us how enthusiastically they respond to the Office, which so many priests and religious find a burden rather

---

* The chapters of *Moment of Christ* are drawn from these talks.

than refreshment. Similarly with the Eucharist; in celebrating Mass four times a week rather than daily we avoid the danger of institutionalizing it as a routine. However deep or reverent one's faith, mechanical responses can accrue and deaden the innate sense of wonder and mystery which we need to make the liturgy not only worshipful but instructive. With this schedule everyone in the community looks forward to the Eucharist with an appreciation of its being a gift rather than a right. The half-hour of meditation after communion not only ensures the reverent enactment of the rites but also clarifies the mystery of the Mass as a sacrament, signifying externally the reality of the indwelling Spirit and, in so doing, forming the participants into the Body of Christ's Spirit.

Many of the meditation groups around the world have been started by oblates of the monastery. As a form of association with a monastic community, oblation is as old as Christian monasticism itself. From the days of our first oblates we realized that this form of lay association with our monastery was unusually strong and creative, because of the depth of the spiritual bond created in meditation. Our oblates associated themselves with us for real and personally important reasons, growing directly out of their own spiritual discipline. They share the pilgrimage with us and, as part of their pilgrimage is communicating it to others, they share in our work and often take imaginative initiatives.

Numbering about three hundred and extending across North America, Europe, Australia and Africa, this fellowship of oblates brings together eighteen and eighty-year-olds, conservatives and liberals, laity and clergy. As they share in the experience of the Spirit in our daily life, it becomes for us all an exciting manifestation of what Christian community truly is.

For several years, on Saturday mornings, a group of children has been meeting at the Priory for meditation. This has reinforced our conviction that meditation is indeed 'for everyone' and that the problems we find in learning to meditate later in life would be much lessened if we were taught earlier.

Although most of the teaching at the monastery takes place at the weekly groups and in the liturgy, there are also visits from special groups. Among these are groups of theology students who often express their concern about the absence of a practical spiritual training in their studies. Father John was

233

once asked to give a series of meditation group meetings at the Faculty of Religious Studies at McGill University. I remember one session during which an ambulance siren sounded during the meditation period. The theology professor who had come with his class asked the obvious question: during this time of prayer shouldn't we have stopped saying the mantra and instead prayed for the person being taken to hospital? Father John's response was that in a real sense we were doing this by saying the mantra, because we were entering the Spirit, the prayer of Jesus, who is the one mediator for all. The practical simplicity of meditation opens up a theology of much-needed spiritual depth.

At the heart of this extended fellowship of meditation, united by the 'Communitas' tapes and the newsletters as well as by personal visits, is the monastic community. Now numbering eight, it has grown through the usual trials and tests of all growth. Two of the novices who came into the new house with us in 1980 left within a few months. But their place was taken by others, some of whom came in different capacities, like the former Anglican bishop of Ontario, who became a resident ecumenical oblate and now pursues his work for Christian unity throughout the world.

Other events in the life of our community, from the summer of 1980 to December 1982, are indicated briefly in the opening section of each chapter; these are summaries of the 'news items' which preceded the teaching part of Father John's letters.

Father John continued to speak to the Monday and Tuesday night groups until about six weeks before his death on 30 December 1982. His last teaching letter, of 8 December and the short foreword for *Moment of Christ*, which he wrote during those weeks, speak with an authority and clarity for which his whole life had been a preparation. He used to say we must live well as a preparation for dying well.

To be with him as he died, during those months, was an experience of the transformation of flesh into spirit. In the expansion of the community and the work into which he breathed his spirit, Father John lives more fully than ever, because he lives no longer but Christ lives in him.

1

Silence of Real Knowledge

Among those coming to visit and share our life during the summer of 1980 were an increasing number asking about a monastic vocation.

Father John spoke on meditation at a wide variety of gatherings in Montreal and the United States, mirroring the many dimensions of community life that were manifesting themselves.

The ordination of Brother Laurence Freeman was a milestone in the development of community. The motherhouse of the Congregation of Notre Dame was needed to receive the large numbers who attended – symbolizing what had been achieved and what was yet to come.

One of the challenges we all face is to be continually sensitive to the unfolding of God's plan in our lives: to give free and open assent to the destiny his love is shaping for us. It is so easy to lose that sensitivity. So much of our life is dominated by the mechanical, by the response that is expected or demanded of us, by attempts to predict or anticipate growth, that we are always in danger of losing contact with life as a mystery – and so with life itself. When we cease to respond to life with wonder we begin to understand it merely as a problem, a series of complicated interlocking processes. But our life is whole. And the wholeness is both its mystery and its simplicity.

The wholeness of our life is the harmony of our experience, both its inner harmony, the inner sense it persuades us it has, and the harmony with which it resonates, its reality stretching far beyond the frontiers of our limited experience; the reality which we come in time humbly to realize contains our experience. Experience, though, does not become significant experience, our life does not become charged with meaning, until it begins to repeat itself. The meaning and inner purposefulness of our life usually reveals itself in the pattern of our experience; every pattern is the projection of creative repetition. But of course the pattern is never completed. At least, it can only be said to be complete within the infinite space of God's inner expansion, where all is both new and familiar – eternity. Any fixed pattern we try to impose on our life falsifies the truth of the mystery that is eternally present and so unpredictable. Rigidity is an attempt to evade the challenge our life constantly places before us to remain continually open to the unfolding of our destiny. It is fear of the expanding interiority of truth that tempts us into trying to protect the ground gained rather than pushing the frontiers further, to self-cultivation rather than selfless exploration. Our insensitivity to the mystery of life can wrap itself around us like a strangling vine, stifling the circulation of our spirit and making us ever more closed in upon an examination of our own pain. In the outward circumstances of our life this lingering spiritual death is manifested in the diminishing returns of our attempts at self-distraction, in the deepening fear of boredom. The kingdom of the ego is a grey world without laughter.

If we live merely within the perspective of a fixed pattern, from day to day, we are wasting our deepest response to life on what is passing away. We have not engaged with life on the level at which things endure. To remain thus unaware of the eternal that unfolds itself within our lives out of our inmost being, is the saddest fate that can befall anyone. And the great Christian insight is that this is a fate that need have no power over us. 'Fear not, for I have overcome the world.' Whatever else befalls us the divine perspective can be a redeeming reality for us because all possible human experience, all reality, has been shot through with Christ's redeeming love. We are each of us called to know within this perspective, to be ourselves wholly penetrated with his consciousness, and we are so called simply because we are human and our destiny is to become fully human.

Our gift of spiritual knowledge, our capacity to know by participation, is our gift of life. Whatever our experience may be, it recalls us to the grounding realization that we are and, in contacting this ground of our being – the consciousness that we simply are – we are filled with joy: and the consciousness that Being is Joy once more transforms the pattern of our experience. 'Though our outward humanity is in decay, day by day we are inwardly renewed' (2 Cor. 4:16). Each time we meditate we return to this grounding consciousness of Being, and each time we return to the changing pattern of our life more firmly rooted in our being and so more able to perceive life as mystery and to communicate this perception in joy to others. Our ability to see this is itself the gift of our creation – the gift that is being given with ever-increasing generosity moment by moment. Our creation is ever expanding in harmony with the overflowing love occurring in the secret depths of the Father's timeless mystery. As his being fills our being, our heart is purified and we are led deeper into the vision of God that is his own infinitely generous self-knowledge.

This gift of vision is the wonder of our creation. The perspective with which we are empowered to see is the reality within which we live and move and have our being. It is not a gift we possess but one that we receive and, in returning, receive again more fully. That is why, however long we have been meditating, we meditate without demands and without expectation. Thus the knowledge that God has created us to share in takes possession of us – in a way without our knowing it, yet the consciousness we gain is complete as the self-consciousness we lose could never be. We live no longer but Christ lives fully in us.

Christ is light. He is the light that gives range and depth to our vision. He is also, in his fully realized human consciousness, the eyes with which we see the Father in the divine perspective. Without his light our vision would be tied to the partial dimension and our spirit could not soar above itself into the infinite liberty and crystal clarity of the unified state. Our consciousness would, however wonderful, remain an observer on the periphery of his space, unfulfilled by union with his consciousness, unco-ordinated with his Body. Without his Spirit dwelling in our mortal bodies and opening up the infinite dimension within our spirit, we would be like men restricted by their own innate limitations from moving freely in the liberty they have been given. But the light that transforms our weakness, that makes our limitations the crucible in which his power is brought to perfection, has been freely given, poured into our heart as the pure effulgence of the Father, for Christ is the radiance of the Father. The light we need to empower our vision is not less than this radiance, the glory of God itself. 'For the same God who said, "Out of darkness let light shine," has caused his light to shine within us, to give us the light of revelation – the revelation of the glory of God in the face of Jesus Christ' (2 Cor. 4:6).

For those of us humbly treading the pilgrimage of prayer into this experience of light this is the only fundamental knowledge we need. It is the word that summons us out of the fixed pattern and inspires us to align ourselves on the expanding reality, to place our centre of consciousness beyond the limits of our own self-preoccupation and to discover that our centre is in God. How any of us come to begin this journey is not so important as that we do in fact begin. To begin, it is only necessary to enter into one moment of commitment – one chink in the wall of the ego allows in the light that will flow in more and more powerfully and will steadily overcome all that prevents complete translucence. This moment of commitment is always upon us. It is never an absent ideal, a future possibility but always a present reality. The only question is whether we are sufficiently present to ourselves to be able to see it, to hear the invitation and respond. Every moment is the moment because all time has been charged with divine meaning. Our age is the age of Christ, the age of the glory of God, and it awaits the completion of its transformation by our awakening, our realization. 'Now is the acceptable time.'

Our day-to-day life is of vital importance, as this mystery of transformation is worked out in us and through us by the power of Christ. No detail is insignificant if it is seen in the true light because the reassimilation of all creation in Christ is to be complete. And so our hours of prayer are of supreme importance within the continuous expansion of the mystery, if our spirit is to expand in harmony with it and receive the life and light it offers us. Nothing should be allowed to retard this process of expansion or to obscure the power of the light. Indeed, nothing can, except our own heedlessness.

The besetting fault of Christians in every age is that they become so busy about so many things that they forget that only 'one thing is necessary': to be one as he is One. The plan being worked out in the life of each of us is the same as that being realized in all creation, the bringing into unity with Christ of

238

all that is. It is a unity that lies beyond our capacity to describe. No part of us is left outside the final mystery of oneness. This oneness is at the same time the primal simplicity of being, the unrefracted consciousness of innocence, and the highest point of evolutionary creation, the omega point that is the genesis of infinite growth. We do not, however, need to be able to describe or even understand this mystery in which our own deepest life-process and inner meaning is rooted. All we need is to have begun to experience this plan as a fully personal reality in our own heart, to have known our creation in its dimension of mystery and to have rejoiced in this knowledge of the One who is One.

We will then have begun to know, and our daily meditation will confirm and deepen the knowledge, that the first sphere of this great movement into unity is the achievement of wholeness within ourselves. As the mantra roots itself in our being it gently but surely draws all the distracted and scattered parts of our being together. It calms and disciplines the unruliness of our mind, the tree filled with the chattering monkeys. It takes us beyond our self-centred attachment to our own moods and feelings, beyond all desire including spiritual desire. It takes us too through the turbulent periods in which our unconscious fears or anxieties are run off, often disappearing for ever without our knowing what they were. Through all this the mantra leads us into the discipline that allows us to be silent – and it is in the silence that our spirit naturally expands. From day to day also our inner confidence in the reality of our own being is deepened and the fear that we are slipping into non-being or that we do not exist at all, which are the besetting fears of our time, are exorcised. The unfolding of our own harmony is the experience of wonder and beauty that allows us to recognize the wonder and beauty of all creation. The wonder is that we are becoming fully conscious of our own creation, knowing that we are being brought to completion. Yet we are not as it were witnesses at our own creation. We are at one with our creator and the uncovering of our own harmony serves to set up a resonance with the source of all harmony. To find our own centre is the reverse of becoming self-centred. It is to awaken to the centre beyond ourselves, whence we are created and to which we return with Christ, the

239

centre where we find ourselves and him in that experience of communion we call the Kingdom.

I spend much of my time talking with good people who would agree with this at the level of theory and yet are often reluctant to set out on the pilgrimage that realizes it in practice. The ideas and the language we use to express them can become so intoxicating in themselves that they make the pilgrimage, in its wonderful but relentless ordinariness, seem by contrast very mundane. Our distracted need for novelty is better satisfied by the wares of the spiritual supermarket than by the simple labour asked of us in the garden of our daily meditation. We need to be recalled to the practical simplicity of the way in which the mystery of life is made real for us, or rather perhaps how we are made real in the mystery. We are recalled in so many ways it is difficult to understand how the tradition that teaches us this simplicity is so often read, preached and lectured on and yet so rarely followed. The teaching of every major Christian source points to the same set of simple truths: our way into the mystery of life is the way of becoming centred in God, the way of prayer. For John Cassian it was prayer as the way of poverty, a becoming 'grandly poor' in the utter simplicity of the single verse. For the *Cloud of Unknowing*, too, it is prayer as a journey of progressive simplification, a going beyond all words and thoughts in the stark simplicity of the one little word. It seems to me more and more that any talking about prayer that does not recognize that the talking must come to an end and the practice of it begin soon has little value in leading us into the actual experience of the mystery. The gospel itself lies across our theorizing paths at every turn with its implacable injunction to 'become as little children'. In the mantra we have a means that is at one with our end: a way that is simple and absolute. Our daily fidelity to meditation and our fidelity to the mantra throughout the meditation is the sign that we have heard and attended the gospel's call. Each day that rests on the twin pillars of the morning and evening meditation is a step on the pilgrimage from theory into reality, from idea into experience as we turn aside from all complexity, all trivial concerns, simply to be one in Him, with Him and through Him.

The silence releases the power of the glory of God in our heart. Indeed we find the silence itself as a power within us, the power of the Spirit who in silence is loving to all, and the silence we find through the poverty of our mantra. As we approach that profound silence reigning in our heart that is the Spirit, we know that it is itself the light, the glory that beckons us onwards. And as we pass more fully into the transforming aura of this silence the greater becomes our wonder, the deeper our joy that we are on this pilgrimage at all.

There are days in our lives, days of epiphany, when the unfolding revelation takes on a wholly incarnate form and the plan of the mystery is made visible. On such days what seems the toil and labour of the pilgrimage gives way to enfleshed grace. The centre of the pattern dilates and touches us with a sureness beyond the power of any pattern of words or experience to contain. Such a day for our Community was June the 8th, 1980, the Feast of Corpus Christi, the Body of Christ, when Laurence Freeman was ordained to the sacred priesthood.

Understanding can only emerge from within if we begin by accepting that there are many things we cannot understand or can at least apprehend only very dimly. The deepest Christian experience can only be entered upon when the wisdom of this humility has dawned upon us, because only then are we in a position to allow the mind of Christ full realization in our consciousness. Only then can we understand that we know the Father only by means of our union with Christ. Only thus can we 'know it though it is beyond knowledge'. The power of the sacraments is such an area where we can know fully only if we know with him and through him, allowing him to know us. We can talk of the Body of Christ. We can talk of the Priesthood of Christ, but our talk can never plumb the depth of the mystery for it cannot take us into the vision of that divine perspective that is opened up by silence.

Our own intimate involvement and participation in God's self-revelation fills us with an awe that demands silence as the truest and most natural response. It is such a deep involvement that the mystery is closer to us than our own words and ideas about it. It is not simply that God is drawing us closer to himself by the revelation of his plan, it is rather that in Christ we are participating in the eternal meaning of the communion of love that is God. Man is not meant to be a mere onlooker at this mystery. When the Creator, on the ceiling of the Sistine Chapel, passes his life into Adam he looks into his inmost

241

depths and from them he receives man's awakened recognition. God knows himself in man – not as we might hear the echo of our voice in a hollow chamber, but in the full wonder and liberty of his own being. The full flow of the divine current is earthed in man and it fills him with the brilliance and beauty of the Spirit itself.

The sacraments are dynamic manifestations of the 'joy of Being' earthed in man; and so they continually remind us, through the ordinary fabric of our experience, that our potential is to be wholly transfigured by the power of God passing through us and bringing us to the fullness of our creation.

The great moments in which our minds and hearts advance into this fullness are always moments of silence. The moment of silence in the ordination ceremony is the actual sacramental moment of power when we allow all that our words and rituals have prepared us to receive to dilate in the sacred space in which we have gathered and to fill us. It is a still moment, full of energy, the loving energy of God delighting in the realization of his plan for those he has called. In the stillness we are filled with a reverential fear, but it is a fear that flows into supreme confidence in the presence of him who discloses himself to us in love. Everyone present is turned in the same direction, drawn and at the same time liberated by the power that unveils a reality encompassing the bishop, the priests, the new priest and everyone assisting but that goes beyond all into the mystery of God in whom space and time subsist. It is one of those moments of transcendence when we are taken beyond ourselves and yet are never more truly the person we are called to be.

The sacrament of Holy Orders, like all sacraments, is an outward sign, a sign of an inner reality that is pure openness to God and the power of his love. In the generosity of that openness there comes an end to all the barriers preventing the free flow of that power. The knowledge of the reality of the universal communion that his love ensures expands, and we know that all things are held together by love. Because this is the inner dynamic of the sacrament we celebrated with Bishop Crowley in the Chapel of the mother house of the Congregation de Notre Dame here in Montreal it is no idle thing to say that all our friends were there with us, as Laurence was led deeper into the mystery of creation.

Every life is charged with meaning from within. Every

pattern we try to impose on our experience from outside inevitably falsifies the truth. This is the dangerous quality of language, for whatever we say about the mystery of God expanding in our life, or of meditation itself, misses the wholeness of the truth and usually its simplicity. One aspect of the mystery usually gets ignored or distorted as we talk about another. In talking of meditation as the way we lose our life, go beyond our self-consciousness into the clear light and open space of Christ's consciousness, we often distract attention from the profound degree to which we find our life, discover the unique and abiding gift of our own being in its union with God. We talk too of silence as the natural medium in which this discovery is made, but in talking of it we suggest that it is a negative value, the privation of sound and image. That is why the experience of silence is so vital for any right understanding of it. Only in entering the mystery of silence in meditation can we understand that, though it certainly demands faith and discipline, it is the silence of love, of unqualified and unconditional acceptance. It is the silence which proceeds from the overcoming of time and space; limiting patterns of the mind dissolve when all has been said and understanding has begun to flourish in communion.

To begin to understand this from our own experience it is only necessary that we begin to commit ourselves to it as the truth. Confirmation then follows our commitment. In the external features of our life we begin to see reality in the perspective that only centrality (being rooted in our centre) can give. Our vision, our understanding, expands from within this centre where our mind rests in silence in meditation. Let your mind rest in the heart, say the Upanishads. Set your mind on the kingdom before everything else and all else will be given to you as well, says the Gospel. The fact that we are, in our most real being, rooted in the silence of this centre seems to us the most elusive truth of our life. But the problem is our distractedness, our possessiveness. In fact the Spirit waits patiently for us in its own eternal stillness. Our pilgrimage of meditation teaches us that in spirit and in truth we are there already, with our Father who has called us to be there, who created us to be there and who loves us to be there.

Our awakening to this reality is the expansion of our spirit. With expansion comes liberty, the liberty of spirit that pushes forward the range of our limited consciousness by union with the human consciousness of Jesus dwelling with the infinite space of his love in our human heart. Yet there he dwells with the most perfect respect for our freedom, for the destiny being shaped for us in the bosom of his Father and our Father. The liberty is our capacity to enter with undivided consciousness into this destiny and to know it as the perfection of the mystery of love. This knowledge is not theory or speculation but contact with the most immediate and personal reality. We are not meditating long before our eyes begin to open upon epiphanies of love in our life that before we were too short-sighted to perceive or not generous enough to receive.

The mystery of faith is that liberty is the fruit of rootedness. Our materialistic, egocentric values dispute this, seeing freedom as the absence of commitment, freedom *from* ties or responsibilities. This is the negative protection temporarily offered by the ego as it demands the fruit before the flower. But while our ego is being melted away and our desire dissolved in the faithfulness of our meditation the kingdom dawns. The mantra leads us into the rootedness that bears fruit beyond our imagining. Through all the directions of our pilgrimage the simple faith of our single word keeps us homed on our only destination, the only destination there is, the unshakeable reality of the Father's love. There we enter upon the infinite expansion of heart that liberates us once for all from all narrowness, all insensitivity, all the shadows of the ego.

Our language will only frustrate us unless it leads us back into the refining silence. This is why it has to be a language of opposites, trying to be truthful to the freshness and eternal simplicity of the paradoxes in which we see our spirit expand beyond the fixed patterns. But the mind cannot know this as a separate reality, to analyse, remember, quantify. The mind is itself transformed by this knowledge – the knowledge proceeding from the heart's silence that only the heart can know at source. The knowledge of love is only knowable in love's transformation. Our mind finds its peace through being still in the heart, and in that union of our own being we awaken to a greater union still of which this is but a sacrament – the union of all in Christ who transforms all by the grace and power of his union with our Father.

2

Absolute Gift

In the summer of 1980 we were offered a large house and estate which wonderfully answered our needs. The house stands in three acres of wooded garden on the slopes of Mount Royal, only a few minutes from central Montreal. Four young men had recently come to be novices at the Priory – this giving a special sense of providential design to the move.

Our guests included several missionaries en route to or from their assignments. Meditating with them reinforced our conviction that the way of meditation is a way for all walks of life and vocations even, indeed especially, for the more active.

The oblate community continued to expand, with new members from across Canada, the United States and Europe. In Toronto great interest in the work of the Community led to an invitation, from a large network of meditation groups associated with the Priory, to Father John to speak there in November.

During the summer Father John went to Ireland, where he gave meditation-retreats to the Benedictines at Kylemore and the Dominicans in Drogheda. Later he gave a retreat to the Benedictines at St Louis Priory, Missouri.

Shortly before our move from Avenue de Vendôme, we received His Holiness the Dalai Lama, after an inter-faith service at the cathedral. As a fellow monk he meditated with us after the midday Office, and at lunch he presented Father John with the traditional white silk scarf of Buddhist esteem.

There is a deep and urgent need in our society to recover the true experience of spirit. By 'true' I mean an experience that is fully personal, really authenticated by the engagement of our whole person. It is not enough to be moved by another's spiritual experience. It is not enough to approach the dimension of spirit merely with part of our being, whether that part is intellectual or emotional. The fullness of the spiritual experience to which we are each summoned requires not less than everything we are.

I would like to put before you an aspect of this conviction which was emphasized for us this summer as we meditated with our missionary guests – men and women who meditate daily through lives of active and often very courageous service, and with the Dalai Lama, spiritual leader of one of the world's oldest and largest contemplative monastic orders.

Meditation, as the way of a life centred faithfully and with discipline on prayer, is our way into this true experience of spirit, of *the* Spirit. As anyone who follows this way soon comes to know for himself, its demand upon us increases with each step we take along the pilgrimage. As our capacity to receive the revelation increases so too does the natural impulse we feel to make our response, our openness, more generous, more unpossessive. The strange and wonderful thing is that this demand is unlike any other demand made upon us. Most demands upon us seem to limit our freedom, but this demand is nothing less than an invitation to enter into full liberty of spirit – the liberty we enjoy when we are turned away from self. What seems the demand for absolute surrender is in fact the opportunity for the infinite realization of our potential. But to understand this we cannot flinch from the fact that the demand is absolute and consequently so must our response be.

So used are we to what is relative rather than absolute, so used are we to making compromises, that it often seems that the absolute response is an ideal rather than a practical possibility. 'It would be nice if we could but it just isn't realistic.' The urgent need facing the Church is to awaken to the fact that not only is it realistic but it is the only way to come into contact with reality. The Church has no less need than the rest of society to recover the true experience of spirit as the central priority in its life if it is to be true to itself, its Lord and its vocation. Only if it has personally recovered this knowledge in lived experience can it point the way forward to the fundamental truth of the human mystery which is the mystery of Christ. The absolute commitment required was described by the early Church as faith – faith in the utter reality of God's revelation in Jesus.

The challenge to the Church is the same one facing all men

246

and women – to understand that the absolute is the only realism. For those who have begun to awaken to the mystery of Christ it is perhaps easier to understand how practical is the absolute because what they are awakening to is the mystery of the incarnation of the one who says 'I am'. The Spirit dwells in us as absolute gift, unconditionally. It dwells in us in our ordinary humanity, a humanity that is weak, vain or silly, that knows failure, mistakes and false starts. Yet it persists within us with the complete commitment of love. It dwells within us through the humanity of Christ and it is through the mutual openness, the union of our consciousness with his that we are empowered to make that absolute response which is the secret meaning of our creation.

Any life which fails to place this mutual openness, which is prayer, at its centre loses its balance as it moves away from its centre of gravity, and it can only fall into one or either extreme of solemnity or triviality. Between these two extremes is the discipline of seriousness, the truly serious approach to life that prepares and sustains us for the response to the absolute. In that response we enter into the experience of pure joy, the joy of being, the joy that underlies everything we are and everything we do. Beginning the journey of meditation is to begin to understand that it is for this joy that we have to learn to prepare ourselves and that our capacity to receive it with open, generous hearts depends upon the generosity of our discipline.

This is why our response to the absolute reality is a matter of absolute ordinariness. We live in a world where it is the extraordinary, the phenomenal, that fascinates and attracts attention, and this is often manifested most of all among religious people. Underlying this kind of sensationalism and cult of novelty is a loss of faith in the mystery of life as it is given to us, as absolute gift, to live and to live in its fullness. What has been lost is essential to the survival of the contemplative experience at the heart of each human life and of human society – the sense of the wholeness of life. The mystery of life is its wholeness and the wholeness of life is the mystery that continually deepens the perspective of our consciousness.

If meditation seems to people to be an unrealistic, non-incarnational dimension to our spiritual life it can only be because the experience of this mystery of wholeness has been lost or has become merely notional. The truth of the Incarnation is that the absolute reality of God has touched and indeed become One with the variable, contingent reality of man. God became man so that man might become God, as the early Fathers of the Church express it. Staggering as this revelation is and feeble though our capacity may be to receive it, it is all worked out through the ordinariness of our human person and the ordinariness of our human life. And for this reason we meditate as an ordinary reality of our daily life, every morning and every evening. It is part of the routine of our daily life, but unlike the other, largely unconscious parts of that routine our times of meditation are moments of ever deeper wakefulness, ever fuller consciousness.

The growing sense of unreality that is overtaking our society often leads people to an intense self-consciousness about the more mundane routines of life, like diet or exercise. The tendency of such self-consciousness is to spread to every other part of our life and for this reason a hyper self-consciousness about food is not infrequently associated with intense self-consciousness about 'methods of spiritual realization'. The tragedy of this type of self-consciousness is that it has its origin in a loss of the experience of pure consciousness and though it is an attempt to recover that experience it is an attempt doomed by its very nature to be counter-productive. The simple truth is that to enter into undivided consciousness, into purity of heart, we have to leave our self-consciousness behind. He who loves his life will lose it.

There comes a point in time after we have begun to meditate when the self-conscious novelty of it wears thin and the ordinariness of it begins to appear. It is, ironically, at this moment when our self-consciousness is beginning to fade and the experience of wholeness begins to emerge that many people give up. The power needed to continue and to allow the mystery to dilate at the centre of our being is again what we call faith. What the Church has always known is that faith is pure gift. The power that enables us to travel deeper into the ordinariness of meditation is fully personal, calls forth from us a mature acceptance, but it is not our own in any possessive or self-dependent sense. We know it as the faith Jesus himself communicates to us through his consciousness dwelling undividedly within us and among us. We receive this power from this source deep in the centre of our spirit where his Spirit dwells. We receive it too from the word of faith spoken to us in innumerable ways by our fellow men, both saints and sinners, the human community of the faithful.

Hearing the word of faith is to experience a challenge addressed to our whole person to realize our wholeness. It is a challenge we can find many ways of postponing. Our lives are busy, distracted. They are designed by social pressure and indeed by our own fear of stillness to be very busy. How many people, seeing a spare time in their average day or a spare evening in their average week, react automatically by looking for some activity to fill it? Our contemporary conditioning tries to make it second nature for us to believe that if we are not doing something we will cease to be. Our being, we are encouraged to believe, depends on our activity.

It is this delusion that causes us to lose our spiritual centre, both personally and as a society. It is a fundamental inversion of reality. It is *not* necessary to do in order to be. In fact, it is only if we can first learn to be that we become fit for all doing.

The danger of this truth is that it seems abstract and so, by our current values, impractical. It remains, that is to say, what for so many Christians the Gospel can remain – a beautiful theory. In the spiritual life, a life committed to reality, all theories are dangerous because they can so easily become means of keeping our minds busy while the whole person lives at one remove from reality. Theories are either applied idealistically to ordinary life and produce extremism, an inflexible lack of humanity, or they are isolated from ordinary life to produce a destructive sense of alienation and inauthenticity. The fundamental truths of a life lived in reality are discovered through and grounded in our ordinary lives.

Among so many people of all traditions who have lost a living ordinary relationship with the spiritual, an 'ideal' like meditation can seem in just this way true but impractical – something at best to be practised in one's rare spare moments. It is one of the great dangers of religious people that they can feel so at home in their verbal formulas and their rituals that they fail to recognize such an absolutely fundamental value of the spiritual life as silence. The most refreshing and encouraging aspect of the inter-faith service held to greet the Dalai Lama in the cathedral in Montreal was precisely the recognition of this value by several thousand people of different traditions when we meditated together in deep silence for about twenty minutes. It was at the same time an absolute and an ordinary occasion, a realization of unity in spirit.

Our lives are not only busy, they are usually noisy. But if our life is to be charged with meaning, to have depth and to be a true growth in consciousness we have to be rooted in silence, rooted in the spirit, in the mystery whose depth can never be plumbed and whose meaning is found only in the consummation of union. We are each called to enter with wonder into this mystery with our whole being, in the total immediacy of the present moment which is the eternal moment of God. To be touched with this wonder is to be made reverent and so to know in the absolute certainty that belongs to our own experience that the energy of creation, the power of love, dwells in the human heart in silence and in the stillness of pure consciousness. The meaning of our own awakening in this power of creation, the meaning of our being is simply to open our consciousness to its source. The source to which we have awakened is our goal. Every aspect of our life, our leisure or our work, relates directly to this meaning. Nothing in our life is without the significance of this spiritual relation and that is why the greatest sacrilege in any human life is triviality. When we have understood this and committed ourselves to understanding it more deeply an entirely new perception of the essential harmony between Being and Action begins to dawn.

The fundamental aspect of this perception is that the apparent opposition between the two is essentially only verbal. Our thinking classifies and divides but our concrete experience unifies. To be truly open to the spiritual reality, through our ordinary practice of meditation, reveals to us the mystery of God as pure activity. Pure stillness, silence, are not inactive. They are harmonized energy, energy that has reached its highest and destined goal, and in this harmony the power and meaning of all movement is contained. The stillness of God into which we enter through our own stillness is the focal point, the centre and source of all activity. Our own stillness is the divine stillness precisely because our centre is in God. The ordinariness of meditation reveals to us as a lived knowledge what thought alone could never convince us of – that Being is pure Action.

Meditation is in no way isolated from the meaning of our

ordinary activity. Our set times of meditation, our fidelity to the saying of our mantra from the beginning to the end of these times, constitute the essence of our activities because meditation is our realization of Being, of pure action. Meditation is pure activity. It is action in the sense that it is the positive, purposeful deployment of energy, an ordering and focusing of all the energies that make up the mystery of our personhood. It cannot be a merely passive state, because what is both energetic and still is at the highest point of action, energy incandescent – consciousness. We know this in very immediate experience, the experience of persevering in our journey up the mountainside. The faith demanded of us by the pilgrimage requires the quite unpassive qualities of courage, perseverance and commitment.

Meditation is pure action that purifies all our other activities. It is pure because it is selfless, wholly other-centred. Most of our activities, our hopes and plans are carried out with a predominant concern for results, for their material worthwhileness. At its worst this concern is mere self-interest, egoism at its most intense. But any concern for results, for the fruit of action, betrays a possessiveness or attachment which disturbs the harmony of the energies deployed in the activity. In meditating day by day, however, humbly and ordinarily, beginning our pilgrimage at the point we have received the gift of faith to begin, wherever that may be, we set out into the mystery of selfless, other-centred activity. We may indeed begin meditating with a superficial concern for results, trying to estimate if our investment of time and energy is justified by returns in knowledge or 'extraordinary' experience. Perhaps anyone formed by our society is conditioned to begin in this way. But the ordinary practice of meditation purifies us of this spiritual materialism, and as we enter into the direct experience of Being, of pure action, we find all our other activities progressively, radically, purified of egoism. To put this more simply – because meditation leads us into the experience of love at the centre of our being, it makes us in our ordinary lives and relationships more loving persons. Meditation teaches us what theology alone could not convince us of, that Being is Love.

It is so vital for the redemption of our society from the constricting and complex self-consciousness into which it has fallen, that this fully personal knowledge of Being, of Being as purity of motive, as love, be recovered. It can only be redeemed and restored to whole, other-centred consciousness if enough people enter into the pilgrimage that this knowledge demands. Our society can return to sanity, to wholeness and true consciousness only if enough people within it undertake the journey to reality, to the renunciation of self-consciousness, to love. Only in this way can our life be integrally transformed by the power of love that is the Spirit. Our life is a holistic growth, a movement into a wholeness that is infinitely greater than ourselves and yet that contains and fulfils us. Any such growth must have a centre, and if we could find that centre we would have found both our point of departure and our point of convergence. Where then is this focal point of the whole life, where we find both the spiritual reality from which we come into consciousness and the faith that empowers us to embrace it – the reality in which our consciousness is infinitely expanded because it awakens to the mind of Christ with which it is in a union of love?

We know that in terms of the mystery of our own being this focal point is the heart where we are one in body and spirit. But in terms of our daily, ordinary life it is the centrality of meditation in our day, the two periods of meditation on which every day is balanced. The heart of our ordinary life is prayer. The great wonder and joy of knowing this is that the purity of our meditation, our purity of heart, purifies and unifies all our activity, bringing it all into true harmony, into the dynamic state of other-centredness, into the condition of truly loving service. The selflessness of the mantra progressively liberates us from all self-centredness, profoundly summons us into the mystery of the wholeness of life.

To enter into our wholeness is to enter into our selfhood, and this is to enter into God. It is only in this movement of love that our life can find its true spiritual focus and direction. Only thus can it become a wholehearted service of the Lord of Life.

So let me encourage you with what St Benedict calls 'the support of many brethren' in your daily commitment to this journey. In understanding its ordinariness you will awaken to its absoluteness, and then you will know the infinite enrichment of your whole life that is the work of the liberating power of love. Liberated from self-centredness in order to become ourselves, we are led into the experience of communion in which Being and Action are One, the communion of love that is Spirit, the selfsame Spirit dwelling within each of us. We have only to begin the journey and to remain faithful to our beginning.

3

Preparing for Birth

Preparing for the first Christmas in our new home, the Community was very aware of its own experience of growth, indeed of a second birth. There was little time for self-reflection, however, in the work of settling in and keeping warm in a house that was large and beautiful but not too well insulated. Even amid the bustle of moving-day itself we had all stopped at noon for the usual meditation. Through the busy weeks and months ahead the stillness of these times would underpin our life ever more securely.

The new house soon began to fill up with guests and community members. Evening groups on Mondays and Tuesdays seemed almost immediately to expand to fill the larger room. Many new oblates were received, including one from Germany who was to introduce our work there and translate the books into German. Our first oblate and dear friend, Rosie Lovat, made her final oblation, while sharing with us our last days at Avenue de Vendôme and our first, very active weeks on Pine Avenue.

On 13 December three of our novices received the monastic habit. We rejoiced because they had recognized the place where they are called to live in freedom, to develop it and to communicate it to others.

With all the materialistic pressures involved in Christmas today we can easily think of it as a period of hectic preparation, a day of celebration and a brief aftermath. We can forget that it is more than a feast. It is a season. And like all seasons its essence is a cycle of preparation, achievement and then the incorporation of what has been achieved into the larger season of which it is a part, the season of our life.

As the four-week period of preparation for Christmas draws

to a close and we approach the feast itself I would like you to know that we all wish you much joy and deeper peace as we are led more deeply into the mystery of the Lord's birth. Our period of preparation for celebrating the mystery is itself a joyful time, because there is a quietly deepening understanding of whose birth it is we celebrate and just how eternal an event is involved. Each year, it seems to me, the mystery of this birth becomes greater and yet the greater it grows the closer it seems to come to us. In a society that has lost so much of its capacity for peace and so much of the peacefulness needed to prepare quietly for anything, we run the risk of being left only with the worship of the instantly visible, the immediately possessed, of being left finally only with the dryness of the instantly forgotten. Then a liturgical season of preparation, so much part of the deeper rhythms of our spirit, becomes not just a religious but a psychological anachronism. Yet so much depends upon our being prepared, on our having firsthand experience of being ready. If we are to know the truly spiritual quality of Christmas, the meaning of our celebration and ritual at home or in worshipping communities, we have to know what it means to enter into the space where celebration becomes possible with prepared and peaceful hearts. This is one thing our daily pilgrimage of meditation teaches us from within. On that simple and humble journey we know what it means to make space in our heart, to prepare the heart for its great celebration of life. As we prepare, and as our more materialistic expectations and possessiveness drop away, it dawns on us that the event we are preparing for has preceded us. The great liturgy has begun in spirit and in truth.

So often we have the experience and miss the meaning. Later we can know the hollowness of disappointment at what was merely said or done, the external signs that did not connect us with underlying realities. This is the sad result of being unprepared, of being committed to the superficial. Once, though, we have begun to find our true relation in depth, the whole of our experience becomes pulled into meaningful patterns. It is only necessary for us to prepare our hearts to be prepared for everything.

Perhaps one of the reasons that Christmas can continue to mean so much to us spiritually, despite all the materialism and busyness which accompanies it, is that it continues to remind us of our innocence. Too often, however, our understanding of innocence is romantic rather than Christian. We think of a period of 'lost innocence' and so are filled with that great enemy of maturity, sentimentality, and that great enemy of prayer, nostalgia. In any season the balance and clarity of our spiritual response to life can so easily be disturbed by emotional self-indulgence, by the cultivation or indulgence of an image of self; these are the ways by which we stifle our true sensitivity and capacity for empathy with others. Instead of the game of regretting a lost innocence we are called to realize our present innocence, the potential we have right here and now for a direct response. We must cease trying to limit the mystery to forms contained by ready-made formulae of interpretation, by our attempt to 'make sense out of life', which too often means committing the nonsense of trying to control life by devitalizing it. The true character of innocence, however, is energy, adaptability and a wonder that derives its power from within an expanding mystery. If we could begin to know ourselves as naturally innocent in this actual present, we would be preparing to enter not just into the full experience of the Christmas season but of our whole life.

What does it really mean to know ourselves to be innocent? To answer this I think we have really only to look into our own experience. In a moment of pure sensitivity to beauty, when we are suddenly struck with wonder at the sheer power of love to create a new world, or when we are led, beyond our expectations, to set another's interests before our own – in such ways we have precious insights into the real nature of things and into our own real nature. Our elaborate theories and systems simply crumble before the power of the actual experience, one that is so evident, so simple it defies adequate verbal expression. It can indeed only be communicated by sharing the experience-in-itself. Any description of it alienates it from the authenticity of the present when we try to treat it as observable. Whatever can be observed or objectified in this way is static, and it is the nature of the true, the innocent, to be wholly dynamic. It is in this dimension of innocence, the state of a pure consciousness, an undivided heart, that we know the joy we sometimes call liberty of spirit, when we are realizing our potential for self-transcendence. The exhilaration is to know the goodness of the mystery of life unfolding itself in an infinite generosity through our whole self. We sense then the extraordinary inter-relatedness of the mystery, the way our life is connected intimately with the lives of others and all together woven into the great mystery, extending far beyond our imaginations or intellects, whereby all things are being brought into unity in Christ. These are ineffable glimpses of the supreme reality, of supreme love, but at the same time they are absolutely ordinary. We know that no amount of contrivance or experimentation, no kind of fascination with the out-of-the ordinary could have led us into so natural, so real, so simple and so whole a way of being. It is not so much that we see or understand something new as that we *are* someone new, or rather the old person led mysteriously to completion. Reality is not made, certainly not made by us. To be real is to know in our ordinary lives what philosophers or theologians can make sound difficult or pompous, that to be is to be joyous, because Being is bliss: that to be is to be simple – because Being is ONE.

We know only because we are known. We understand only because we are understood. This is the great Christian insight into the human mystery: 'This is the love I speak of, not our love for God but his love for us in sending his Son.' To be innocent is then only to live in accord with this truth of our being. It is to be able to receive a gift with delight, with generosity and without possessiveness. A child's wonder and happiness at Christmas is very rightly seen as a sacrament of its real meaning. It is with the same simplicity that we should receive the supreme gift we receive in the love of Jesus.

The only problem is of our own making, that the outward sign is so rarely seen for its true meaning and so rarely followed through to its inward reality. At Christmas, as at so many times of our life, we are encouraged to remain at the surface level, and without the challenge to sink our roots deeper into reality we drift discontentedly between desire and disappointment. Our society's infatuation with the new, the novel, keeps us well supplied with objects of desire and with distractions to cope temporarily with disappointment. We need a truly spiritual response to life to be able to escape from this *samsara*, this round of death and rebirth. We need it to be able to make use of the innocence we already possess. Because, although we may have known such moments or periods of truth, though we may have strands of clarity and joy running through our life in the form of relationships or gifts, of creativity or service, too often these are not integrated into the unity of our life. They are not linked to the living centre. If we are not deeply inserted into the reality that sustains us in this centre then we inevitably lack any essential unity. We are parts waiting to be made whole. Only to dare to go beyond the superficial, however, is to encounter in a realm of faith not just a beautiful idea, not a fascinating image, not a reflection of our own self-consciousness but Oneness itself. In that encounter our own essential unity is touched awake and we discover that all is one and we are one with the all within the great, simple truth of Christ – the one who is one with the Father – our Father.

But it is easy to remain convinced of our 'lost innocence'. We can do so for several reasons and so slip into that divided consciousness and self-rejection that are so characteristic of our time. One of the reasons for this condition of sadness, of half-life, is, as I have said, because we are so inclined to live in the past, to look for our emotional or spiritual resources in past experiences instead of taking the risk of leaving the past behind and becoming poor once more in the present. We carry so many of the false riches of the past around with us that we do not have hands free to receive the real, living gifts being offered to us. The past can indeed exert a terrible fascination upon us, conscious and unconscious. It can lure us with the gratification of endless self-reflection. One of the ego's most enervating pleasures is regret. And another, very similar reason for our belief in the 'lost innocence' is our obsession with the future. We can invest ourselves so exclusively in future plans and dreams, imagining what might happen, trying to control what we think should happen. In either case the present, where the real is, where the essence of life and the simple secret of joy await us, goes unnoticed, and so we are closed to the God who is ever NOW.

There is something both absurd and tragic about the consciousness that misses the present moment and drifts rootless in the shadows of past or through the fabrications of the future. Its condition is one of self-alienation, and the longer it remains separated from itself the more tired it becomes, the more exhausted by its imprisonment in the self-reflecting self-consciousness of the ego. I have often thought that what many people identify in themselves (with the terrible inaccuracy of egoism) as guilt, their loss of innocence, is usually not so much the weight of their sin as the oppression of their boredom, their lifelessness. Boredom with self, with others, with the hope that the presence of God unfailingly sets before us as an option within our reach, proceeds from an implosion of spiritual energy that it is precisely the invitation of prayer to reverse. The greatest task the Church faces today is to extend that invitation convincingly and as widely, as universally as her purpose demands, and to present it persuasively as an invitation addressed to every man and woman in the ordinary circumstances of their life. Christmas is the feast of the divine explosion – the love of God revealed in the poverty of Christ.

Loneliness, self-rejection, the boredom that the early monks called 'acedia', these are perhaps the most virulent diseases of the modern world and the ones that pose a social threat as much as a spiritual crisis. Indeed the more we proceed, the more it seems that the crisis of our spiritual life is the great and fundamental crisis of society. If our Christian communities are vital, if they have experienced a present reality of the transcendence of their faith, if they are praying communities rooted in the actual reality of the living Christ, then it is to this crisis that they can and should address themselves. If they lack these essential Christian qualities they will fall prey to the egoism our social conditioning has come to encourage. They will become concerned with their image, their success rate, their numbers, their own psychologies. But these are not the concerns of a Christian community. A Christian community has indeed only one concern – to set its mind upon the Kingdom before all else, and all the rest will be given in the measure needed and the way best suited. To set our minds upon the Kingdom, not just as individuals but as integral parts of a community, that is the simple single-mindedness that best describes our true and present state of innocence.

The authentic Christian response in any situation is to address itself not so much to the symptoms as to the causes. This does not mean we adopt a theoretical charity. On the contrary, our compassion and concern are all the more practical because they are directed by a realistic estimate of the underlying causes. And so, in the alienation, the spiritual and mental suffering of so many around us, we see not economic or socio-

logical cases but human beings of an infinite value and lovableness capable of being restored to their true relation with themselves, with others, with God. It is our belief in the curability
of the disease that has gripped our society that makes our
practice of compassion so faith-filled and our faith so
compassionate. We know, because we ourselves are being
cured, that if the slightest aperture can be made in the wall of
a closed spirit the love of God can enter and work wonders
beyond our imagining.

The Christian's experience of this love working the wonder
of God in his own heart means that he is not offering merely
temporary relief, a panacea or a distraction. He is communicating a diagnosis of life that carries within it the power to
cure, a life-giving word. It is a powerful, an awesome message
and a precious responsibility. We cannot pretend that the cure
does not entail a certain rigour, that the way to freedom does
not lie through commitment, and to absolute freedom through
absolute commitment. We can say that the power of this
process comes from beyond us but has taken up its dwelling in
the human heart and that for every one surrender we can make
in that sacred space we win a thousand victories.

To show the way into this space our communities must be
on the way themselves, travelling into the experience of their
own innocence as epiphanies of the Kingdom. The journey
they have to undertake is from materialism to a new-found
sense of the essential quality of life, its spiritual quality
discovered in its ordinariness; from the boredom of
consumerism to the vitality of our full humanity. The frame of
the journey is the central commitment to prayer that really
brings the community to birth in the first place. Until that is
made, the community is little more than a group waiting to
begin the journey, reading timetables and travel-guides,
discussing routes. But it is a journey that cannot be predicted.
It is one that is made wholly in the present; every day we travel
a little deeper into the fullness of God's presence. Ultimately,
it is a journey we may postpone but not one that we can decide
not to make. It is a simple journey, not an easy one nor a
difficult one. Once begun, there are so many strengths given
to us. It is one that attracts fellow-travellers, the greatest
strength. One who begins alone will be joined by others and
in that mystery of communion the Church is reborn, rekindled

in many quiet corners of the earth. However small the corner, it is born in its fullness because Christ is born there, humble, vulnerable, fully human, and in those very qualities bringing us the fullness of the Father's love. And this is why the authentic Christian community, like Jesus himself, has always had an influence out of all proportion to its size and material power. The Kingdom, realized in the innocence of a community persevering in prayer, may not conquer the world but it can love the world and redeem it by its love.

Generalities, of course, can be great enemies of true religion. Blake was wiser when he spoke of the 'holiness of minute particulars'. The restoration of the world to the experience of its own innocence, to the capacity to delight in the gift of life without attempting to possess it, the achievement of a free-flowing spirit – all this is made real not in the media, not in programmes or courses but in the minute particular of the heart. To begin its realization we have to undertake a work, a daily labour, of preparing our heart, of clearing space within it. This is the simple, humble and above all entirely practical work of our daily meditation. Each morning and evening we make space for the kingdom to expand a little further firstly within us and then through us. And it is our mantra, our faithful and continuous recitation of the mantra, that is the little tool clearing the space that opens to infinity.

One of the fears I most often encounter in people beginning to meditate as a daily pilgrimage is that the journey to their own heart, to this infinite space, may take them into isolation, away from the comfort and familiarity of the known into the unknown. This is an understandable initial fear. To leave behind the superficial is what we often mean by leaving behind the familiar and this can create a sense of emptiness as we become exposed to greater depth and more substantial reality. It takes time for us to adjust to this new sense of belonging, of a new relatedness that seems to set all our relations in a new order. Our coming home can seem like homelessness. Reflect a little this Christmas on the homelessness of the stable at Bethlehem.

In time we realize that in this new experience of innocence, of delight in the gift of life, we are leaving childishness behind and entering into the full maturity that Jesus enjoys in the Father, the fullness of his love that enters and expands within

261

our hearts in the Spirit. It is not only now, at the beginning of the pilgrimage, that we need the human love and inspiration of others. But it is now when we encounter an unfamiliarly wide horizon that we have a special need for the power of community with others. Our openness to them expands our sensitivity in turn to their needs. And as the mantra leads us ever further from self-centredness we turn more generously to others and receive their support in return. Indeed, our love for others is the only truly Christian way of measuring our progress on the pilgrimage of prayer.

To those of you who have recently begun to meditate I would like to send you especially much love and encouragement. The commitment this journey calls from us at first is unfamiliar. It requires faith, perhaps a certain recklessness to begin. But once we have begun, it is the nature of God, the nature of love to sweep us along, teaching us by experience that our commitment is to reality, that our discipline is the springboard to freedom. The fear that the journey is 'away from,' rather than 'towards' is only disproved by experience. This is a journey where ultimately only experience counts. The words or writings of others can add only a little light to the wholly actual, wholly present and wholly personal reality that lives in your heart and in my heart. Miraculously we can enter this experience together and discover communion just where communication seemed to break down.

The journey to our own heart is a journey into every heart. And in the first light of the real we see that this is the communion which is the kingdom Jesus was born to establish and in which he is born again in every human heart to realize. What we have left behind is loneliness, confusion, isolation. What we have found is communion, sureness, love. Our way is simplicity and fidelity. The simplicity of the mantra. Our fidelity to our daily meditation. As we travel this way we are drawn closer together by the same power of love that unites us.

4

Belief and Faith

After Christmas the coach house on the monastery grounds was converted into a guest house for women and married couples. We continued to receive many guests, particularly from Europe, where groups were continuously forming and multiplying.

Bishop Henry Hill, one of our first oblates, resigned from the Anglican Diocese of Ontario and came to live in the community as a resident ecumenical oblate.

As our society becomes increasingly less religious its need for the authentically spiritual intensifies. As the religious and social support systems fail, we are faced with the urgency of the ultimate challenge to the meaning and value of life.

I think this is best expressed in Christian terms as the essential difference between belief and faith. A great deal of ink – and blood – have been spilled through the Christian centuries over beliefs. And even today, in an age not of faith but of scepticism and anxiety, what we believe, or think we believe, can still be a source of division, estrangement and religious self-importance. How often though does the violence with which men assert or defend their beliefs betray an attempt to convince themselves that they do really believe or that their beliefs are authentic? The spectre of our actual unbelief can be so frightening that we can be plunged into extreme, self-contradictory ways of imposing our beliefs on others rather than simply, peacefully, living them ourselves. There is another extreme reaction to the uneasy suspicion we have about our lack of true conviction – that is, not arrogance but indifference. Feeling our own inauthenticity we evade it by collapsing into the emotions it creates, fatalism or egocentric pessimism. But whatever the extreme, bigotry or lukewarmness, the source is the fear of the gap between what we believe and what we experience. And we know that, if this gap makes us inauthentic, our message – even if it is the gospel – can convince no one unless it has so convinced us that we are transformed by it.

Wherever this fear of our own unbelief grips the Church then what should be a joyful, tolerant and compassionate community united in celebrating the wonder of a common transcendent experience becomes instead either a lifeless observer of formal routines or an intolerant, pompous agent of repression. From our historical perspective we can look back on a Church that has been both of these. In fact, because of the complex and volatile society we inhabit, we can probably find both extremes of Christian unbelief in different areas of the same Church today.

It is an ever-present danger, because the life-force of the Christian tradition is so precarious, so personal and so delicate. It cannot be compromised or diluted without ceasing to be what it is and becoming instead mere pious wordiness or arrogant religiosity. And yet this life-force that St Paul calls the Spirit – the Spirit we must neither sadden nor stifle – is a power of irresistible joy and peace, if only we allow ourselves to be. If we can only find the way simply to be, ourselves, then this power within us dilates and absorbs us. Then we can become what we can so often and so self-consciously talk of being, apostles of the reality that is Christ, communicators of the living energy of his gospel.

One of the great ironies of history is that men have never been able to institutionalize this energy, because no experience of reality can be known except by direct, spontaneous participation. Yet it is only too easy to codify, formalize and institutionalize the inauthentic experience, the memory of a brief glimpse of reality's light. It is this memory, many times removed from direct experience, that passes into the codified beliefs passed on by societies to successive generations.

This gap between the authentic experience and the received memory can become the chasm between honesty and hypocrisy, and this is a possibility that underlies the religious practice of every tradition. It is the gap, simply, between our credal statements and our experience. In a positive light, this gap is our opportunity for growth and development in reality if we can accept it realistically, which is to say in a spirit of humility. We do, after all, know more than we can prove. This gap exists

264

for us all simply because we are born into a long, rich and complex tradition. But to accept a belief is only ever a first step, not, as the agonizers of doubt have thought, the final one. The tradition conveys beliefs to us almost automatically. It would be difficult to say we could ever *choose* to believe, for example. But if this tradition is a living and truly spiritual one, then it will also demand that these beliefs become realized, become grounded in our own experience. The supreme test of any tradition, of its authenticity, is the degree to which it demands this realization of all those who follow it, and not simply the select or esoteric few. And this is the supreme, ultimate importance of the Christian tradition in human history – that it demands, or rather offers, this personal authentication to all mankind. The Gospel is minimally credal. It is not obsessed with right beliefs and wrong beliefs but advances the uncompromisingly personal truth of its message – because the message is the person of Jesus. He does not call us to believe or to do but, first of all, to be. If in the first place we can be with him, then we are fit for all doing, all believing.

However, in a negative light this gap between belief and experience can become a limbo of unreality that is only too easily institutionalized. It can even attract us in the way un-reality does, because it is well-populated by those who have agreed not to tell the truth to each other – the world of complacent piety or of intolerant self-righteousness. A place of slow dying and protracted suffering, it defends the half-life that masquerades as truth. But there is no reason why anyone should settle for half-life. We are called to fullness of life and that fullness has not to be achieved, but only realized, only accepted. We accept it by entering upon this journey of faith across the gap between belief and experience. And on that journey we are purified in the darkness of faith, beyond belief. We make the transition to the deeper level of reality by letting go of all the words, concepts and images that tie us to memory, to the past. Instead we enter the extraordinary purity of the present moment. Entering humbly, realistically, into the reality of our own incompleteness teaches us the wonder of our capacity for infinite growth. But to be taught we have first to learn to be dispossessed. Blessed are the poor in spirit.

Vast numbers of men and women over the centuries, including whole societies, have affirmed their belief in Jesus and his gospel. Our whole Western culture is permeated by this belief even now that those who do still personally believe are probably in a minority. Why, then, has this not transformed the world? This is a vital question for us to understand, and we can only adequately face it as a society or as a Church if we can face it as personal, accepting our personal responsibility for the authenticity of Christian belief at large. A good part of the answer, I think, is that we have glibly confused belief and faith. We have thought that we could convince others that the Gospel is truth by means of our beliefs alone. Those others we called, significantly, non-believers.

Our beliefs tend to be stronger than our faith if we have not yet understood that faith – unconditional, open-hearted commitment – is the fundamental level of our being and of our participation in the mystery of the Spirit's life. What we call belief is the tip of an iceberg, most of whose substance is invisible. Faith makes up the greater and more essential part of our commitment to the person of Christ – the person who is universally present in the energy of his love for all men, all creation, and who is the invisible reality we celebrate and enflesh in our lives and with our whole being. Faith is the invisible but wholly realistic condition of being that allows us to share in the mystery of Christ's self-communication. As a condition of our being, faith is a power. A power within us that communicates itself to others as it is being set free within our own hearts.

The Letter to the Hebrews describes how it is faith that helps us to perceive that the visible comes forth from the invisible. It is our beliefs that are the visible expressions of our faith, our personal commitment to the person of Jesus. But because they are expressions they find form transiently in words, concepts and images. The sense of inauthenticity that can so often over-take the religious mind is frequently due to the fact that we treat the transient as if it were enduring – we overtax the resources of what is finite and changeable. The forms in which our beliefs exist and in which they are expressed are always in the process of passing away – the mind has here no abiding city; only in the heart can we find the enduring reign of God. Whatever has form, like our beliefs or bodies, is always in transition to a new form. Our beliefs are always seeking new definitions, new words to express themselves. When I studied theology our belief in the Eucharist was summed up in the word 'transubstantiation'. Since then many new words, even words like 'transfinalization' and 'transignification', have been proposed as more apt expressions of the mystery of the Eucharist – a mystery we can experience in faith but never solve in words. As words change, and even as the meaning of words change, so in a sense our beliefs change, develop. The fact that we ourselves are changing, being changed by life, means that our beliefs must similarly grow, mature and become more attuned to the mystery that is greater than they are. But what endures, changes only by becoming more perfectly what it always is, is our faith. It does so pre-eminently in pace with our commitment to meditation, the journey of faith. Because in that commitment, each morning and evening, we acknowledge the absolute priority of faith and do so by repeatedly emptying out of it all that is transient, all that is passing away – all words, ideas and images. The language and creative context of faith is silence. We know from our human relationships how much faith we need to have in a person to be silent with them. We know that our faith in a person is deepened by such silence. This too is the dynamic of our silence in meditation – realizing God's love for us expressed in the love of Jesus, deepening our faith in his love. In this silence we are invited to enter into the enduring reality where Becoming is embraced by Being. What is visible passes away, what is invisible endures.

Because of Jesus and the communication of his Being to us, we know that this reality is no abstract, platonic idea. It is a fully personal, wholly incarnate reality. The person of Jesus is the revelation of the person of God. And the gospel, which is the continuation and extension of his teaching and presence, is the revelation of the priority of the personal over all secondary, institutional forms. The extraordinary discovery that is the goal of each person's pilgrimage is that the ultimate completion of each person is effected in Jesus. We are all made one with him who is one with God. To call this a 'relationship' with Jesus only inadequately expresses the wonder of the union that is being realized in the power of our faith in him and his love for us. It is a relationship with Jesus but it is also a participation in his life at source. The deeper our journey of faith takes us into reality the more evidently it appears that this life is the life of God. That life itself is what we call the Trinity, the explosion of love that is the Being of God, the God who is the ground of all Being. And because God is this infinitely uncontainable energy of love, because he simply is love, he seeks himself beyond himself. In obedience to the dynamic of his own being, he seeks the Other to whom he can give himself, into whom he can empty himself. For Jesus, we are that Other. He has sent the Spirit to dwell in our hearts.

The wonder of this is so overwhelming it must make us humble. But it also makes us confident. It is the personal vocation of each of us to experience this wonder in the immediacy of faith, to share, as St Peter tells us, in the very Being of God. But to experience this wonder we have to let go of all secondary forms and expressions. We have to pass definitively beyond beliefs to faith. In the condition of faith we are drawn into the ever-expanding self-knowledge of God. We know him only with his own self-knowledge. We know ourselves and all others only in him. It is only very inadequately expressed as a relationship. The mutual presence and self-communication that is the love-force of the Trinity transcends difference but does not obliterate distinction. In the same way our relationship with God in Jesus is infinitely greater than the dialogue of two self-contained individuals. There is achieved between us a common consciousness, a single ground of being. And this we call love.

Any of the many mysteries of love that make up this reality and point to it is the fruit of faith rather than belief. With those we love we have a mysterious bond, something so close it is indefinable. It is a mutual commitment to each other's unique-ness and an unconditional acceptance of our inalienable communion. This is how we are loved by God and how we are empowered to return that love within the reality of his own Being. The wonder of love is that it always creates its own universe, transforming the mundane and finite into a world of meaning and mystery radiant everywhere with a light that originates deep within our own spirit. This new creation gener-ated by love is built up into an expanding universe by the power of faith – unconditional commitment to what is real but unseen.

The world desperately needs men and women filled with this faith. It is faith that is both the precondition and the medium for the communication of any personal reality. The Gospel as the ultimate revelation of the personal is, as St Paul expresses it, a way that begins and ends in faith. Perhaps never more than today has the world needed a Church filled with men and women of faith – their 'eyes fixed on Jesus', the Invisible One among us, as the Letter to the Hebrews puts it. If it is to respond to this need the Church must sink its consciousness deeper than its beliefs and into the roots of faith – that is, into the consciousness of Jesus. We can do this only at the bedrock of our being where the pure consciousness of Jesus fills and sustains us. In a real sense Jesus himself is our faith, just as the person we love is really our love.

As a church we are not travel agents handing out brochures to places we have never visited. We are explorers of a country without frontiers, one we discover little by little not to be a place but a person. We are not communicating a script, because we are neither actors nor audience. In harmony with this Person and in the light shed everywhere by the reality of Jesus all roles have been burned away, leaving only persons open to each other in love – this is the Church.

To meditate is to accept this exploration of the universe of God as the supreme meaning and authentication of our live. It is to be rooted in faith – like Abraham obeying the call to go out to a land destined for himself and his heirs and leaving home without knowing where he was to go. After you have been meditating even for a short while you understand that our commitment in faith to this reality is always deepening. There is always the home, the familiar ground of our ideas and plans and dreams, to leave behind us as we move more surely towards the heart of reality.

The price we pay for a gospel of absolute power is absolute commitment. As we sit to meditate each day we encounter and are made one with this power at a level of reality deeper than that of belief – more enduring than that of the images and concepts of belief. And as we rise from meditation to commit ourselves with greater generosity to the responsibilities of our lives, we bring the power of this purer reality into every part of our ordinary life. It is through our meditation that in a real way we put our faith into practice.

We are called to believe in Jesus. But our belief summons us to something greater, to faith in him. Our faith then becomes our potential to resonate with him, to be in harmony with him who is in harmony with God. It is a source of wonder and deep gratitude that we have found the way to place ourselves within this harmony. And the way is the way of the mantra, the harmonic of our faith. It includes our belief but sets us free from all the limitations imposed on us by the images and words of belief. It bridges the gap between belief and experience because it is the bridge of faith, the sacrament of faith. Travelling across that gap, going beyond ourselves as Jesus has gone before us and calls us to follow him, we awaken in the heart of reality, in Jesus, who himself is fully awake within the heart of God.

As we prepare to enter another Lent let us keep one another in our hearts. This is a time of conversion – a time to turn from what is passing away in order to be at one with him who is eternal.

5

The Present Christ

During the spring of 1981 one of the great enrichments of our communal life and theological reflection derived, as usual, from the Benedictine charism of hospitality. Guests came primarily to meditate with us, but they also shared in the manual work of the day and observed the prescribed periods of Lectio *(spiritual reading).*

Bishop Crowley paid us one of his regular and very welcome visits. We knew it was not common for a bishop to understand so sympathetically what a monastery is about. His clear and far-seeing vision of the Church of the future made him not only open to development in the tradition but an agent of change.

Father Laurence visited several meditation groups and communities in England, France and Germany and spent time in Trosly-Breuil, the headquarters of L'Arche, Jean Vanier's communities for mentally handicapped people. In Germany he visited our oblates in Würzburg who have been taking the teaching of meditation into the university there. Returning to Montreal he took over the editorship of Monastic Studies, *a journal of monastic theology and scholarship formerly edited from Mount Saviour Monastery.*

The work of the community was extended into the wider scale of the publishing world through the appearance of Word into Silence *published by Darton Longman and Todd in England and Paulist Press in the States. With 'Communitas' a new medium for the teaching was launched. This is a series of cassettes, ten a year, of talks given by Father John to the weekly meditation groups meeting at the monastery. (The series continues to provide an inspiring record of a great teacher's work week by week.) Out of this, too, came a fuller sense of the extended community that had already, silently, come into being.*

271

We celebrated the Easter liturgies of Holy Saturday night here with our resident guests and those who had come to join us from outside. During the Vigil it was made very clear to us in a fresh way how much the mystery of Christ consists in his nearness to us. Whatever is distant is merely strange or foreign, not truly mysterious. If, for example, we objectify something or someone we can always admire it but its essential identity is alienated precisely because we have distanced it so far from ourselves. In relation to it we remain mutually isolated and as a result fundamentally unchanged by what we 'contemplate'. But if, in the presence of the mystery of God, instead of objectifying it, we are humble enough in its proximity to be one with it; if we can allow our being to resonate finely with the mystery, then we ourselves are changed and we enter quite another and more creative mode of being. The agent of all objectification, all distancing and alienation is the ego. It is the subliminal voice in our consciousness that urges us to be separate, even from what we worship or love. The fading of this voice of the tempter is the dawning of the reality which we find as we enter the Kingdom of Heaven. It is a reality we can only discover in union, only through union.

We know something or someone *fully* when we simultaneously experience and understand – that is when subject and object are transcended in full knowledge in the state of union. We can only fully understand the closeness of Christ to us from within this egoless state of union. In other words we can only know him with his own knowledge. The knowledge that is love is something more than what we generally think of as a 'relationship', something more achieved than what we think of as a dialogue, and something more incarnate and tangible than what we consider an 'idea'. The deeply moving symbols of the Vigil bring this home to us by pointing beyond themselves and beyond ourselves to a realm of meaning where not even the profoundest symbol, word or gesture can express the fullness of the reality of Christ – for that is a reality known in a deep understanding so infinitely intimate that it transcends both sign and ego and becomes both personal and universal. When we bless the fire at the beginning of the Vigil we become part of a pre-historic dimension of humanity; appropriately and mysteriously we begin the night's re-enactment of man's redemption with a memorial dating from the dawn of human consciousness. The fire we light burns right into our deepest atavistic memory. And then, in the kindling of the Paschal Candle from this same fire we are returned to the presentness of Christ in all time.

Similarly, when later in the evening around the altar we bless the baptismal water, we recreate a primary symbol of the source of life and consciousness, full of meaning too as an agent of purification and clarification. And by immersing the candle in the water we enact the unique synthesis that has occurred in Christ. We are again transferred from a distant mode of being to an encounter with what is immediate and present. For what the symbols remind us of is that the flame of the Christ consciousness has come to dwell in our hearts – for 'we possess the mind of Christ' (1 Cor. 2:16).

The presentness of Christ to us is, as it were, contained within his presentness in all time. As Christian thinkers have realized from the beginning, the redemptive love of Jesus universalized for mankind on the Cross and occupying the centre of all consciousness through the Resurrection, travels both backwards and forwards through space and time, uniting every human consciousness in him. From this moment, in and out of time, man has been plunged into a radically new way of being within the mystery of God. He has been touched by a ray of reality that has opened his eyes to the ambiance within which he lives and moves and has his being. He is now empowered to be with God in a quite unprecedented way, by participating directly and wholly in the plenitude of God's Being. For one thing, he is absolved from the necessity of regarding this Being as an external reality, an object of his devotional or intellectual interest. And so, man is no longer obliged to objectify his source – an objectification that alienated him from it and that we call 'sin'. Christ's forgiveness of our sin is not the reprieve of a judge but the embrace of a lover. Our redemption is our being brought near – so near, in Christ, that we can no longer focus on God as an external object with the mind's eye but are instead taken beyond all images to be in the presence of the truth, revealed in silence; the eye with which we see is the eye that sees us. Our vision itself is Christ.

We are absolved from the need to objectify God, to talk to him, to appease or petition him. 'Your father knows what your needs are before you ask him.' From that eternal moment when

273

Jesus awoke to his union with the Father, all humanity has passed out of the stage of its spiritual infancy. In one moment it has evolved into maturity, the 'full stature' of Christ. And that moment is to be found in the centre of our own heart where his spirit dwells, like a seed buried in the ground. Finding that moment is the work of our meditation, a joyful and vitalizing work because we travel to the heart's centre in a faith that knows the moment is already born and born for imperishability. And once we have known this fully, through union and in union, our whole being, life and time is rediscovered, united in the wholeness that is our holiness, and all within this moment.

It is not just that we are absolved from the necessity of considering ourselves and God in a dualistic way. It is that we are summoned not to. The time has come, indeed it is already here, when we are summoned to worship God in spirit and in truth. We cannot persist in the dualism of our spiritual infancy and remain in the truth. The indwelling Spirit of Christ is not just a gift, a special offer, a grace we can accept or decline. It is a reality, the door into the sheepfold. As such it is a summons, an inherent power within our destiny to come to completion. But the wonder is that the summons is a summons made by love and that it educates us to itself with an infinite gentleness.

But the gentleness is purposeful and determined, linked to the movement of all creative energy in creation back to its source. The energy of the Christ-Spirit is unquenchable and so ultimately unavoidable. In the ordinariness of our daily life, it is steadily, wonderfully present to us. There is more than just a symbolic meaning, I think, in the fact that the power of the Resurrection reaches us in the springtime of the year while we are rediscovering all the energies of growth in nature, energies that are also intense and cosmic and yet creative of such delicate marvels of earth's beauty.

The essence of the human condition is that it is a condition of growth in all its aspects. In the measurable aspects of our life the growth is contained within the cycle of birth and decline: we bud, blossom and fade. But the profounder dimensions of our life are not measurable, not conditioned by time or space, and in those the growth is of an infinite potential. For us, as for all life that grows, growth can occur only in union. Like all

274

developing realities, tending towards a destined fulfilment of their being, we need roots to connect us unitively with the source of life's energy. For man, in his essential nature, the root is Christ and the source of life is the Father. Our union with Christ, the mingling of his consciousness with ours at the entirely human level, is the heart of the mystery of our life – the mystery to which all growth, finite and infinite is an awakening. Perhaps the greatest mystery is that even the most finite, the cycle of birth and decline, is fundamentally changed by the power of this union. The Resurrection is the saving of the whole man, heart, mind, spirit and corruptible body. The power of this affirmation of the divineness of the human condition is that the life of the Father flows into us through our rootedness in Christ and the channel of its communication is the human consciousness of Jesus, wholly open to the reality of God and dwelling at one with us and within us. His openness to the Father in his human consciousness is the condition that allows us to realize our union with the Father through him in *our* human consciousness. With him, we travel beyond ourselves, beyond himself into the heart of God – this is transcendence realized.

'All that the Father has is mine,' Jesus told his disciples, and he has revealed to us everything he has heard from the Father (John 15:16; 16:15). It is as a result of this oneness of Father and Son and of the Son's oneness with us that we are able to stand in the truth. The innate restlessness of man in his condition of growth is the consequence of his having an expanding capacity to be in the truth, to be one with the truth. He is impelled by the inner expansiveness of his own being to align himself to his destiny and to enter the simplicity of the egoless state which growth demands – the need to let go of the past and to venture upon what is to come without desire or resistance. We are restless for the truth; above all, the truth of our own being, for there we can be sure we are not encountering an image or theory of truth, but truth incarnate – what we instinctively recognize as reality. The revelation of the Father to us that occurs in union with the consciousness of Jesus is the fundamental authenticity of human life. Without contact with this source of being we remain rootless, meaningless, theoretical and static. Without the touch of truth we stay as imaginary creatures, struggling to make fantasy or intellect substitute for the real. But this is an unbearable, negative restlessness, for the attraction towards the truth is the deepest characteristic of the human spirit. In our innate movement towards the real and the true, we are more deeply in touch with ourselves than in the more superficial (and common) movement towards fantasy. In the centre of our being where, until we travel there, we think we are most closed in upon ourselves, there is an opening towards a wholeness that is infinite, towards God. It is here we encounter the utter simplicity of our contact with truth, where the revelation of the Father becomes actual. The Greek for truth is *alētheia*; it means a revealing, an uncovering. To find the truth we need not images but an open heart.

The mystery of Christ reveals man's new involvement in the truth and it makes us wonderfully, terribly present to God. Even our rituals and symbols cannot distance him who has drawn so near to us. He is God with us, Emmanuel. And yet, if we can learn to be with him, to awaken to union, then his closeness to us is not a source of fear but of peace. 'He himself is our peace' – a peace that is both the fulfilment and harmonization of all creative energy, beyond our ordinary understanding. The harmony is achieved when we have taken the step of faith into the silence in which the truth resides, the step from image to reality. In the marvellous dispensation of God we have only to take the first step for us to be swept along by his power for the rest of the way. That is why we discover that the truth we yearn for is not a cold platonic wisdom but a movement of love. The indwelling of the Spirit of Christ is itself the whole of this movement of life resolved into a Person and it lingers within us with the ache of love until it evokes a fully personal response.

The presentness of Christ to us in this way is our transition from image to reality, from idea to Person. We are the 'heirs of the prophets'. In the new modality of being that has the risen Christ as its definitive and universal centre, all symbols find their resolution. Even the most sacred and potent symbol is only a stage in the revelation of a reality that is already one with us. That is why we are now called to 'worship the Father in spirit and in truth': because in the immediacy of Christ's presence this oneness is manifest. In direct communion 'to be with' is 'to be in love'. An early Christian writer put it very simply: 'Who bows to the statue of the King when the King himself is present?'

I think this is what makes the Christian revelation so mysteriously contemporary in every age, so innately 'modern'. Perhaps what we call the modern consciousness is in fact the Christic consciousness of union, and maybe we first encounter it in the spirit of the pages of the New Testament when Peter, in the portico of Solomon, declares with the irrefutable authority that comes from a transcendent experience 'and so said all the prophets from Samuel onwards; with one voice they all predicted this present time' (Acts 3:24).

The faith of the Christic consciousness contains this extraordinary sense of having reached the fullness of time. When it is repeated as a mere theological formula it inevitably sounds astonishingly arrogant. But spoken out of the experience of the Spirit who inspired the prophets to imagine such a time it becomes mysteriously persuasive and strangely non-controversial. 'All these things that happened to them were symbolic and were recorded for our benefit as a warning. For upon us the fulfilment of the ages has come' (1 Cor. 10:11).

To hear this proclaimed with authority is to be awakened to an unexpected experience – not merely to the presentness of Christ in time and in our own lifetime but also to the fraternity of all mankind that this creates. We recognize our solidarity as men because we stand together, in the same place and in the same time before the same mystery. This is why 'he himself is our peace'.

The sense that we are already at the convergence point for the destined growth of all consciousness in creation back to the Creator is intoxicating. But it carries with it also a profound sense of responsibility. If we are no longer in the infancy of mankind then we are summoned, personally not anonymously, to a maturity of spirit that we often (such is the appeal of the unreal) prefer to postpone rather than realize. But the end of a period of preparation becomes immediately the beginning of a time of perfecting and we are, each of us, summoned to reach this perfection. Our vocation is no less than to be holy – not 'holier than thou' but as holy as God in whose fullness of being we already share (2 Pet. 1:4).

The reality Jesus has uncovered for us is the new age of Presence. It demands a correspondingly new understanding of

277

how we share in the Trinitarian mystery. Because of the new Christic consciousness we can understand in a way that is disturbingly personal and universal, that we do not so much exist in relation to God as subsist within God – he is the ground of our being. We are called to know and to know fully, not just notionally, that nothing can be outside the ground of all Being that God is. And so, in the light of Christ, prayer is not talking-to but being-with.

In the past, recent as well as distant, man has thought of himself as a creature summoned to surrender himself to his Creator. He has been dominated by a sense of the infinite superiority of the divine mystery to himself. This sense of the distance of the untouchable God does not lead us into the experience of transcendence, of being swept out of ourselves, beyond ourselves into the mystery in which we have our being, but rather, so often, it leads into fear of what is so far beyond our control and yet so powerful over us. Man's prayer in this condition of non-growth becomes a psychological means of coping with a fear that is perhaps our most fundamental terror – the fear of ceasing to be. However great our sufferings or disappointments we are always more deeply and chaotically terrified by the prospect of extinction. And, if our knowledge of God stops short at this fear of his power over all being, we can see him only as a threat to our being, our conscious survival. So, our prayer comes to be a way of pleasing or placating him, and in petitioning him we hope to 'turn his anger from us'. But all the time the fear has us in the vice of paralysis.

This is God as Creator. But Jesus opens up God to us as Abba, Father. And, in this most personal yet universal of revelations, our dependence upon God is changed from being a source of terror into a source of infinite joy and wonder. We are because God is. God is our being and so our being is good, as he is. We have nothing to fear of such goodness because of the perfect love that is his goodness; the Trinity's explosive creativity burns away all fear. And so, the ground of man's most haunting fear – of isolation and the extinction to which all isolation leads – is revealed as illusory. The dream-world created by the ego and the source of all our sense of isolation, fear and loneliness, the world that is itself only a terrible mistake, an absurd mis-rendering image of reality, is dissolved by the sheer power of God's love.

Prayer, in the Christian vision of reality, is the way we experience that the basic condition of man is not separateness but communion, *being-with*. This indeed is the Christic consciousness of love, both commanding and empowering us to *be-with* everyone out of the harmony of our own basic experience of communion. 'Love one another as I have loved you.' In giving us his whole self Jesus authenticates this teaching with an absolute and final authority. In the light of this teaching, of this self-giving and of the consciousness that is communicated we can no longer seriously think of ourselves as summoned to 'surrender' to God. In any surrender we retain the human failure to dissolve the illusion of dualism. There remains an I to surrender, a Thou to be surrendered to. And in the light of the reality of God it matters little whether such dualism is retained due to fear or false piety. The result in either case is a kind of spiritual schizophrenia. We cannot surrender to the one with whom we are already united.

But we can awaken to and realize our empathy. In the Christic consciousness, and most urgently for modern man trying to come to terms with this new being, our relationship with the divine has to be understood in terms of empathy.

It is true that to realize this empathy a type of surrender is involved – this is the dynamic process of any experience of love where self is lost in the other. But it is not surrender *to*; it is surrender *of* – the surrender of isolation, fear, possessiveness, self-centredness, all the demons bred in the breeding-ground of the ego. It is the surrender, the letting-go of this reflected self, the false image projected in self-consciousness that we fear. But if we can, even for a moment (the first step of faith), move aside from the distorted field of vision of the ego then we look upon the selflessness of love with unimaginable wonder and excitement. But the knot that seems to hold us is a paradox, a strange compulsion, for we are frightened to lose our fear.

This is evident in a short while to anyone who has begun to meditate. He becomes aware almost simultaneously of the extraordinary new perspective on reality that opens up and of the strange insistence we can have to remain within the narrow world of the ego. But he realizes too that the way forward is the way of poverty. We enter into the freedom of poverty of the mantra. And this is simultaneously the loss of fear and the winning of freedom. It is always difficult to communicate this to people who are not meditating. Yet it has to be communicated. There is a strangely apostolic dynamic in this deep interior poverty of the Christ-spirit. Somehow, as Jesus recognized and commanded, it must be told; and somehow, provided that the poverty is generously enough embraced, it does communicate itself.

The most frequent objection is that this is not what Jesus meant by loss of self or that this is not Christianity but a form of monism. I can only think that if Jesus meant a 'partial loss of self' he would have said so and that the mystery of Jesus is precisely his oneness with God and his oneness with us. But we cannot understand what he meant by saying 'the Father and I are one' unless we can enter into the living experience of our oneness with him. To enter that experience is our prayer and it is an entry into the prayer of Jesus. The koan of the saying, 'the Father and I are one' is unresolvable but it dilates beyond the confines of logic in the experience of the Spirit, the bond of oneness between Father and the Son, the prayer of Jesus, our prayer.

'The Spirit prays within us.' It is this Spirit who is the guarantee of the fundamentally positive dynamic of laying down our life, of leaving self behind. There are other forms of selflessness which are not positive – self-rejection, the abandonment of self to mass-hysteria or anonymous forms of the denial of life. But these are precisely those forms of surrendering-to that only intensify the anguish of isolation. In meditation, on the other hand, we embrace the entire naturalness of the surrender of isolation and we do so in the power of the Spirit of oneness, the Spirit of love. The error we made in the past was that it seemed we had to be thinking about this Spirit if it were to be there to help us. But of course the Spirit is unceasingly present and potent within us and by its silence calls us into its own unified consciousness. The irony is that while we are trying to conjure it up by thinking about it or by imagining what it would be like to experience it, we ourselves are not present to the Spirit. That is why the first step in faith is to stop thinking about God at the time of prayer. We have instead to believe – not just mentally but with the whole of our being that makes belief into faith – that he is with us and we in him. 'Dwell in me as I in you.'

The path of meditation is the path of faith and the sacrament of faith is our silence. The door to silence is the mantra. It is not then long before we begin to understand that the loss of self involved is not abnegation but empathy, not an extinction of individuality but a communion of persons. For as we become more deeply rooted in the ground of our being we have our being clarified and affirmed in the purifying silence of the mystery present to us in our heart.

The power of the Resurrection collects the whole of time and space into a single, universal focus. Within our own hearts a cosmos has also been radically transformed by this same power, brought to the single point of a pure and limitless love. We are no longer outside creation or outside God, because through the power that dwells in the open space in the centre of our being we pass beyond ourselves into his fullness of being. To do this we have to be simple enough to be rooted in reality, and faithful enough to stay on our pilgrimage and to meditate each morning and evening. Then we realize our union with our point of origin. Our destination and our companion are one. 'I call you servants no longer; a servant does not know what his master is about. I have called you friends because I have disclosed to you everything I have heard from my Father.' It is this that makes the pilgrimage possible for us all.

6

Sacramental Vision

Month by month we continued to hear of the ongoing develop-
ment of meditation groups in Toronto and Ottawa. In May,
Father John visited these Canadian centres to meditate with them
and encourage them on the journey.

In Montreal we continued to be amazed by the richness and
unpredictability of community. The stroke suffered by one of
our older oblates deepened for us St Benedict's words on the
care of the sick, in whom, he said, we see Christ. Another oblate,
who had come with us from the lay community in England,
married and moved to an apartment near to the monastery. This
was for him the beginning of a dimension of the community that
later developed in physical proximity to the monastery.

After conducting visitations and presiding over an abbatial
election in an Irish Benedictine monastery, Father John visited
an old friend, Mgr Tom Fehily, who had begun meditation
groups in Dublin. Returning to Canada he led an important
session on meditation for a large assembly of sisters in eastern
Canada.

Greetings in the Lord. Today we have been celebrating the
Feast of St Benedict and it seems a suitable date to send this
letter out to so many of you who share with us his vision
and achievement. His understanding of the Christian life as a
commitment to ordinary reality rooted in the contemplative
experience has inspired and continues to inspire people in many
different walks of life and following different vocations to the
one God. I remember some years ago hearing an old monk
quoting a description of monastic generosity that seemed to be
wonderfully apt: 'on things of no account an unaccountable
zeal bestowing'. It is the particular that reveals the universal,
and a commitment to perfection in all we do for its own sake

that enables us to leave ourselves behind. The genius of Benedict's vision is that whereas this approach could so easily become fanatical, he renders it humane, compassionate and tolerant – truly Christian. The enduring power of his vision is its humanity. So often a religious vision of life can lose its human focus, but for Benedict it was through the humanity of Jesus and our own humanity that we enter the divine mystery.

I returned from Ireland in June in time to celebrate Corpus Christi with the Community. Annual feasts like this have an important part in clarifying the Christian rhythm of our life. They can never become routine, because they can never be celebrated in the same way – provided that we have ourselves grown in the interval between the celebrations. Like the Mass itself, the great feasts are expressions of a mystery that we are continually growing into; and so, our outward rites and forms, though remaining the same, are always conveying some deeper, clearer aspect of the mystery. Provided that we are committed to this continuous penetration of the mystery, our rituals can never become routines and the mystery can never become mechanical. A feast like Corpus Christi gives us a regular opportunity to focus, within the liturgical mystery itself, the way our thought and experience have developed. And it does this, as all liturgical action does, by helping us to bring our thought and experience into deeper harmony. This is something we have to be open to, especially in regard to the Eucharist, which focuses our whole religious, sacramental life, as well as providing us with a vital source of the strength we need to remain faithful to the pilgrimage.

The general experience of someone who has been meditating for a while is that the Mass becomes both more meaningful and more of a mystery. This becomes especially clear when, as in this monastery, there is an opportunity to integrate the celebration of Mass with meditation, meditating after the communion. It brings home, in a very powerful way, the true purpose of all the words and rituals we use in worship – not to communicate something *to* God but to prepare ourselves to enter communion *with* him. All religious words point and lead to the silence of a spirit attentive to the presence of God.

The Mass is a supreme symbol of the Christian mystery of Incarnation. It teaches us, in a concrete and tangible form, that reality is incarnate, not conceptual. And it reminds us that it is as we are that we are to make the commitment to this reality – fallible and fickle human beings, redeemed by a power both greater than ourselves and totally committed to us. The extra-ordinary revelation of the gospel is the absolute value of the ordinary and the potential of the ordinary, to be transfigured by the divine power, the universal energy of love. A life that is structured within the discipline of our morning and evening meditation is rooted in the reality of this power and so is always being transformed and penetrated by it. What we might at first seem to 'lose' by sacrificing the time for meditation in the course of a demanding day, is not worth comparing with what we gain. We indeed *re*gain even what we lose, both because of the sense of clarity and order which meditation gives us in our ordinary decision-making, and because of the sharpened sense of the value of time and our growing incapacity to waste or use it trivially. But above and beyond this, a light is shed on our life and radiates through it, that reveals it in its true meaning and sacredness. Our meditation deepens our appreciation of the Mass because it refines our perception of our own life as a sacrament of the love of God.

Meditation highlights even the most ordinary and routine parts of life and draws out their hidden sacramental value. The source of most discontentedness and frustration is just that this value has been lost to man and, looking at his life and work in search of meaning, he can find nothing but a series of self-referring values turned in upon themselves. The search for meaning is the search for the sacramental nature of the ordinary and immediate. This mysterious nature, the value given to it by its divine origin, is there. It is not our creation. It is not even our own meaning reflected back to us by creation. The things and processes of the world have a meaning, a value of their own and this is why we can be transported by a sense of wonder at the beauty of creation and feel ourselves rendered more meaningful by being part of it. But the direction given to us by our own meaning and purpose points us directly towards the originating centre of all meaning, to the Creator. His reality is absolute because in him, the inherent meaning of all creation is focused and realized. In him, we live and move and have our being. This is why we cannot awaken to God without awakening in wonder and compassion to the reality of mankind, both in general and in the particular persons who are for us

284

the sacraments of God's personal mystery and with whom we turn towards his central presence. The sacramental value of these persons and of all the processes and things of our life lead us back to this Presence. Modern man is so often sad because he thinks this value has been lost. The truth is that neither we nor creation have lost the divine radiance. But we have lost the faculty of seeing it. To be saved is to regain it, and our redemption is achieved because we now see all creation with the vision of Christ and, extraordinary though it may seem, we see more – with the vision of Christ we see into the divine Mystery itself.

St Benedict reminded his followers (in chapter 19 of the Rule), that the divine Presence is everywhere. The maturing of our spirit, in the course of our life, is simply our growth in this capacity to see this Presence in every part of our being and experience. To see it is not possible unless we are prepared to become one with what we see, just as we are one with the power of seeing. Our union with Christ is our way into union with the Father. This process of unification is the deepest mystery of our life and the greatest power in creation. It is detectable only imperfectly and in localized areas. We cannot stand back on a spectator's bench and watch the process at work, because we are not the centre of the process and even our own centre, our objectifying consciousness, is being unified. All this, the process of 'oneing', is the work of the Spirit. It is the Spirit itself, at one with his own work as he is with the Father and the Son, from whom he proceeds. The shape and form of this process varies according to the material with which it is involved, but it is the same Spirit working in all and through all. It is the Spirit crying 'Abba' in our heart and leading us into union with the Father through the Son. It is the Spirit who unites the bread and wine with the body and blood of Christ and who unites those who stand around his altar with each other and with him.

The Spirit is the spirit of God who is love. One of the discoveries made through the experience of love is that we truly find our own innerness in the other and that we ourselves become the temple of their interiority. This is the loss of self-centredness and the restoration to real selfhood in the beloved. Another way of putting it, is to say that the division we assume to be so definite between the inner and outer worlds is simply dissolved, gradually perhaps, but no less surely for being gradual, by the reality of the power of love. The energy we employed to maintain this illusion of dividedness is transformed into the liberty of spirit and joyfulness that characterizes the person 'in love.'

We see reality as divided into inner and outer worlds because we ourselves are divided. The accumulative force of our meditation heals this wound in our consciousness and the effect of healing is to make whole. More and more we are allowed to see reality as a continuous whole and, as we become one with ourselves, we are no longer spectators watching the world and ourselves through cracked spectacles. What is the power that restores us to this sense and knowledge of the wholeness of ourselves and of reality and of the harmony between the self and creation? It is the power of the wholeness itself, the uninterrupted presence of God in all persons and all things. To experience God as Creator is to experience the liberation that every encounter with truth – with things as they really are – provokes. And we know him as Creator and creating, when we encounter reality in our ordinary experience as having a divine centre and meaning. This again means all reality because reality cannot be divided. There is not a 'religious' area of our life where this vision is seen and other areas where it is not. To see it is to see it everywhere. The religious response to life is a response based on wonder and on a sense of the incompleted potential of life as we are living it. As the roots of the word imply, religion *relinks* us to the power that brings life to its destined fullness, which is its wholeness. The different parts of our ordinary experience are then no longer alienated from each other. We are empowered to see one area of our experience in terms of other areas. We see with the vision of God. And we see in both the 'abstract' and 'concrete' manifestations of reality, the same presence of God shining with supreme, benevolent simplicity.

The presence of God can never be a partial revelation of his love. Wherever he is, he is wholly present – unlike man's ability to be only 'half-there', such is man's divided and distracted nature. We know this only too well from the sad experience of being with someone who is evidently not present to us as we are to them; or of ourselves being unable to concentrate on what we are engaged upon. To meditate is to know the value

286

of being able to pay complete attention to whatever we are doing or to whomever we are with. Learning to do this through our simple fidelity to the mantra is a real entry into the sharing in the being of God, which St Peter says is our fundamental call. For God is turned with complete and undivided attention to us in Christ. Wholly turned toward us, he is wholly loving. That is why we do not say just that God is loving but that *God is love*. To be wholly loving is to *be* love.

If God were in any degree self-centred – if he were not wholly attentive and concentrated in his movement of love – then we would be able to analyse, to objectify him, to know him as an external manifestation of reality. Then men would be able to 'see God and live'. But as it is, his *completeness* allows us to know him only by participation in his own self-knowledge, which is itself an ever-flowing stream of self-transcendence, creative *other-centredness*. To enter the life of the Trinity through our union with the Son, is far from settling down to the contemplation of a finished picture. It is to be swept out of the sideroads of our self-centredness into the living stream of God's eternal creative love.

We could never recognize the presence of God in the reality in which we find ourselves if we did not already 'possess' that presence; or, to put it better, if he did not already know himself and us in our human heart. 'The love I speak of is not our love for God but his love for us.' We are touched into consciousness by his presence; his spirit is breathed into us. Then we awaken with a growing wonder, awe and joyful confidence in our own reality to his presence around us. We are incapable of seeing reality until we ourselves are realized, made real by his presence. To know ourselves is to know God in us, to know God is to know ourselves in him. It is this dynamic of growth in consciousness, that is profoundly reciprocal, that underlies the central paradox of the revelation of Jesus – a revelation of the nature of the reality that we find our life in the losing of it. The expansion of the frontiers of our being by our growth into the mind of Christ is a centrifugal process, proceeding from the centre of our being outwards. The way we make this journey 'outwards' is by the 'interior' journey of meditation.

In the Eucharist we have a real and living symbol of the unity of the interior and exterior aspects of reality. But what is the special quality of the 'real presence' of Christ in the

Eucharist? It is not that the presence of God-in-Christ is less real in other dimensions of life. God cannot be more or less present, as he is indivisible; but we can, of course, be more or less open to his Presence due to our dividedness. It is rather that in the Eucharist we meet a fully human sign and realization of Christ's universal presence. We call this manifestation *real* because our grasp of reality is stronger at the level of human encounter; the experience of human love is the necessary first stage for the realization of the true nature of love as God himself. 'The glory of God is man fully alive.' In the Eucharist, we encounter the human love of Jesus, fully humanized and so fully realized and integral with the reality of God who is love. Having loved wholly he becomes love, and in the Eucharist we meet, not any effect or reflection of Christ, but his own person, given to us and universally present in its unique and particular human nature. We enter communion with the one who is the fully human sacrament and incarnation of God.

To talk of the universal presence of God in creation is an attempt to emphasize his concrete reality in matter and spirit, to remind us that created reality is always incarnate and unlimited. But it can become an abstract way of talking. We cannot after all really imagine *all* creation. Yet, out of a primary experience of love, we do believe. We commit ourselves to the vision of reality this experience initiates. To believe without imagining is faith. It is faith that is the basis of every degree of the knowledge of God. The meaning of the reality of the Eucharist is only available to one who is in this condition of faith.

If it is the nature of God to be universal, it is the ordinary nature of man to be particular. We know this because we have to make choices (and our fundamental choice is the assent to the gift of our own being). God, however, does not have to select, as all options coexist in his realized present moment. Man, in our as yet unrealized finitude, expresses the divine universality through the particular, and the particular is the creation of choice. The mystery of the Eucharist is the human mystery of Jesus choosing the particular meal of the Passover, with its particular (but universally meaningful) symbols of bread and wine, to express the universality, the divinity, of his love for his human brothers and sisters.

So, in a profoundly moving way, the Eucharist is the

expression of the weakness of man, his finitude. Some *one* thing had to be chosen to express what was universal. This is itself a manifestation of the tragic nature of our finitude, but it is wonderfully appropriate when we see it as forming part of the larger mystery of which the Last Supper was an effective symbol. This larger mystery is the Cross; or rather the acceptance of the Cross as the particular point where the love of Christ and his consequent vulnerability would reach its apogee. The silence of the Cross stirs an essential question in the heart of every man and woman. How did the finitude and weakness of the man Jesus break through to universal presence and power?

Limited and vulnerable Jesus was, like us. But he made what man alone cannot make – a complete and integral gift of self. His love for man was inherent in his fidelity to truth and this was his commitment of self to others. This is what makes him still the *man for others*. The completeness of this commitment was, of course, the love of God for man working in Jesus. It was not that he merely co-operated with this love, but he was one with it and was so in the beginning. True man and true God.

The folly of the Cross is the wisdom of God. Entire and unlimited as was the spirit of Jesus in accepting the Cross, it was still necessary that the Cross was an experience of final failure, defeat and death. But in the radiance of his integrity, the finality of the Cross becomes transformed into something of eternal meaning. It shows, to those who see it with faith, that the integral spirit not only survives death but is glorified, realized through death. The Cross is the extreme point of the development of human finitude, of man's being limited by the particular. But by the completeness, the wholeness of Jesus' commitment to this particular, it becomes the *universal* means of man's liberation into the reality of God.

In the Eucharist we encounter the frailty of the human, the immediacy and the ordinariness of the bread and wine and of the fallible, fickle human beings who constitute the community which itself is a vital part of the sacrament. We ourselves, as St Augustine said, are upon the paten that the priest raises to the Father. We also encounter the Cross. We die with Christ. But we do so in the power of the Resurrection which sheds its light both backwards upon the Cross and forwards upon the

289

gathering together of all creation in Christ. The Cross remains a particular moment of complete human weakness. The Resurrection does not negate the tragedy of the Cross. But, like all moments, it is charged with the Presence, the power of God, realized in the Resurrection.

As the Mass transforms the ordinary into the mysterious (without betraying its particularity or frailty), so our meditation leads us from the particular to the universal (without betraying our wholeness or the strange gift of our mortality). No part of our life is left untransformed by meditation, because we meditate from the centre outwards and, as we travel deeper into this centre, the outward is transformed and unified with the inward mystery of God's presence. The mantra thus consecrates our whole life and, like the sacramental mystery of the Eucharist, it becomes an outward sign of an inner reality whose full realization is known only in faith.

Around the eucharistic table there are no observers, only participants. If anyone is there to observe themselves or others, then their presence is not real. The Lord is still present to them – for 'if we are faithless he remains faithful for he cannot deny himself'. And the complete and unconditional fidelity of his being present to us exposes us to a power of love that must eventually impel us to turn our self-centred attention outwards to him who dwells in silence and love within us.

This is the dynamic power of our stillness in meditation. The part of our consciousness that is looking for results, searching for experience or calculating spiritual progress is simply not part of this movement towards God. That this part of us is of no significant power is a discovery we make on the pilgrimage. His Presence to us is stronger than our absence from him. All we need do is to enter the condition of faith that is our integral openness to his Presence. By our faithfulness to the mantra, our incarnate movement of faith, we thus allow the power of his indwelling Presence to radiate outwards, to be realized by our fully personal acceptance. Thus, we ourselves are made real by reality. Just as the Eucharistic community is made one by faith in the Body and Blood of Christ, so our personal inner unity is realized by the simple faith we bring to each of our particular times of meditation. And from that inner unity, we move outwards to realize our unity with others in the mystery of God.

Just as we see the presence of God in Creation because he is present within us, so we see reality because we are made real. And we are made real by his presence. The wholeness of God is such that it is only necessary to *be* in his presence in order to be transformed. It is vital that we learn to *be*. To learn it, most of us have to accept the ascesis of unlearning a great deal, both about God and ourselves. We have so complicated the simple truth we learn in meditation – that it is the wholly natural movement of our spirit to rise above all self-centredness by opening our consciousness to God *in the mind of Christ*.

The impersonal and materialistic assumptions our society creates in our attitude to life have done great harm to our understanding of the reality of prayer and to our capacity to pray. Above all they have replaced the value of *presence* with the idea of *function* – it is not what a person is but what he does that counts. The truth is that the value of action consists in the quality of being. Our experience of love is always contradicting the false assumptions, but they remain deep-rooted attitudes of the modern consciousness. Meditation challenges it at root, because when we meditate we are not trying to do anything: we are simply attending to the reality of the divine Presence and learning to be in that Presence.

We learn a little each step we take, each time we meditate, every morning and evening. More deeply we discover that to *be* is not to be isolated, but to be realized *in communion*. The Presence of Christ is eternally present to us and we grow in our capacity to be present to him. In that realization of mutual presence, of communion, the divine transcendence occurs and we are swept away from the netherworld of self-centredness into the infinite energy and complete fulfilment of the reality who is love. We send you encouragement and support in the commitment you are making to this journey into the reality of God. We keep you present in our heart and ask you to hold us in yours.

7

The Christian Crisis

In August Father Laurence conducted a retreat in Buffalo, New York, and another at Queen's University in Kingston, Ontario, in October. He also taught a course on the history and practice of meditation at Marianapolis College here in Montreal.

The first twelve of Father John's newsletters were published by Crossroads in New York under the title Letters from the Heart; Christian Monasticism and the Renewal of Community. *We were also preparing a pamphlet on conducting or starting a meditation group which contains a list of the groups around the world.*

Guests continued to arrive, enriching the community with a wealth of personal experience. Among them were the whole House of Bishops of the Anglican Church in Canada headed by Archbishop Ted Scott, the Primate.

We received several new oblates, and meditation groups continued to flourish in New York, Toronto, Montreal, Vermont and England.

It seems to me that the basic challenge facing the Christian Church is also a most vitalizing opportunity. This is the challenge and chance we have of putting before our contemporaries what we might describe as the basic Christian experience.

That may seem obvious enough until we distinguish between the basic experience and the superficial experience. The redemptive liberating power of Christ is announced at the superficial level but it is communicated, shared and known at the basic level of our being. This does not mean that the superficial levels of life are unimportant: our essential life and work is inseparable from our spiritual journey. But the superficial quickly becomes trivial, an empty sign, unless it is continually springing out of the depths of our spirit, where our whole being is centred, renewed and daily refreshed. It is peculiarly easy for religious-minded people to live superficially, alienated from the depth of the reality which they claim to be experiencing and proclaiming. The awareness of the perennial need to be authentically in touch with the experience of that depth is one of the essential insights of the teaching of Jesus and of the whole Christian tradition. To be a disciple of this Master means to be constantly mindful of the depth that lies beyond the surface, of the spiritual power that lies beyond religious authority, of the living person who lies beyond all theology and philosophy.

It is instructive to see how essentially Christian this sense of depth is. Look at the Letter to the Hebrews and listen to how curiously modern it sounds. 'Let us then stop discussing the rudiments of Christianity. We ought not to be laying over again the foundations of faith in God . . . Let us advance towards maturity, and so we shall, if God permits' (6:1,3). One can be quite sincere living off the ideas and images of our faith but, as our ordinary experience is constantly reminding us, sincerity alone is not ultimately satisfying. Our call as Christians is a call beyond thought and image and sincerity to that essential encounter with Reality, the encounter with Reality itself, and it is this encounter which makes us authentic. We are not only called, but are empowered to respond, because of the unique and fundamental transformation of our consciousness that has occurred as a result of the life of Jesus. The consciousness of a fully human being has opened in love to the infinite mystery of God. It has been swept out of itself into God but without ceasing to be itself. The mystery of the Incarnation means that Jesus remains fully human, fully alive to us and to the Father in his glorified state. And so it is through his human consciousness that we can make that same journey into authenticity: our call is to be realized by being bathed in the light of that reality, the reality that has glorified him. This is not only possible; it is, in a personal way for each of us, unavoidable – or avoided only at the cost of a wasted life. What the Letter to the Hebrews calls maturity, what St John calls 'the fullness of life', St Peter 'our sharing in the very being of God', St Paul 'the strength and power of his spirit in your inner being': all this is what modern man is desperately seeking. He is seeking to be made 'real'.

There is a general sense in our society, I think, of the loss of power. The energy crisis we're all so familiar with is really a superficial expression of this deeper-rooted sense of the loss of spiritual power. Both physically and spiritually there is more than an element of absurdity in the 'crisis'. We talk of the energy crisis while at the same time we are the most wasteful and mindlessly over-productive generation ever to walk the earth. And we talk of the loss of spiritual power while we are, each of us, despite the powers of depersonalization that affect us, a temple of the living Spirit. Yet, the prevailing awareness of our time which underlies our experience and our fear of chaos is that our sources of power are running down. Not far below the surface of our frenetic activity and endless distractions is the fear that this is just as true of the spiritual and moral spheres as it is of the physical and social and economic spheres.

Of course there is a deep and complex interdependence between these areas. The visible surface of our lives is even more than a reflection of the state of things in the depths. It is part of the depths in the sense that our whole identity is the integration of everything we are. Moral choices are not the only criterion of our godliness but they are a vital expression of our oneness with the power that motivates a truly Christian morality – the power of love. That is why a Christian vision is one that sees surface and depths in the way that they do really correspond. Personal experience, as well as the larger condition of our society, should bear this out. It is little less than amazing that the social chaos that follows in the wake of economic crisis should so closely mirror the moral confusion that follows on the loss of spiritual power.

Our sense of an overriding crisis is realistic only if we foresee no chance of affecting the outward march of events through an interior change of direction. If, as the Christian vision claims, the external is intimately linked to the internal (surely this is what the Incarnation is about), a purification of our interior reality should result in the harmonization of external reality also. The social dream of the Gospel is one where charity, not exploitation, marks the relationships between people, where generosity rather than possessiveness controls the economy, where freedom not fear colours the psychological atmosphere. It is the dream, only partially and sporadically come true in some Christian communities, of a revolution. But a Christian revolution is a revolution that must be energized by centrifugal forces – forces that radiate from the personal centre outwards. This is an ascending movement of liberation and expansion – not like most revolutions, a descending movement of aggression and constriction. The process that initiates this centrifugal revolution described in the Gospels is conversion, the interior, depth-turning change of the basic orientation of our being from self to beyond self.

Every conversion is a rediscovery of our true self and of our real participation in the Reality of God and is so much greater than our own limited potential reality. Every conversion – and, as St Benedict understood it, our whole Christian life is a conversion, a turning to God – is a further degree of awakening. The embedded momentum of our being urges us forwards towards full wakefulness.

> Awake, sleeper, rise from the dead
> And Christ will shine upon you. (Eph. 5:14)

To awaken is to open our eyes, and we open them, as St Benedict said, 'to the divinizing light'. What we see transforms what we are.

Each time we meditate we take a step further into this wakefulness, this state of being in light. And the more fully we integrate the basic Christian experience into our ordinary daily life the more deeply wakeful we become. This makes our life a journey of discovery, an exploration, a constantly renewed miracle of created vitality. To meditate is to put an end to dullness, to fear, and above all to pettiness. What is vital is that we are really on this journey, not just thinking about the journey or talking about it. A peculiar danger for religious people is to believe that because they are so religious they have all the answers taped. The frightful arrogance of the religious egoist is to believe that he has arrived before he has even started. It is easy to read about wakefulness, to have elaborate and, as far as they go, accurate ideas about enlightenment, and yet all the while to be fast asleep. The man who is awake knows without doubt he is awake. But the man who is dreaming also believes he is awake. In that state, the images of a dream convince us that they are the realities we know as real when we are awake. We enter wakefulness, as the meditator knows, by letting go of the images and by learning to wait for the Reality – for 'Christ to shine upon you'.

This is the basic Christian experience I was speaking of. It is perennial, unchanging, but also it is new in every generation and unique for every individual and unique every time we meditate. Every time we meditate we enter into the vitalizing creative presence of God. It is its manifold uniqueness that gives us our common ground, our oneness in him. This is the basis of all Christian community. The dynamic of the experience is always conversion, a turning from self to the Other, a rediscovery of a realm beyond ourselves and yet in which we have our own real and unique place. The dream image we let go of is of a universe revolving around us as its centre. The reality revealed – and the burden of illusion lifted – is the revelation that we are in our own unique and indispensable place in the universe, a universe that is centred in God, and which is permeated by his presence, for his centre is everywhere.

This rediscovery has a particular colouring in every time and place. Today the rediscovery we need is not primarily a religious one. We don't need, in the first place, to recover our identity in any superficial religious sense with any superficial religious demarcations – for example as good Baptists, Anglicans, Catholics or even Atheists. What we need is an experience of depth, to fill the surface with identity, with meaning, purpose and shape once again. This experience ensues when we make contact with our own inner spiritual nature, when we enter the structure of reality as it is established in our deepest centre, where the Spirit of God, God in all his fullness, dwells in love. Out of that contact – and the word is 'contact' much more than 'contemplation' – arises a deeply rooted and sane spiritual sense that will naturally communicate itself in the whole gamut of our religious, social, interpersonal and personal living responses to reality.

The call to modern man, the call to all of us, is to become spiritual, and to become spiritual we have to learn to leave behind our official religious selves – that is, to leave behind the Pharisee that lurks inside all of us – because, as Jesus has told us, we have to leave behind our whole self. All images of ourselves coming as they do out of the fevered brain of the ego, have to be renounced and transcended if we are to become one with ourselves, with God, with our brethren – that is, to become truly human, truly real, truly humble. Our images of God must similarly fall away. We must not be idol-worshippers. Curiously, what we find is that they fall away as our images of self fall away, which suggests what I suppose we always guessed anyway, that our images of God were really images of ourselves. In this wonderful process of coming into the full light of Reality, of falling away from illusion, a great silence emerges from the centre. We feel ourselves engulfed in the eternal silence of God. We are no longer talking to God or worse, talking to ourselves. We are learning to be – to be with God, to be in God.

That is why it is so important for all of us to learn to be still. In that stillness we learn to remain with the energy that arises from the contact we have made with our own spiritual nature. The phenomenon of so much contemporary 'spirituality' is not of a pilgrimage to the centre, but more like a raid mission that descends suddenly, plunders what can be got in the form of spiritual experience or insight, and then immediately retreats behind the walls of the religious ego. There is all the difference in the world – the difference between reality and illusion – between the pilgrim and the nomad. The pilgrim stays on the journey, steadily and selflessly, focused not on emotional or intellectual satisfaction but upon the goal, the goal that leads us, the goal who is Christ. This is true Christian conversion, the revolution that Christ taught and exemplified in his own person. It is what makes our beliefs credible – to ourselves and to others because it makes us credible. The steadiness – firmness, rootedness as St Paul described it – is the guarantee of our sanity. Our seriousness about the journey guarantees its joyfulness.

On the spiritual journey it takes more energy to be still than to run. I suppose most people spend so much of their waking hours rushing from one thing to another that they are afraid of stillness and of silence. A certain existential panic can overtake us when we first face the stillness, when we first enter into this state of pure being. But if we can once find the courage to face this silence, we enter into the peace that is beyond all understanding. No doubt it is easier to learn this in a balanced and stable society. In a turbulent and confused world there are so many more deceptive voices, so many calls for our attention.

But the Christian vision is uncompromising in its sanity, its rejection of extremism, in its invitation to each of us to have the courage to become ourselves and not merely to respond to some image of ourselves that is imposed upon us from outside. And the Christian vision proclaims to us that not only is this possible but the resources to achieve it are given to us, given to us in the power that is placed in our hearts as a result of the redemptive love of Jesus Christ. The Christian message is a message of limitless hope, because of the limitless generosity of Christ. But we would be foolish not to recognize that there is a certain austerity to the message too. Listen again to the Letter to the Hebrews: 'When men have once been enlightened, when they have had a taste of the heavenly gift . . . and after all this have fallen away, it is impossible to bring them again to repentance' (6:4, 6).

It is not that God withdraws his gift, as it were in pique; I think what the writer of the Letter to the Hebrews means is that, if we persist in treating ourselves trivially, we can mortally damage our capacity to receive the divine gift. The call to meditate every day of our lives is simply the call to take the words of Jesus seriously. We take them seriously by turning to his presence in our hearts every morning and every evening of our lives as our first responsibility.

We trivialize ourselves if we set limits to the energy available to us for this inner journey – the journey to our own heart, to the presence of Christ within us, and the journey beyond with Christ to the Father. The power source from which we draw our dynamism for this journey is inexhaustible, as St Paul tells us, 'It can be measured by nothing less than the power that God exercised in raising Jesus from the dead.' This power was exercised in the root of Christ's being, and Christ's presence is to be found in the root of our human being. The transformation that this exercise of the power of God brought about – 'the glory of the Resurrection' – was effected in the depth of the being of humanity as a whole. What each of us must realize is that in the depth of our soul we have died and we have been raised to new life in Christ. The basic challenge of our existence is to be open to the life of Christ. To be open to this life we must become fully alive. Only life can respond to life. Only in the loving attention of our own deep openness to Christ can we recognize that this life is the energy of the whole of creation, the energy of the Creator, the energy of love.

We can describe the journey as a journey from self-consciousness (the prismatic distraction and narrowness of the ego) to self-awareness (the clarified and expansive knowledge of our participation in reality). The Church itself is called to be a special sign of this transformation of consciousness. It is called beyond concern for its own image, its own success or its own influence. The Church is only itself when it is aware that it is the conscious presence of Christ in this world. This consciousness is the basis of its transcendent nature that can never be wholly institutionalized. The Church has always been vitalized and always will be vitalized by men and women who have the courage to tread this austere way, the way beyond self into the consciousness of Christ. The tradition that preserves, nurtures and communicates this awareness of God in Christ is the tradition of the Spirit present in the Church, enlivening the Church. All this suggests to us the primacy of the Spirit over the letter. Letters can only build up into the living Word that the Church must utter in every generation if the energy of new life is set free to enliven the letter, and this new life must be set free in the depths of our hearts. As Christians, we must speak a living Word to our contemporaries. It must be a Word that is authoritative, not authoritarian, a Word that is not sectarian, but is truly catholic. We can only speak this Word when we are alive with the life of Christ. The Church as envisioned in the New Testament is primarily a community of vitalized and enlightened brethren, illumined and charged with a life beyond their own – a life arising from the power of the risen Christ. The writers of the New Testament everywhere call on the early Christians to be open to this power. We in our turn, carrying on a tradition greater than ourselves, must call on our contemporaries to enter the dynamism of the marriage between God and humanity in Christ. But we can only do so when we ourselves have undertaken the pilgrimage to this union by our own selfless commitment to the pilgrimage.

What each of us must learn in the experience of our meditation is that the power for the pilgrimage is in fact inexhaustibly present. It takes only one step of faith for us to know that from our own experience. The important thing to remember is that one faltering but actual step is more valuable than any number of journeys performed in the imagination. As beginners we have to accept a certain distance between what we say externally, what we seek externally – and what we are internally. As we begin to tread the path that unites surface and depth, we have to recognize that we are limited, that we are sinners. What all this means is that we must understand that although we are setting out, we are only setting out, we have not yet arrived. Nothing is more likely to make us arrogant than to imagine that we have arrived before we have actually left. Leave we must. When we reflect on the necessity of this commitment it illumines the real opportunity and responsibility we have. Christ is consciously present in time only to the degree that we, his sons and daughters, open our minds and hearts to him in this world, only to the degree that we have undertaken the commitment to be real, to be still, to persist in reality. When we do embrace this commitment, the Church becomes in the first place not an institution, not an organization, not a hierarchy but the Body of Christ, filled in its every limb with his vital and vitalizing power. Not only filled with his power but – in the way of all conscious life – alive to that life in full self-awareness.

All this remains potential energy – not the kinetic energy which the Resurrection is – until we find the way to realize it. Commitment to the reality of Christ is in effect commitment to prayer. Prayer is our empathy with the consciousness of Christ, and in that empathy we know that his consciousness is of his infinite love for the Father, and of the Father's infinite love for him. Man's openness to this consciousness (the Spirit praying within us) sweeps us out of ourselves beyond ourselves into that stream of power flowing from the human heart and mind of Christ to the Father – to his Father – to our Father. Implanted in our human depths this stream is within time. So we return to our times of meditation each day, lest within the cares and concerns of time we forget the Supreme Reality in which we have our being, in which our being is rooted. As we do so faithfully and simply, as we follow the pilgrimage, we discover that the stream will carry us beyond time, beyond all division, and beyond all limitation into the now – into the infinite liberty of God. Unless we know the ordinariness of the way of prayer we fail to know the sublimity of its goal. Never forget the importance of the daily return each morning and each evening.

The essence of the Christian message is knowing this love and this power – although, as St Paul says, 'It is beyond knowledge.' So we must know it with a knowledge greater than our own knowledge because it is beyond the capacity of mere human knowledge. We must know this with the consciousness of Christ himself. This is the basic redemptive Christian experience.

The invitation we have is to be open, available to this experience. There are two elements to this. First, we must hear the Word of the Gospel, and this is not perhaps as easy as it sounds. There are many competing voices clamouring for our attention – most of them encouraged by our own egotistical spirit. But the Word of the Gospel is a call to sanity and, as such, it remains steady and strong in its utterance. The second step, once we have become silent and steady, and enough ourselves to hear it, is to 'remain within the Revelation'.

For all this we need the full resources of our humanity balanced and integrated. We need the strength and encouragement of the love of others in their humanity. But our deepest need is for the inexhaustible power of the love of Christ, the love of his human consciousness pervaded by the Light of the Father. The miracle of Christianity is that this need is already met. This power dwells within us, so far exceeding our need that contact with it sweeps us out of ourselves beyond anything we could have imagined or desired, into the reality that is the Kingdom. In the first step we take towards this power, his Kingdom begins to overtake us, to come to birth within us.

8

Self-will and Divine Will

New Year 1982 started with the simple profession of Paul Geraghty, who became the first monk professed for our Community, a sign for us all of our ever-deepening commitment into the heart of the Trinitarian Mystery.

As part of his ongoing commitment to the work of Christian unity, Bishop Henry Hill was appointed as the delegate of the Archbishop of Canterbury to visit Churches in the Middle East.

At the ceremony of Brother Paul's Profession, I spoke on the Benedictine vision of life. It is a vision that aims to make life more vital because, for St Benedict, the principal quality needed in a truly Christian life is an ongoing spirit of conversion. When this spirit is present in any life, there follows a continuous turning beyond the limitations of our own isolated and isolating self-will towards the divine will.

If our motivating force is self-will, we live in the prison of our own desires and disappointments. If, on the other hand, we have turned away from this force and are motivated by the divine will, we are swept into a liberty without frontiers in which everything in our experience is transformed into gift with epiphanies.

But those of us trained in a traditional religious vocabulary need to remind ourselves of the infinite liberty that is implied by a phrase like 'the divine will'. It is easy to limit this will by analogy to our own wants and needs and desires. The next step, following logically, but leading into absurdity, is to see the function of prayer as somehow influencing the divine will, trying to make the divine will coincide with our will. It is a good example of how dangerous and illusory any deduction or action becomes, whether in the spiritual or material sphere, when our point of departure is egoism. The actual experience of our potential for egolessness – our meditation – is, therefore, vital for a right ordering of our perspectives on reality. It is only when we begin the journey away from egoism that we can construct a religious language that really does make sense. From the basis of spiritual knowledge we know that to speak of the divine will is not to speak of what God wants – it is to speak of what he is. Then we will know, too, what Dante meant in his great saying, 'In his will is our peace.' What is the divine will? It is, simply, love.

Because St Benedict knew this mystery and lived out of it, his Rule can only be understood if we see the harmonious interdependence that he saw between obedience and love. In his vision monastic obedience was not mature while there was any trace of fear in it. We obey because we listen and respond out of love. This central and centralizing vision serves to align the whole person – body, spirit, mind and heart on the divine reality.

The actual experience of love, not the word, the theological idea or the dream, takes the life of the monk far beyond merely intellectual assent to certain propositions, even further from being a retreat from reality and it makes it instead into a life commitment towards truth, integrity and wholeness. Each of these ideals are deeply and humanly interwoven in the monk's daily life of prayer and work. Because of their fusion, their centredness in his own actual experience, he enjoys what is, perhaps, the essential gift of the monastic vocation – liberty of spirit grounded in wholeness of vision. He is able to commit himself to truth because the experience of love, welling up from within and so simultaneously greeting him from without, teaches him that this is the actual structure of reality. 'Happy are the poor in spirit.' This is the joy the monk knows in seeing how wonderfully simple all is.

Truth, integrity, wholeness. The ancient writers called these 'oneness'. If we fear the power of oneness, the experience of oneness, it is with good cause. It is the power of the living God which no dividedness or disharmony can withstand – and we are, all of us, absurdly attached to our own disunity and alienation. The detachment of the monk is essentially the renunciation of this absurdity which underlies all sin and the sadness and isolation consequent upon it. To pursue this new commitment to the reality of unity, to sense and sanity, requires courage, perhaps indeed a certain passion and recklessness. It requires the strength and flexibility of real humility, the capacity to learn about oneself, to find oneself and the gentleness and rootedness of true faith, the capacity to persevere in commitment to our gentle but uncompromising Lord.

The monk (*monos*) is, therefore, one who is one. One with himself because he can face and pass beyond all interior divisions. One with the brethren, not seeking his own convenience, but constantly turning to the community will, and one with God; the monk only fully becomes himself when lost in this oneness.

Benedict's understanding of conversion is of major importance, not just for monks, but for all who would try to lead a vital, which is to say, expanding Christian life. Our own practice of daily meditation is the essential expression of our commitment to the dynamic of conversion that unites our whole person, our complete life. It is impossible to convey this in words to someone who has not begun to experience it or at least to become aware of the possibility of it through meditation. It is one of the most inexplicable and frustrating limitations of the human condition, that the meaning of spiritual experience cannot adequately be verbalized beyond the community that the experience creates among those following the same path, regardless of who they are or where they are coming from. Of course, the attempt to communicate it is demanded of all in that community and the attempt more effectively succeeds when we realize that the experience is itself self-communication. Such is the Divine nature, which is love.

The self-communication of this redemptive experience progresses as we ourselves are unified by it. To be unified is 'to possess eternal life', as the New Testament puts it. This means that no part of ourselves, no aspect of our total human sensitivity is lost or destroyed.

One of the earliest things we discover when we begin to meditate on a daily basis, is that the practice itself begins to have results throughout our life. The harmonic sounded within us at the time of our meditation sets up sympathetic responses in every aspect of our personality and life. If it were not so – if our meditation were isolated in a spiritual vacuum – then we could be sure that the practice itself was illusory.

It is good to remind ourselves occasionally that meditation is not just another activity or interest in our life. It is so absolutely fundamental or central that we could say that it is, in a real sense, *lifegiving*. All life involves movement, growth, development. A person or an institution begins to die when their commitment to growth begins to wane. This is why our faith is, in effect, the energy that fuels the journey of meditation and, because it is a journey into God, our commitment is to a deep, divine principle of infinite growth. Our journey, like the Gospel itself, as St Paul describes it, begins in faith and ends in faith. Our daily commitment to meditation is the expression and renewal of our faith.

Conversion is to the spiritual life what revolution is to the political life. It is the free, conscious principle that assures freshness, honesty, creativity, all that we mean by integrity. As we all know, the ideal revolution is peaceful. It occurs in a society that recognizes the necessity for change as an indispensable part of the life and growth principle. It understands, also, that all the contributing parts of society, the groups or institutions, which are like the limbs of a body, stand in need of development if they are to meet new situations, new technologies, the new aspirations of man in the face of his own new discoveries. The creative energy activated in one part challenges the response of the whole.

The whole can only respond to the new situation created by an eruption of creativity, a new phase of growth, if it has already some genuine achievement of integrity. If, that is, it has a conscious centre. Unconscious centres are more common, of course – political powers or human hearts that operate by repression, out of fear, rather than by liberation, out of love. But the truly conscious heart – whether the centre of an individual person or of society – can cope with the new energies of growth, because it has already, up to that moment, to some degree harmonized the different forces that make up any organization. The centre is the open space where the paradoxes of being are held in dynamic and wonder-filled suspension. This dynamic suspension of conflict is both the goal of all life-oriented movement and the condition that makes growth, infinite growth, a realistic possibility. Another name for this dynamic suspension of paradox is peace.

The best revolutions are peacefully embraced. An orderly constitutional process of assimilation and advance is created and set in motion out of the great resources of power contained in the peaceful heart. The whole body politic is galvanized by this power. The more conservative and the more progressive forces unite maturely in a creative reassessment of the needs of society. An expansion of the circumferences is demanded by all in concert because the centre has produced more than the whole can absorb.

True revolution is motivated by this deep instinct to maintain, by expansion, the equilibrium between the centre and the circumference, between the parts and the whole. It is motivated, therefore, by a passion for peace. We have not really experienced peace if we think of it as the cessation or absence of violence. It is really the harmony of all the mighty forces that, disunited, lead to violence. Peace is not so much a consolation or an escape as a power in its own right and a rooting principle of reality. Like the word love, we use it loosely and vulgarly.

The social and political influence exerted by single individuals in history, men like Gandhi or Martin Luther King, an influence out of all proportion to their material power, should remind us exactly what it was that Jesus bequeathed us when he breathed on his disciples and spoke the word 'Shalom', peace, over them. Peace is an aspect of the human experience, of the human perception of the infinitely varied mystery of the will, the life, the love of God. It is a form of his energy which, like all energies, take their being from him. As such, it cannot be destroyed but is capable of infinite transformations. The Holy Spirit, which is the universality of God's power, his freedom to take all forms and his freedom from all forms, is therefore, for us, at the same time the love we find welling up in our own inmost heart and the power that impels us to realize equity and peace in our own societies. It is the power of all true peaceful revolution.

In the spiritual life, the same sort of principles apply. We do not approach true conversion of life with any sort of dramatic histrionics. We need the orderly, daily return to that process whereby we alter our angle of vision and so become capable of seeing the basis of all sovereignty. Because we are in a state of continuous conversion, we have never turned fully enough towards God. Each phase of growth clarifies and sharpens our vision further.

Sometimes it is said that conversion is the spiritual law by which we learn to live by the will of God rather than by our own will. In a certain sense this is true enough. But what I think the practice of daily meditation soon reveals to us is that true conversion is much more a matter of learning to love as God loves.

St Paul tells us that there is a light shining in our hearts. St John tells us that this light is the point of divine consciousness, of infinitely pure love, to be found and worshipped in every person – the light that enlightens everyone who comes into this world. This is what it means to be human: to enshrine this unique and universal divine one-pointedness. St Paul and St John are, therefore, precious witnesses, but our own experience must then teach us that everything and everyone is enlightened by this same point that we find in ourselves – we must discover in a real sense that we are ourselves. We must become our real selves. The divine love is the originating and sustaining power of all creation and all consciousness. Our hopes for peace are not vain, because this experience of God, in the light of Christ that shines within us, brings us peace, unifies us, harmonizes our interior forces and satisfies our every desire, beyond the power of the imagination or heart to conceive.

Our life has to be a pursuit of wisdom because wisdom requires of us that we learn to live out of this light, this energy. To be wise is to be always in harmony with it and always vitalized by it. To slip out of this harmony, to descend from wisdom to mere cleverness is to begin to slide down the slope that ends in the hell of non-being. This slipping way is the reverse process of conversion. So, whenever a person is travelling in this reverse direction, he perhaps sees everything that a person in conversion sees, but does so in reverse, as mirror images of reality; whereas conversion leads us through love and life, its opposite creates non-love – the magician egoism, which leads through to non-being. Love is always creative; non-love is death-dealing. Conversion is commitment to the creativity of love. But to be turned towards non-love, egoism, is to be enthralled by the fascination for death. We find this in individuals as well as in societies. In both cases, material prosperity or production is no yardstick of true creativity. The only trustworthy measure is the depth of peace flowing from the centre that harmonizes all its parts in love.

307

Conversion requires in all of us significant readjustments in our life, in our angle of vision. These readjustments can be thought of but they cannot be effected by the power of thought. They can only be integrated into our life from the creative power that we find in our centre. That is why we best understand meditation, not as a process of self-improvement, nor as a tool we employ for desired ends, but rather as a process of learning, a process of wonder and deepening humility. We learn, above all, that God is the centre, the universal centre and the source of all that is. Everything begins in him and everything returns to him.

This, of course, is obvious enough but it becomes more challenging when we examine our own practice. The light which enables us to do this is provided by our meditation – here, as always, the touchstone is the degree to which we are living out the consequences of our meditation. How then do we live our lives, in fact? How do we arrive at our daily decisions?

Isn't it often the case that, in practice, the centre we align ourselves upon is ourselves? Seeing ourselves as the centre of the universe, we take our decisions, more or less, solely on the basis of how they will advance our own comfort, amusement or self-fulfilment. This self-centredness is our isolation – more terrible than any physical solitary confinement cell in the worst prison.

But, as we begin to break through our own egoism, we find that we certainly have a point of centredness, a place of our own but not the central place. Our destiny is to find our own insertion point in the cosmic reality of God's love. Only then can we love as he loves because only then can we be who we are. The power to love is only present in those who know or have begun to know who they are. This self-knowledge is not our own achievement or creation. It is potential for full being, created in the creative movement of God's love for us. We have being and we are persons capable of loving – which is to say, living the divine life, sharing the divine nature – because we are loved. This first step in conversion is, therefore, not renunciation, asceticism or any kind of suffering. It is allowing ourselves to be loved. If so many people never really begin the journey, it is because they have never drawn the curtains of their spirit and allowed the light of love to illumine their darkened hearts. There would be no greater tragedy than to die with such a curtained, untouched heart.

Once we are stabilized in our insertion point, we can come to the truth that sets us free, propelling us always further into the infinite liberty of God. It is the truth about him, the truth about ourselves and the truth of all that is. We can only see this truth with clarity of vision and in its totality if we are rooted and grounded in him. Otherwise, we see only aspects of things, unrelated to their convergent centre. So, in this fractured vision, we can never make valid judgements about the ultimate significance of the parts we see. Jesus has told us he is the truth; he is also the way because in him our vision is healed and focused. Through his life we can find our way into the place destined for us by his love.

Meditation is of such importance because we can only come to the truth if we have the confidence to face it. This confidence arises from the encounter with pure love in our own hearts. The really important thing to know in life – for life – is that he is and that he is love. It may be of some preparatory use to know also that we are sinners. But it is much more necessary to know and to know clearly, truthfully, that our sins are of no account. They cannot even exist in the light of his love, because they are entirely blotted out, burned away by that pure light.

It is very simple. The most important task of any life that would respond fully to its potential is that we come into this light to be purified, to be made real, to discover our own divine potential. The term 'enlightenment' is used widely today, and for those of us who follow in the footsteps of Christ, it is an important term. We can only see with his light. What we see transforms who we are. We become, as St John tells us 'like him'.

Perhaps the most valuable first lesson to learn is that the coming of Jesus, which we celebrated at Christmas, has transformed the ordinary. If we can see this clearly, we can see our own spiritual journey, our own religious practice, our personal life, all shot through with the transforming potentiality of Christ's redemptive love. In order to see this clearly, we have to understand how ordinary meditation is. Just as breathing is necessary for bodily life, so meditation is necessary for the development and sustenance of our spiritual life. To say the mantra is a very ordinary thing. It is of the same order as eating, breathing, sleeping. It remains esoteric only to those who have not yet undertaken the journey. To those who have begun, it is as ordinary and as wonderful as daylight. Like the other functions necessary for a balanced and healthy life, it requires a regular, daily commitment. But it is unique among these functions. It is the great integrating function wherein all our other processes are held in balance and aligned on the centre. Achieving, or realizing, the balance is the first step. From there on, we progress steadily into the heart of the divine Mystery.

The Church has a vital role to play in the world in calling people to this divinizing work. As far as I can see, very many of our non-religious, those we call secular, contemporaries are longing to hear this good news but we can only speak the enlightening word to them if we ourselves are on the Way. The Church has an unparalleled spiritual opportunity in this time, but it can rise to it only if we can find enough Christians to take Christ at his Word: 'Anyone who wishes to be a follower of mine must leave self behind' (Mark 8:34).

The faithful saying of our mantra is our response to this call of Jesus. It is work – the work of God. Above all, meditation is an all-out onslaught on egoism, on isolation and on sadness. It is an affirmation of consciousness and life through the experience of love. The Christian vision demands a community that is created and vitalized in the mind of Christ. The message this community must communicate is that it is possible for all of us to become alive with the life of Christ. It is not only possible, it is the destiny of each one of us.

The way to this vitalizing Christianity – a Christianity which is a light for the nations, the salt of the world and a power for peace – is the way of prayer: the prayer that is not our prayer but is the prayer of Jesus himself. That prayer is, even now as you read this, flowing in our hearts. Our meditation is our full acceptance of this ontological reality – the full acceptance of the gift of our own being and of the Being of God, fully embodied in Jesus. Our prayer in this vision is our life force.

9

A Way of Vision

*Father Laurence returned from a six-week visit during January
and February to Tanzania, where he gave a series of retreats
and workshops on meditation. He was greatly gladdened by the
many positive responses among both the African people and
European missionaries. On his way back he visited Germany,
where he conducted a seminar on contemplative prayer at the
University of Würzburg, organized by the oblates there.*

*During the early part of 1982 several groups visited the monas-
tery, ranging from the Knights of Colombus to a group from
the Church of the Advent. A long-term guest, Dom Michael
Hall from St Anselm's in Washington, D.C., participated in an
ecumenical Lenten evening in St Bruno. We were also delighted
to receive a visit from Father George Maloney, author of several
books on prayer. We continued to receive new oblates in Toronto
and Montreal.*

*Rose Lovat, our first oblate, was with us in March. She and
Sister Madeleine Simon organized a meeting of the groups in
London. From that meeting Father John went to Liverpool and
Manchester to address the groups there and then on to Dublin
to give a talk.*

Easter was a full and joyful time for all of us here, and a time
when we united to reflect upon the deepest mysteries of our
life. We celebrate Easter liturgically over a few days but we
discover its meaning only in a lifetime. Each year I hear these
words of St Paul read out during the ceremonies and their
significance seems to become both sharper and more real,
urgent and yet more mysterious, each year. 'By baptism we
were buried with him, and lay dead, in order that, as Christ
was raised from the dead in the splendour of the Father, so

also we might set our feet upon the new path of life' (Rom. 6:4).

To know this is to be a Christian, not just a member of a church or sect but a joyful personal disciple. It is to know that this new path of life is already opened up for us because of the energies set free among all humanity by the Resurrection. From our point of view we may see only the same tired, worn, old paths but if this Resurrection energy has touched us, if we have touched it in our hearts, the new path of life stands out brilliant and dominant, transcending all the old ways. As the snows of winter melted in our garden here a carpet of brown and withered leaves from last fall was exposed. As we started to rake them away we found that the earth was covered with young green shoots pushing up from the earth with an irrepressible energy – the energy of new life. We have to penetrate beyond the surface to make contact with the new life of the Resurrection.

The Resurrection is the eternal sign of our invitation to share in the glory, the complete realization of Christ. Just what does this new Resurrection-life mean? Does it have personal meaning for each of us or is it like a news item that everyone talks about and no one feels involved in? We find the answer, I think, in the New Testament accounts of the Resurrection. They all make it transparently clear that the risen Jesus could only be seen and recognized with the eyes of faith. 'She turned around and saw Jesus standing there, but did not recognize him . . . Jesus said, "Mary". She turned to him and said, "Rabbuni!" (which is Hebrew for "My Master") (John 20:14–16).

In the profoundly real and symbolic atmosphere of this encounter there is a marvellously condensed account of the human response to the Resurrection. We hear and see the Good News, but until the moment that it engages our absolute attention, by name, we fail to recognize it. When we do, all thought of self evaporates in the overwhelming joy of the reality so much greater than us, that can call us into itself. Mary is described as 'turning' twice, in this brief episode. For all of us there is this two-fold conversion that unfolds throughout a lifetime, the total conversion that demands absolute harmony of mind and heart.

Each of us needs this clarified vision that enables us to recog-

312

nize what we see. Without this new dimension of faith we can only fail to see and to recognize the risen Christ within the creation he now pervades. Finding the power of vision which lets us see what is there, lets us see what is, requires of us the wisdom to penetrate the shell of reality, to go beyond appearances. This does not mean rejecting the ordinary or cultivating an esoteric 'essential' spirituality. Far from it. To go that route would be to remain locked at the most superficial of all levels of reality: the vanity of the self-centred consciousness, the egoism of the alienated 'me'. Penetrating the appearance of things means rediscovering in childlike wonder the divine and mysterious correspondence between appearance and meaning, between the mortal and the immortal. In the Christian vision of eternal life – which means full realization of all potentiality – nothing is rejected or wasted. Even our most fragile and ephemeral dimension, our body, is to be 'saved' from the entropic processes that so frighten us: so that as St Paul said, 'Our mortal part may be absorbed into life immortal' (2 Cor. 5:4).

We need the wisdom to search into the depths of things. We also need a deepening sensitivity to a dimension of reality which can only be revealed to those who want to see, who are humble enough to cry out with the blind beggar of the Gospel, 'Lord, that I may see.' (Mark 10:51). It is only the blindly arrogant who claim to see enough. Those who are beginning to see are aware of how much more their vision of faith needs to be purified. They know that no man can see God and live. The more we see him the further our self-consciousness contracts and our ego evaporates. To see God is to be absorbed into him. To have the 'eye' of our heart opened by the process of his love is to lose our very sense of the 'I' who sees. This is the sensitivity, the delicacy of spiritual refinement we need in order to see the risen Christ. It is the gentle delicacy that follows the cataclysm of death. It is the spirit of fully selfless love that does not flinch from being transformed into the beloved. 'What we shall be has not yet been disclosed, but we know that when it is disclosed we shall be like him, because we shall see him as he is' (1 John 3:2). There is an immortal power, the 'strength' of God, in this sensitivity. And that is why we cannot enter the new vision without finding a harmony with the basic structure of reality, without being sensitive to the truth that the underpinning reality of everything we see is God.

It is in this sense that meditation is rightly called a way of wisdom, a way of vision. Wisdom is more than the knowledge derived from accumulated experience. Vision is more than the power to visualize. To be wise we must learn to know with the heart. To see we must learn to see with the eyes of the heart – with love.

The only analogy I know of that does justice to this way of wisdom and vision is the analogy of falling in love. When we have fallen in love – and are still falling, still letting go of ourselves – the beloved changes before our eyes while remaining the same in all appearances to others not caught up into this vortex of love. Loving the other deeply and unreservedly, we see them in a new light which burns away (makes us forget) our own self-important isolation and allows the smallest gesture of theirs to reveal to us what no one else can recognize. That is why falling in love is so important for us because it sweeps us out of ourselves and beyond our limitations of fear and pride into the reality of the other. Until we can lose ourselves and find ourselves again in the other I don't believe any of us can ever know what liberty really is.

Profound meditation is of the same order. Our silence, stillness and our fidelity to the simplicity of the mantra serves to lead us away from our isolated self-centred view of life. We are only 'realized' or 'fulfilled' in meditation, because we have ceased to seek or desire realization or fulfilment. We only learn to be joyful, because we have learned not to possess nor to want to possess. The ordinary discipline of our daily meditation increasingly shifts our centre of consciousness from ourselves into the limitless Mystery of God's love. But first a certain effort is needed to root the discipline in our being rather than just into the routine of our day. We need to have it rooted as an interior as well as an external discipline, so that we can carry it with us through the inevitably changing circumstances of life. Even monasteries change their timetables! When the rhythm of the twice-daily meditation becomes part of the fabric of our being, entirely natural and so always renewed and renewing, then our life is being transformed from the centre outwards. Then we are learning to see even the appearances of our ordinary life, work, relationships with the vision of love. The Christian is called to see all reality with the eyes of Christ.

Because we are so used to remaining at the superficial levels of life rather than penetrating beyond appearances it can seem unbelievable to us that the way to real vision is the transcendence of all images. It seems to us, on the surface, that without images there is no vision, just as without thought there is no consciousness. What takes us this beyond this shallowness of unbelief? First, perhaps the frustration of shallowness itself, the frustration of finding that year after year we are penetrating no further into the real experience of life, into the real meaning of our own life. St Paul wrote, 'Your world was a world without hope.' This is the dilemma of the contemporary world. But what ultimately makes depth of vision possible is faith: the leap into the unknown, the commitment to the Reality we cannot see. 'What is faith?' the Letter to the Hebrews asked. 'Faith gives substance to our hopes, and makes us certain of realities we do not see' (Heb. 11:1).

The influence of the scientific method on our entire way of responding to life has persuaded us not to believe in, not to commit ourselves to, anything until we can see the proof of it. The method works well enough for the verification of scientific theory but it does not work in the dimension of reality that lies beyond appearances. There we must commit ourselves before we see God, because without that commitment there is no purity of heart, no undivided consciousness, and only the pure of heart can see God. The commitment must be unconditional, innocent of self-interest, childlike, 'a condition of complete simplicity demanding not less than everything'. It only requires a little experience of meditation to understand those words of Dame Julian.

Between the commitment – it can take us years to achieve it – and the vision there is a kind of hiatus. It is a vital interlude – what some men and women of prayer have called a glowing night – because it is here that we experience the loss of self which is the pre-requisite of the unified vision and wisdom to which we are summoned. The waiting is not a time of delay or postponement, as our instant culture would have us believe. It is much rather a time of joyful purification and preparation. It is a time of learning to be ready, ready to be disciplined, so

315

that when the gift is given we will not try to possess it. It is a time of learning, that is, to say the mantra.

The saddest people that I have met in my life have been those who have in one way or another turned back from this vision, from the pursuit of this vision. It is, unfortunately, not enough to see the way or to understand what is demanded. Nor is it enough to become an expert in other people's experience. The only sufficient commitment is the total personal commitment of the childlike heart. As we begin to realize what is involved, all of us are tempted to compromise, to seek consolation in distraction, to turn back because we feel we haven't got what it takes to complete the journey to the other shore. That is why it is so important to remember the humility we need: the faith is the faith of Christ, the power to make the journey is given by him, if we can sufficiently acknowledge our poverty and so accept it.

The sign and the medium of this commitment is silence. By becoming genuinely silent, going beyond all images and thoughts, we quite naturally open the eyes of our heart to the light of infinity. We begin to see reality with a new power of vision, with a sharpness and acuity of vision which is startling and with a profundity which is intoxicating. What do we see? We see knowledge. That is, we see the One who knows that he is. We see oneness everywhere and at all times we know then with his knowledge that 'all must be one' – that is, all divisions must be transcended. We see love which is the supreme unifying power of creation. We see that all 'knowledge' and 'wisdom' are as nothing compared with the supreme all-inclusive Reality of the Love who Is.

When we set out we all imagine we will become wise or knowledgeable or at least that we will 'know' more. Gradually we become aware – a good sense of humour is essential for the journey – that this would be nothing but becoming more clever. At that point we must decide either for cleverness or for true knowledge. Rather than becoming more knowledgeable we become more loving, because everything is revealed to us in love. To see the world unified and to know ourselves as one, means that we are learning to love our neighbour as ourselves and to love God with our whole heart and whole soul. To love is to be *one with*. The infinite mystery of love, its intoxication and its boundless creativity is to discover the freedom that is

316

given us when we love, and then the sheer wonder of discovery that we are loved in return. It is the Trinitarian mystery – Father, Son and Spirit – a mystery of reciprocal love.

We must be wholly committed. We must be ready. The revelation takes place in the moment of God's choosing: the co-mingling of the eternal with time. The Incarnation in each personal life is as it unfolds in its destined congruity with the one Incarnation, the one Resurrection. The only ultimate tragedy in life would be not to be ready for this moment of love, to be distracted at the time of revelation in which all time is transcended.

Our meditation and our daily recommitment to it is our setting out on the path of faith, which is the preparation of our heart for this moment. Day by day we leave all egoism behind and shed all divisions. We meditate in deepening silence in the humble acknowledgement that everything we can learn or experience is in the direct gift of God. Underpinning the journey and underpinning our deepening commitment is the simple acknowledgement that God is God, God is one, God is love. The moment of revelation is our entry into the eternal now of God. And so the revelation encapsulates, unifies all time. It unifies our whole life 'before' and 'after', just as the one Incarnation, the one Crucifixion, the one Resurrection embraces past and future in the eternal present. At this moment we recognize what we have been seeing. We know that we are called – by name, personally – into the ocean of oneness towards God. And we recognize the call because it comes from one of ourselves who has attained this oneness. It comes from our Brother, Jesus, our Lord, our Guide.

May his oneness, the power of his Resurrection inspire strength and guide our pilgrimage.

10

Parts of a Whole

We were delighted to be visited by the Abbot Primate of the Benedictine Confederation, who was visiting monasteries in North America. He spoke to us at Mass and we then introduced him to our many friends who have been such a support to us since we arrived in Montreal.

Bishop Henry Hill left us to visit Orthodox Churches in the Middle East and went on to Cairo. In June Father John had a most warm and encouraging visit with our groups in London, Liverpool and Manchester. In Ireland he went to see the sisters at Kylemore, and he then made a day of retreat with our Dublin groups at the Convent of the Sisters of Charity at Glenmaroon in Dublin.

Meeting and meditating with so many who follow the extraordinary and wonderful pilgrimage in the usual course of their ordinary daily lives makes me see more clearly than ever before the true nature of this journey we are making together. We know it as a journey of faith, of expanding capacity to love and to be loved; and so also as an expanding vision of reality. And we know it too as a way that demands more and more faith. Mountains get steeper the closer you approach the summit and the path narrows. But so also the view becomes vaster, more inspiring and more humbling, strengthening us for the deeper commitment required of us for the last stages of the climb.

We know too that our journey is a way of solitude. True, it is the end to loneliness and isolation. And the solitude becomes the real material of integrity which the love of God transforms into communion, into belonging and relatedness at every level of our lives. But still it is an ascesis, a continual purification, an on-going refining in the fire of love.

We best understand the true nature of solitude when we have

318

the opportunity of meditating regularly with a group. And what struck me so clearly in England and in Ireland is that this journey is a wholly personal journey. Each one of us bears the responsibility of responding to the call personally, committing ourselves personally. No one – neither parent, friend or church – can absolve us of this ultimate personal responsibility for accepting fully the gift of our own being and, by accepting it, for bringing it to its fruition in the mystery of its source and goal – the infinite love of God. But it is not, for all that, a journey we make alone. The Father of Lies, the ego, often makes his best converts among the most religious of us. Religious people are so prone to self-importance, self-fixation, self-dramatization. They can approach their spiritual progress or direction or vocation so self-centredly, so solemnly that the life of their religious response is stifled and becomes an inward-turning search for perfection, happiness or spiritual success.

The most vulnerable area of our spiritual journey in regard to the ego's ubiquitous assaults is that place where we choose between solitude and loneliness as the context of the journey. It is a real and crucial choice and one that has to be continuously reaffirmed by many of the decisions that life throws out, challenging us to self-transcendence, selfless love. So many – and it is the cause of the sadness and desperation of our age – choose to be lonely in the crowd rather than find communion in solitude. The community of the faithful, the monastery, the meditation group, the spiritual family, each one of these is the vital element in preparing us for this most important of decisions. Alone we can hardly see it, because when we are isolated we cannot see beyond ourselves: this is the terrible delusion of self-centredness. But in contact with others we awaken to the deeper truth of our being that we are meant to see, and so we learn to travel beyond ourselves. This is why meditating regularly, whether daily or weekly, with the same group or community is such a source of healthy sustenance to our pilgrimage. We cannot maintain the delusion of an isolated pilgrimage when we are present with others. And yet, this very physical and spiritual presence recalls us to a deeper personal commitment to stillness, to silence and to fidelity. The group or community similarly signals the end to all false heroism and self-dramatization. Being in touch with the ordinary failings and limitations of others puts our response and fidelity into the perspective which we need for balance and harmony in our life. In the presence of others we know ourselves.

The Christian life summons us to loss of self and we lose ourselves in the love we have for others. One of the Desert Fathers returned from his hermitage to the community speaking of the dangers of spiritual pride when separated from others, and then he added, 'There, when I was alone, whose feet could I wash?' The life of charity, of practical other-centredness is not only an experience of the experience of Christ. It is the great stabilizing and enriching element for all who would find a contemplative dimension to life. The great decisions that place us deeper in reality or thrust us further out into lonely illusion are not the decisions between extremes. They are the decisions that are the hardest to make for they are the ones that keep us on the path we are already treading, that make us more centred, deeper rooted. One of the fears people often feel as they go deeper is that their options are diminishing, the ways of escape are getting fewer. The narrowing of the road is a cause for joy because it is a sign we are approaching our goal. I was deeply moved and inspired by the groups I met with in England and Ireland. They showed me the importance of seeing the pilgrimage of meditation in terms of spiritual health and psychological balance rather than as something esoteric or precious. They showed me too how desperately our society needs men and women seriously committed to persevering on this Way to the Absolute. The ordinariness of the weekly meetings, the simplicity of their organization actually highlights the sublimity of the pilgrimage these people are following. They are truly leaving self behind and entering into the infinity of God's love.

A person does not start to meditate because he feels it will help society. Perhaps he even regards his meditation as his ration of personal self-concern over and above what he does in the rest of his life to benefit others. But after some experience of the nature of meditation and of the profound (though often silent and at first inconspicuous) change it makes in one's life, we all begin to see things differently. Our progress on the pilgrimage clarifies, through lived experience, what we mean by saying that 'being is prior to action' or that the significance and quality of what we do depends upon our capacity for simply *being*. This remains a philosophical proposition before we have begun to meditate, but (as with so many other ideas of our faith) contact with our own reality transforms static theory into the wonder of personal discovery. The more fully we open our eyes to the fundamental and all-pervasive mystery of being, the more clearly we see the true place and nature of all activity. The same clarifying process transforms our view of the pilgrimage as well.

We all begin the pilgrimage with a certain degree of egoism, self-centredness, seeing everything in its relation to ourselves. In effect, we see ourselves as the centre of the universe. This applies even to our meditation itself when we begin. But as we progress we lose this self-centred tendency of our perception and we become more other-centred in our understanding. We see that even our meditation itself can *only* be other-centred. That is, concerned not primarily with ourselves but the other who is, who was and who always will be with us: our brother, guide and Lord, the Christ whose centre is simultaneously in God and in us.

Somebody asked me at one of the meetings how meditation fitted in with the vision of the whole human race in its movement back to God through evolution and through free will. Is the Christian one of the elect, the tiny minority from among all races and generations who will awaken to God? And if so, does that mean that the Christian meditator is one on the inner track among the elect? It is an important question.

Every day I am more amazed at the range and variety of people who really *hear* the message of the teaching about meditation, who hear it from some deep and perhaps unsuspected stillness within themselves. And I am even more inspired that so many remain faithful to the discipline and the fidelity that makes the hearing really significant. They are people of all ages and backgrounds, educational, social and religious. But they have all discovered a common centre, Christ, who lives in their hearts and in the heart of all creation.

It would not be easy to generalize about what else they have in common. It is certainly nothing as superficial as an I.Q. rating or an interest in things religious. The wonder of the community of those on the pilgrimage is that it is really only their experience of faith that makes them seem the same. And the very wonder is that this faith is pure, unpredictable, invincible and pure gift. That much we know but according to what purpose or design the gift is given we are much less knowledgeable. The phenomenon of God's self-revelation and embodiment among mankind is the purest of mysteries, knowable but beyond understanding. To know it is to be made real and to be set at peace. To strive to understand it is to strive vainly to go beyond the limits of what is the specifically human reality.

Nevertheless, although this may seem to be pointing towards a spiritual elitism it actually reinforces the solidarity, the interdependence and equality of the whole human family. Precisely because our capacity to *hear* and to *respond*, the capacity we call faith, *is* pure inexplicable gift, it is no cause for pride. Because the source of the gift is God, it cannot be purely arbitrary or without meaning.

The meaning is this: by hearing and responding, by pursuing the call to poverty of spirit and purity of heart, we discover that within the depths of our being we fulfil our part of the divine plan for the whole of mankind. The mantra is, as experience proves, an act of pure love, universal love. Everyone who meditates faithfully through all the personal storms and challenges of their personal life begins to know this. They come also to know that they are meditating through the crises and tragedies of their world. Indeed the further they go on their way, the closer they realize they are to the Whole which is more than the sum of its parts. It is so because the Spirit moves among it, giving it that completion, that redemption which is the centre of God's design. The communion we discover in the solitude of our own hearing and responding is not only communion with ourselves. That is perhaps the first sign we have of it – a deeper personal harmony and freedom. But it persists beyond, to the communion we share with all men and women, with all the dead and all the living and the yet unborn. With them we share the great and mysterious gift of life in the flesh and in the Spirit. And as we awaken to this deeper and higher sense of wholeness we sense the ultimate all-embracing communion which contains all this and of which these are epiphanies. The communion we have with God and the communion within God – this is the great truth we encounter. All we can say in the end is what we said at the beginning – that the meaning of life is the mystery of love.

Because of our incorporation in the whole – an incorporation that has both material and spiritual dimensions – every experience in the human family influences the whole. This is why St Paul calls the early Christians 'to weep with those who weep and to rejoice with those who rejoice'. Violence, injustice, and all suffering anywhere within the Body of Christ affects and implicates us all. The reality is that we are not isolated. We are one with the One. We are one with all.

And yet we are more than component cells in a huge organism. We are each of us given a unique and essential place within the infinite mystery of God. We each of us have a personal call to *hear* and to *respond*, and if we fail then the whole is impoverished.

In breaking through the walls of egoism and fear that so often encase our hearts, the light makes that beam itself universal. The mystery of love is that we become what we delight to gaze upon, and so when we have opened our hearts to this light we become light. We still are ourselves, for God does not remove his gifts – they are given in his eternal present moment. But we are transfigured, burning with a light brighter than ourselves and however dark is the world we are in, this light cannot be extinguished.

To judge only by appearances, materialistic or institutional, one might be tempted to say that the Body of Christ is being broken down in our world. But it is in fact being built up! Often in very human, unexceptional incarnations which testify to a power beyond themselves, beyond appearances, beyond all materialistic notions of success. I felt this very strongly meeting with so many meditators in England and Ireland where individual fidelity and group witness were open doors for the transfigured light of Christ in homes, schools, factories, offices and hospitals. In all these places the human consciousness of Christ made its appearance in the human consciousness of those who seek him daily in all humility. In London and in Dublin where our groups had a whole day together many people came to me afterwards and said how extraordinarily happy and peaceful the day had been, and what a power of love they had felt flowing around them. We are, all of us, moving towards the love, and the light is moving towards us. But we are, none of us, trying to possess the light for ourselves. It is 'the' light rather than 'my' light. And there is only one enlightenment – the opening of the human consciousness of Jesus in that light because he is incorporate in our humanity. We are, all of us, affected by that enlightenment. Indeed his light is what we call our redemption. We are redeemed in the light of his love.

To try too exclusively to understand this might lead us to pride. To *know* it in the ordinary fidelity of our pilgrimage is to be rendered humble by the sheer wonder of it. We each of us have a unique and urgent responsibility to know it. Once we hear, we must respond as fully, as generously as we are called to. For when the light and the kingdom dawn in our hearts, it then touches all we touch. We must not fear the dawn, for the light must dawn and burst and expand in our hearts until it becomes the full dawn of the Resurrection.

11

Beyond Memory

The highlight of summer 1982 was a holiday we had together as a community in Nova Scotia. We stayed, through the generosity of the sisters of the Congregation of Notre Dame, in their house on Iona, a lonely island of the Bras d'Or Lakes.

During the summer and early autumn three new groups started in New York City and New Jersey. We received new oblates from Toronto, Los Angeles, Boston, Calgary and Montreal. At our last oblate meeting we were pleasantly surprised to discover that the oblates had organized a fifth anniversary party for us and had invited a large number of old and new friends.

Early in October Father John spoke to the Palliative Care International Conference at its meeting here in Montreal. There were a thousand or so participants whose work is to look after the terminally ill. It was a wonderful opportunity to speak to a large group of sensitive and caring people on the importance of meditation as the Way. It was at this time that Father John became aware of his own approaching death.

In talking to the Conference on the care of the dying I tried to show them that meditation is a way of growth and development. In a real sense it is the way of growth because what we are growing into through meditation is life itself. It makes us more full of life and therefore more fully alive. Although meditation obviously has some characteristics in common with our other experiences of growth and development (as, for example, the pain that accompanies all growth), it is different from these other experiences, which we usually perceive as growth into greater complexity. But meditation is growth into greater unity, into greater simplicity.

Unity is freedom. Whoever has realized his own essential oneness can easily pass into the reality of his unity with others.

And this realization of oneness is the *raison d'être* of all consciousness. Unless we are on the way to this realization our life lacks meaning and we live our life as if it were a battle against discontent rather than as a celebration of joy in the fact that we *are*. The only ultimate tragedy in our life would be never to realize any part of this oneness and to remain bound by our limitations. The only significant limitations in life are, therefore, those which retard our entry into full unity. In a materialistic view we regard as limitations whatever restricts our freedom of action – illness, poverty, misunderstandings beyond our control. Naturally these imperfections have to be combatted by our life-force and our innate love of goodness. But we can be ill, poor, misunderstood and still be free. We can suffer these forms of external limitation and still be joyful in the gift of our being. We can be restricted in our ability to move, even to communicate and yet still be in communion, *in unity*. The really dangerous limitations are those that arise not from our physical dimension but from our egoism, our preference for isolation, our self-centredness, the reification of self, others and God.

Meditation is a gentle way of growing into the freedom that is beyond all limitations of this dangerous kind. It is not magical. Meditation does restore us to a deeper harmony of body and spirit, but it always remains an essentially *spiritual* growth. All growth is a form of healing. Not just a retrospective healing of past wounds but it propels the whole person we are *now* into greater wholeness, the health we are created for. And so we can say that meditation is a growth beyond limitations that prevents us from being whole, entire, in 'divine health'.

Once we pass a limitation that has previously held us back we discover that we are free from it for all eternity. We are no longer dominated by the fear or the narrowness that limitations impose on us and which can seem, while we are in their power, to be immovable. Time is so precious for us because we must use the unique opportunity time gives us to grow as completely as we can beyond all limitations. Time used for liberation prepares us to enter into eternity as persons who are essentially free to *be* fully alive. What we call eternal life is the state of perfect oneness, and it demands that all those who enter this unity are personally free to do so – free to be, free of self-consciousness, free to love, free to commit ourselves without reserve.

The process of growth into freedom is an essential aspect of the divine dimension of human life and consciousness. God is the one who is infinite growth, infinite and perfect freedom. He is the one who is complete. As I have suggested before, divine perfection is not a static achievement. That is why it is not something that we can contemplate as a fixed object within horizons of our own making. God is quite other than the monumental image we so often picture him as being. He is Person. To be personally complete is simply to be free from all the limitations that restrict us from expansion, and God is precisely the infinite expansion who is perpetually centred in himself. And he is centred in every human consciousness through the unique human consciousness of Jesus. God is complete and he is completeness itself. That is why the state of completeness is always *present*. It is never future or past. God is always now. Our meditation is always concerned with another step into the present moment and it is growth to the degree that we allow ourselves to take this step unconditionally. It is always another step into the eternal *now* of God. Every time we meditate we take another step into the divine life that enlivens, brings to fullness, everyone who opens himself to it by taking this step of turning from self. The paradox we discover in the course of taking this step day by day arises from the divine paradox – a life which is wholly present, wholly without reverie or daydream, where everything is actualized and complete, and yet which is always expanding in self-transcendence. The divine paradox is love.

Like all growth, this entry into the divinizing experience of the present moment involves pain. It is the pain of all maturing. It arises from the need to leave behind us every earlier stage of development, all that we have been, in favour of what we are summoned to become. The transition from time to eternity, which is this growth, is continuous. Every moment is a dying to the past and a rising to a new present in which the past is not rejected – we are who we have become through the experiences of a lifetime – but in which the *memory* of the past is allowed to crumble back into the dust from which it was formed. No *memories* can survive the transition from incompleteness to fulfilment. In a sense the limitations we are talking

327

about are all the limitations imposed and sustained by memory. We have to forget, to *unknow* everything we have been if we are to bring ourselves to completeness. Much of the difficulty involved in overcoming the limitations imposed by memory is that we have to learn to let go, of not just part of ourselves, but the whole of our self-consciousness. We can only become fully present to the now of the divine moment if we can leave the past behind totally.

What we try to do is to maintain observation points, base camps along every stage of our development. Each of these little camps is an outpost of the central H.Q. of the ego. Each of them becomes a link in the chain of command stretching down from the ego into every corner of our life as part of the ego's attempt to bring all life within its sway and to cast its net over our whole consciousness. At each of these observation points we are tempted to hang on to part of ourselves on the brink of the new stage of growth. But if we opt for this, then instead of our life becoming an experience of accumulative growth, we find our lives contracting. Instead of finding that there is more and more space of consciousness to fill by our accepting the gift of Being and love, we will find that the net of self-consciousness will tighten around us and persuade us there is less and less space to expand into. Our life becomes progress into a cul-de-sac rather than progress across a bridge to the further shore.

At each stage of growth we have to leave all of ourselves behind and go forward, becoming a new creation. Accepting this perspective as a workable theory of life, just believing in it, is not enough. We all know how dry and unsatisfying a state we are in when we have all the right theories (with all the possible variations on them duly categorized and discussed) and still have not found the *practice*. It was of this state that Jesus was speaking when he said that to those who have, more will be given, and to those who have not, even what they think they have will be taken away. It is a hard saying but one whose truth we can all recognize. What is perhaps harder to recognize is just where we are. *To have*, in this saying of Jesus, means to be a follower of the Way, our feet really touching the pilgrim path each step we make. *To have not* is to be buoyed up along the path by theories of the pilgrimage and so to be treading air, marking time and losing time. It is difficult to accept that we may fall into the second category. Our theories can make us impotent and self-important, like people with a car manual but no car. We do not like to admit that we may not have been really making the pilgrimage up to this moment of truth. Yet the humility to accept this, to make a new beginning is demanded (and re-demanded) of us, if our feet are ever to touch the ground. If not, then what we think we have – our theories, which are too inadequate to express any but a part of the whole mystery at any one time – will be swept away from us when reality dawns. It does dawn for all of us, whether we are ready or not, when death removes the superstructure of limitations that we can so easily mistake for reality.

We need to pass through theory into actuality, and this is just what we do each time we meditate. Everything we have been and everything we have done up to that moment is abandoned when we sit down to meditate. The more fully the past is truly abandoned, the more completely renewed we are as we return to the work of our day. Meditation is a continuous breakthrough into the present moment of God. This is why we can begin to understand the mystery of this process of growth only if we see it in the perspective of our whole life. The person who meditates is the person we *are* – the person we become from birth to death – the whole person. Not the isolated image of self we usually identify ourselves with while we are moving in and out of one or other of the phases of our life.

Our growth in and through meditation is not, therefore, restricted to isolated experiences. That is why concern for what we are experiencing from day to day is so counter-productive. Spiritual growth is always growth into union which means growth out of self-consciousness. If we have this essential principle of reality made concrete in our daily fidelity to meditation we are in the happy position of one who enjoys the humble and yet absolute confidence of St Paul's Christian who, 'gifted with the Spirit, can judge the worth of everything'. Rooted in this actualized pilgrimage, we know whether anything advances or retards the growth towards completeness in Christ. Does it make us think more about ourselves or less about ourselves? That is the Christian touchstone.

Monitoring our experiences is an attempt to fix God in time and so to stifle his own expansion – the Spirit. And as soon as we do this, we experience not God but only our own egotistical image of God. Strictly speaking, meditation does not give us any 'experience of God'. *God* does not experience himself; rather, he knows. For him to experience himself would suggest a divided consciousness, a limitation to his own perfect freedom. The knowledge God has of himself is one with himself. His self-knowledge is love.

Meditation takes us into this self-knowledge which is the life of God. It is a life full of the knowledge of the self born from self-transcendence. This is why meditation is an entry into divinization through Jesus. Through our union with him we pass the limitations of division and become one with God. Through him we utterly transcend ourselves, leaving our whole self behind and becoming a new creation in him. Meditation is itself the process of self-transcendence. To the degree that we are transcending self we are divine because we are becoming one with the power of love.

Our spiritual growth can never be seen as an *accumulation* of experiences, rather it is the *transcendence* of all experiences. What we so often call a memorable experience is first and foremost a memory. But in the eternal act of creation which is the life of the Trinitarian God everything is *now*.

We must not become self-important about our self-transcendence. We can occupy the centre of our imaginary universe so completely that it seems to us the world would fall apart if we abdicated from our position at that centre. Of course, the only world that does fall apart is the mirror-image world of egoism. The real world comes into being for us as we ourselves become a new creation.

Small though the relative cosmic impact of our little self-transcendence may be, it has absolute value. The completion and the liberation of the human consciousness is after all the central meaning of the entire mystery of God's creation. So each of us, by our own little liberation, is empowered to become one with him. We must never forget this if we are to remain rooted in the expansion of the divine life, if we are to grow. Each time we sit down to meditate we enter into oneness – the oneness of God who is now, the oneness of God who is love.

We can't really understand this vocation to unity. It is too much for the mind to hold or imagine, except in fragments. But what we can do is to sit down and say our mantra. To do so with humility, fidelity and absolute trust in the goodness of God who calls us beyond every limitation to become like him. He calls us, such is the marvel of the Christian revelation, to expand into his infinity.

The more we contemplate the wonder of our vocation the more humble we must become, the more poor in spirit. We become humble and poor by our fidelity to our mantra. It sometimes seems to us at the beginning that as we make progress we won't have to say the mantra quite so faithfully in the future. But as we do progress, in actuality not in imagination, we discover that we must enter more and more completely into the poverty and fidelity to which the mantra leads us.

12

The Oceans of God

In the later months of 1982 we enjoyed visits from many guests from many places. A nun from Stanbrook Abbey enlivened the Community with her stories about monastic life on both sides of the Atlantic. Other guests included Burkard Schuhmann from Würzburg and Sister Camille Campbell, who has joined us for a year to help run the guest house.

Monastic Studies 13 was published and received a very good welcome. We are happy that it has been possible to revive this excellent journal of monastic scholarship and to continue its high standards.

We had a special weekend at the monastery during which artists, poets, sculptors and musicians who meditate with us shared their work and discussed the spiritual value of art. Having meditation as the common bond between all the participants seemed to assure a real foundation for the exchange that took place.

In London, Sister Madeleine Simon started a 'Christian Meditation Centre' from which she distributes the newsletters, runs several meditation groups and organizes a focal point for advice and resources for all the meditation groups in England.

A collection of the first twelve of these newsletters was published, under the title Letters from the Heart, *by Crossroads, New York, and distributed in England by the S.P.C.K. The introduction gives a history of the beginnings of the Montreal community with some thoughts on the emergence of a contemporary monasticism rooted in the tradition of 'pure prayer'.*

[Father John gave these news items in this his last newsletter; it gives his definitive teaching on a Christian's readiness for death.]

At Christmastime we become more sharply aware of the

mysterious blend of the ordinary and the sublime in the monastic life and indeed all life that is really Christian. It is important, though, to see it as a blend not as an opposition.

It is tempting to treat the birth of Christ as something romantically outside the full meaning of his life, something pre-Christian. In the rich and beautiful gospel accounts of his birth we can be tempted to see this part of his life as merely consoling or idyllic. But it is part of the human mystery that nothing is outside the Mystery. By the Incarnation God accepted this aspect of the human condition and so the birth and childhood of Christ are part of the mystery of his life – a life that culminated on the cross and reached its transcendent completion in the Resurrection and Ascension.

Our meditation teaches us how fully every part of us has to be involved in the radical conversion of our life. It teaches us that we have to put our whole heart into this work of the Spirit if we are genuinely to respond to the call to leave the shallows and enter into the deep, direct knowledge that marks a life lived in the mystery of God. Then everything in our life acquires this depth dimension of divine Presence. We are foolish to look for 'signs' on the way – it is a form of spiritual materialism that Jesus rebuked – because if we *are* on the way, which means in the Mystery, in the bright cloud of God's presence, then all things are signs. Everything mediates the love of God.

There is, of course, literary art in the infancy narratives of Luke and Matthew. But this does not mean that the details of the birth of Christ were not charged with wonder and mystery for those who were involved in it. The parents of Jesus 'wondered' at what was being said about him. And Mary teaches us how this experience of wonder is to be assimilated by 'treasuring these things in her heart'. The 'heart' is that focal point in our being where we can simply be in the Mystery without trying to explain or dissect it. A mystery analyzed becomes merely another problem. It must be apprehended whole and entire. And that is why we, who are called to apprehend it, must ourselves be made one in heart and mind.

The mystery surrounding Jesus was perceptible from the beginning of his life. Not until his death and resurrection was it capable of being fully apprehended, fully known. Because not until then was it complete. Our life does not achieve full unity until it transcends itself and all limitations by passing through death. This is why we do not fully comprehend the mystery of Christ, in which we enter the mystery of God, until our life is complete. We begin to enter it as soon as our consciousness begins to stir into vital perception and to learn the laws of reality by learning to love and be loved. But we are always learning, always preparing for the fullness that comes to us all. Until the life of Jesus passed through death and returned in the Resurrection this completion was a source of terror or despair to the human race. Now it has been transformed. For what seemed a dead-end has now been revealed to the eyes of faith as a bridge. This is the hidden significance of the birth of Jesus, his growth through infancy and manhood and his supreme sacrifice of self on the Cross. In our beginning is our end. And so in the birth of Jesus death already began to be transformed. All the intuitions shared by those involved in his birth and his early life were fulfilled in his ministry and the paschal mystery. His life, like every human life, has a hidden and mysterious unity. End and beginning are two ends of the string of life held in the mystery of God and joined together in the mystery of Christ.

Our life is a unity because it is centred in the mystery of God. But to know its unity we have to see beyond ourselves and with a perspective greater than we generally see with, when self-interest is our dominant concern. Only when we have begun to turn from self-interest and self-consciousness does this larger perspective begin to open.

Another way of saying that our vision expands is to say that we come to see beyond mere appearances, into the depth and significance of things. Not just the depth and significance in relation to ourselves is involved but depth in relation to the whole of which we are part. This is the way of true self-knowledge and it is why true self-knowledge is identical with true humility. Meditation opens up for us this precious form of knowledge, and it is what enables us to pass beyond mere objectivity – merely looking at the mystery of God as observers – and to enter the mystery itself. This knowledge becomes *wisdom* once we have entered the cloud of the mystery and when we know no longer by analysis and definition but by participation in the life and spirit of Christ.

So we learn by the path of meditation what cannot be learned otherwise, what is unknowable as long as we hesitate to become real pilgrims of the spirit. Following this path is a fundamental requirement of the Christian life which must be a life lived out of the depths rather than the shallows. This is why Christian discipleship is the completion of the human condition. In this condition man always seeks the *complete action*, something that will call forth all his powers simultaneously, focus and unify all the dimensions of his being. Until we have found this action we are restless, always mastered by distraction or desire masquerading as the reality which only this perfect action can lead us into.

Naturally, if we are truly human we know that this action is love. Only when we live in and out of love do we know that miraculous harmony and integration of our whole being which makes us fully human. This is always a practical rather than idyllic state: I mean that the human condition is always made up of frailties and imperfections, either of personality or environment. The Incarnation of God in the human condition, however, absorbs all these faults and accidents in such a way that they can no longer prevent us from the fullness of love. The saint is not super-human but fully human.

Every part of us, including our faults and failures, must be included in our commitment to the pilgrimage into this fullness. Nothing real is excluded from the kingdom of heaven. Realistic, human wholeness is the accumulative experience of staying on our pilgrimage. Gradually the separate compartments of our life coalesce. The room dividers are taken down and we find that our heart is not a prison made up of a thousand individual cells but a great chamber filled with the light of God whose walls are constantly being pushed back.

Meditation expands our *knowledge* of God because, in leading us into self-knowledge, it propels us beyond self-consciousness. We know God to the degree that we forget ourselves. This is the paradox and the risk of prayer. It is not enough to study the paradox because, like love, it can only be known when it is lived firsthand. Once we have begun to live it we can read the great human testimonies of the spirit – the New Testament and the spiritual classics – from within the same experience. Until then, however, we are merely observers, at best waiting to begin.

It is not an easy paradox to grasp. How *can* one grasp the spirit? It helps though if we reflect on the human manifestation

335

of this essential structure of reality. To love another person involves more than thinking of them, more even than enjoying their company, more even than sacrificing oneself for them. It involves allowing ourselves to be loved by them. This is perhaps the most moving and awe-inspiring mystery of the Incarnation. In becoming human God allows himself to be loved within the human range of love, as ordinarily as any infant, child, adolescent or adult.

The humility of God in allowing himself to be loved in the man Jesus is our cue for recognizing the basic structure of all reality. Our first step in loving God is to allow ourselves to be loved. The grammar of language is misleading here because there is nothing passive about allowing ourselves to be loved. Just as there is nothing passive about turning our attention off ourselves and nothing passive about saying the mantra – which are the ways we allow ourselves to be loved in any human or divine relationship.

Meditation takes us into the basic relationship of our life. It does so because it leads us into the intimacy with God that arises out of the eternal reality of his loving and knowing us. In doing so he calls us into being and *human being* is itself a response to the demand inherent in God's love and knowledge of us. It is the demand that we love and know him. Yet, we can only know him, not as an object of our knowledge, but by participating in his own self-knowledge, his life, his spirit. Thus we are led back to the starting point of our being, his love and knowledge of us. We come to know and love God because we allow him to know and love us. We allow his self-knowledge to become our self-knowledge. This is the alchemy of love.

Knowledge such as this is certain and unshakeable. 'Be rooted and founded in love,' wrote St Paul. Just as the roots of trees hold the soil firm and stop erosion, so it is the roots of love that hold the ground of our being together. They provide the context in which we live and grow. And they each trace back to God as the first root of all being. The roots of love in our life bring us into context with him, with ourselves and with each other. And they show us that to be is to be in connection, each contributing to the other.

Sanity and balance mean knowing the context in which we live. This form of knowledge makes us sensitive to the presence of God in all our surroundings. Meditation teaches us in the only certain way, by experience, that his presence is not external to us. It is interior, the presence that makes up and holds together the ground of our being. So we come no longer to *look* for God's presence in the externals of our life but to *recognize* him in them because our eyes are opened interiorly to his indwelling Spirit. We no longer try to grasp hold of God, to possess him. Rather we are grasped by his presence, interiorly and exteriorly, because we know that his presence is all pervasive and the ground of all that is.

To be possessed by God in this way is the only true freedom. The tyranny of love is the only true relationship. Inevitably we fear this as it develops or emerges during our pilgrimage, because our image of freedom is so different, so naïvely imagined as the freedom to do rather than to be. But if we have the courage to be simple and humble enough to enter this *real* freedom, then we discover in ourselves the power of a faith that is unshakeable. Christian confidence is the discovery of this unshakeability and it is this confidence that underlies Christian compassion, tolerance and acceptance. We are made wonderfully secure in our own existence by this discovery, and out of this security we are empowered to drop our defences and to go out to the other. Our faith is unshakeable, not rigid, because it is one with the ground of our being. Through Christ's union with his disciples his faith becomes their faith and their faith is not an adjunct to their being. It is the breath of their spirit's life.

So, deepening our commitment to this pilgrimage means deepening the knowledge that faith gives birth to in the soul. As Christ is formed in us, as we ourselves live no longer for ourselves but for him and as his spirit breathes the new life of faith into our mortal bodies, we do come to know Christ more deeply. Maybe it sounds arrogant to say we come to know Christ as we persevere in meditation. But the truth is not less than this. We come to know what it is to live every moment, every decision, joy or difficulty from within his presence and so out of the infinite resources of his power – the power of love and compassion, an unshakeable reality.

How do we enter this presence? How can we acquire this 'knowledge that is beyond knowledge'? Because it is the knowledge of unknowing, it is the presence that forms when we allow ourselves to go beyond being present merely to ourselves

337

and instead become present to God – to be known and loved into full being by him. As we are unformed he is formed. We have to learn to forget ourselves. Nothing is simpler to do. It is the condition of full simplicity. Yet nothing – or so it seems – is more difficult for us. It is so easy in theory to accept this. But in practice it is so difficult to live and love as if the other were really more important than ourselves, or as if our first loyalty were really not to self but to the other.

The greatest difficulty is to begin, to take the first step, to launch out into the depth of the reality of God as revealed in Christ. Once we have left the shore of our own self we soon pick up the currents of reality that give us our direction and momentum. The more still and attentive we are, the more sensitively we respond to these currents. And so the more absolute and truly spiritual our faith becomes. By stillness in the spirit we move in the ocean of God. If we have the courage to push off from the shore we cannot fail to find this direction and energy. The further out we travel the stronger the current becomes, and the deeper our faith. For a while the depth of our faith is challenged by the paradox that the horizon of our destination is always receding. *Where are we going with this deeper faith?* Then, gradually we recognize the meaning of the current that guides us and see that the ocean is infinite.

Leaving the shore is the first great challenge, but it is only necessary to *begin* to face the challenge. Even though the challenges may become greater later, we are assured that we shall be given everything we need to face them. We begin by saying the mantra. Saying the mantra is always to be beginning, to be returning to the first step. We learn in time that there is only one step between us and God.

Opening our hearts to the spirit of Christ is the only way into the certain knowledge that that step has been taken. Christ has taken it in himself. He himself *is* the step between God and man because he is God and man. The language we use to express this mystery, the greatest and fundamental mystery of the human race and of all time, is pathetically inadequate – as the theological controversies down through the centuries have shown. No language or concept or metaphor can express the mystery of Christ, because Christ is the full embodiment of God and there can be no adequate expression of God except his own self-expression. The only way to know Christ is to enter his personal mystery, leaving ideas and words behind. We leave them behind in order to enter the silence of full knowledge and love to which meditation is leading each of us.

A New Beginning

At about 8.45 a.m. on 30 December 1982 Father John took the last step of his pilgrimage. He died peacefully in the monastery with several of us around him.

Father John was buried at Mount Saviour Monastery on Monday, 3 January 1983, and a Memorial Mass was held in Montreal on 15 January at the Ascension of Our Lord Church, Westmount, where he and Father Laurence first stayed when they came to Montreal in 1977. Bishop Crowley was the principle concelebrant and the Benedictines from Mount Saviour and Weston Priory were present with us.

'The poverty and joy of our word leads us into the sea of the reality of God and, once there, it keeps us simply in the current of the Spirit and leads us to a place unknown to us where we know ourselves in Him, in His eternal now' (John Main's letter of June 1979). Father John's illness accelerated rapidly after he wrote his last newsletter, and his sudden decline in the last two weeks further prepared us for the mystery of his death. We faced this mystery from out of a strong paradox: the paradox of human sorrow and grief, the bitter loss of his warmth and humour, his strength and gentleness as part of our own ordinary life, his great inspiration and power of clarification and encouragement. Yet all this loss was permeated by the joy of knowing that he had passed through the single focal point of which he had so often spoken, and that he had begun the life of infinite expansion in the love of God for which his work among us prepared him. We felt his absence more deeply than ever before, and yet we had never felt him closer.

Those days were like the experience of the early Christians who wept and rejoiced for their dead and risen Lord. This was because we all die and rise in Christ, and if we are open to his presence in the Resurrection we must therefore be open to the presence of each other as members of his glorified body. In Christ we learn that love is stronger than death.

Over the previous few months there had been an extraordinary surge of witness to the profound effect Father John had on many people's lives. Everyone who had ever been open to his teaching was changed and enriched by his sharing of what he himself had received through his own absolute and courageous, simple and loving openness to the mystery which contains us all. His teaching was and is rooted in the mystery itself, and so it enjoys the life and unpredictable pattern of the mystery. His new life in the Kingdom means new life for the work he began.

We strive to be faithful to the gift his life and teaching gave to us and to so many.

Laurence Freeman OSB

Further Reading on Christian Meditation

By John Main:

Letters from the Heart (New York, Crossroad, 1982)
The Joy of Being: Daily Readings with John Main (London, DLT, 1987)
The Heart of Creation (London, DLT, 1988; New York, Crossroad, 1988)
The Way of Unknowing (London, DLT, 1989; New York, Crossroad, 1989)
Community of Love (London, DLT, 1990)
Word Made Flesh (London, DLT, 1993)

By Laurence Freeman:

Light Within (London, DLT, 1986; New York, Crossroad, 1986)
The Selfless Self (London, DLT, 1989)
A Short Span of Days (Ottawa, Novalis, 1992)
The Meditation Group (London, Medio Media, 1993)

By Paul Harris:

John Main by Those who Knew Him (London, DLT, 1991; Ottawa, Novalis, 1991)
Christian Meditation by Those who Practice it (New Jersey, Dimension, 1993)

By Bede Griffiths:

The New Creation in Christ (London, DLT, 1992)

By Neil McKenty:

In the Stillness Dancing (London, DLT, 1986; New York, Crossroad, 1987). The biography of John Main